THRILLERS

Other Books by John McCarty

The Modern Horror Film: 50 Contemporary Classics
The Complete Films of John Huston
The Official Splatter Movie Guide—Volumes I & II
Deadly Resurrection (a novel)
Splatter Movies: Breaking the Last Taboo of the Screen
Alfred Hitchcock Presents (with Brian Kelleher)
Psychos—80 Years of Mad Movies, Maniacs and Murderous Deeds
The Little Shop of Horrors Book (with Mark Thomas McGee)
You're on Open Line: Inside the Wacky World of Late-Night Talk Radio

THRILLERS

SEVEN DECADES OF CLASSIC FILM SUSPENSE

by John McCarty

A CITADEL PRESS BOOK
PUBLISHED BY CAROL PUBLISHING GROUP

Photo Credits

Circle Films
Columbia Pictures
Continental Distributing
DeLaurentiis Entertainment Group
Embassy Pictures
Hammer Films
Beth Gwinn
International Affiliates
Janus Films
Lorimar Pictures
MGM/UA
National Film Archive—British Film Institute
Orion Pictures
Paramount Pictures
RKO
Turner Entertainment
Twentieth Century-Fox
United Motion Picture Organization
Universal Pictures
Warner Bros.

A Citadel Press Book
Published by Carol Publishing Group

Citadel Press is a registered trademark of Carol Communications, Inc.
Editorial Offices: 600 Madison Avenue, New York, N.Y. 10022
Sales & Distribution Offices: 120 Enterprise Avenue, Secaucus, N.J. 07094
In Canada: Canadian Manda Group, P.O. Box 920, Station U, Toronto, Ontario M8Z 5P9
Queries regarding rights and permissions should be addressed to Carol Publishing Group,
600 Madison Avenue, New York, N.Y. 10022

Carol Publishing Group books are available at special discounts for bulk purchases, for
sales promotions, fund raising, or educational purposes. Special editions can be created
to specifications. For details contact: Special Sales Department, Carol Publishing Group,
120 Enterprise Avenue, Secaucus, N.J. 07094

Designed by *Paul Chevannes*

Manufactured in the United States of America
10 9 8 7 6 5 4 3 2 1

Library of Congress Cataloging-in-Publication Data

McCarty, John, 1944—
        Thrillers : seven decades of classic film suspense / by John
McCarty.
        p. cm.
        "A Citadel Press book."
        ISBN 0-8065-1339-X
        1. Detective and mystery films—History and criticsm. I. Title.
PN1995.9.D4M35 1992
791.43'655—dc20
                                                92-30911
                                                CIP

FOR MY WIFE, CHERYL,
WHO LIKES A GOOD THRILLER

ACKNOWLEDGMENTS

I would like to thank the following people for their help in making this book possible: my tireless agent and fellow film fan, Lori Perkins; my editor, Allan J. Wilson, a big thriller fan himself; Alvin H. Marill at Citadel; Eric Caidin of Hollywood Book & Poster, who always comes through with just the stills I need when I need them; Ken Hanke—for keeping a sharp eye out for certain films I didn't have access to and taping them for me so that I could screen them and refresh myself on them for this book; and a special nod, of course, to the invaluable Ray Cabana, Jr., and John Foster.

CONTENTS

THRILLERS

William Wyler's The Desperate Hours *(1955).*

INTRODUCTION

The first film I remember seeing was a 1949 suspense drama called *The Window*. It was the story of a little boy (Bobby Driscoll) who sees a murder committed by one of his neighbors (Paul Stewart), but because the youngster has a history of spinning tall tales, no one will believe him—except the killer, who proceeds to stalk the boy for seventy-three nail-biting minutes.

An impressionable five-year-old at the time, I experienced three reactions from viewing the film. (1)It scared the pants off me; (2) it triggered a lifelong love of movies; and (3) it made me realize, even at such a young age, that films of relentless, edge-of-your-seat tension and suspense were very much my cup of tea.

And that's what this book is about: thrillers, the cinema of tension and suspense—sensations that people go out of their way to avoid in real life, but have sought out at the movies virtually from the day the medium was born.

People have long enjoyed a good thriller, a generic term born in England where the genre first gained critical as well as popular acceptance as a legitimate literary—and cinematic—art form. Not until relatively recently, however, has the thriller gained similar respect in the United States, where critics have often tended to dismiss the thriller as little more than popular light entertainment, or, at worst, *pulp*. For example, in Great Britain—and Europe—the thrillers of James M. Cain and Jim Thompson have long been appreciated as works of literature, not just popular fiction. In the United States, however, Cain didn't begin to earn critical accolades until the 1970s, during the last years of his life. And the prolific Thompson, who began writing in the 1950s and died in 1979, is only now being hailed as a premier American writer of "serious" not just "hard-boiled" fiction. In the cinema, Alfred Hitchcock, whose career began in the late 1920s, suffered the same experience. Always appreciated in his native England—and Europe—as a serious film artist as well as a slick commercial entertainer, he began to gain critical respect in America only in the 1960s.

In Britain, Europe, and America, there has always been a tendency to use the term thriller quite loosely. It has been applied to everything from the cozy mysteries of Agatha Christie to the cerebral spy yarns of John Le Carré. With all respect to the late Dame Agatha and Mr. Le Carré, however, their works are not "thrillers" in the sense that I define the term. What separates the genuine thriller from a novel or film with the odd suspenseful moment or two is the thriller's singleminded purpose, which is to put the reader or audience on edge and keep them there. In short, the thriller, regardless of whatever thematic and other concerns it may have, is *about* tension. This tension usually arises from the situation into which the characters have been placed—an escape, or dangerous mission, for example—which spurs even more tension as the characters come into conflict with each other or with themselves as the situation reaches critical mass. In other words, the tension in these films is *relentless*—and the reader or audience usually feels it from first page or frame to last.

In cinematic terms, there is also a tendency to link the thriller exclusively with the "crime film." While it is true that many thrillers do fall into the crime film genre, the unique quality of the movie thriller, like its literary counterpart, is its capacity to assume the shape of any genre it wants to. A war film can be a thriller. A Western can be a thriller. And, as Alfred Hitchcock demonstrated time after time, even a romantic comedy can be a thriller. This chameleon aspect of the thriller probably accounts for the reason why thrillers not only have enjoyed great popularity with audiences, but also appeal to very broad demographics within those audiences. In short, they're loved by young and old. As proof of this, more than a few of the films discussed in this book rank among the most financially successful ever made.

A student of such films, I have probed the archives of my memory (and film history) and selected fifty of the most suspenseful, often times nerve-racking, thrillers ever made—which, through this book, I would like to share with you. These are, to my mind, the *best*. These are for the connoisseur: the film fan who truly likes to be put through the wringer.

The selected titles fall into my definition and application of the term thriller. They represent many different kinds of thrillers from many different nations throughout the whole of film history. There are political thrillers like *Twilight's Last Gleaming*, *The China Syndrome*, and *All The President's Men*—the latter a remarkable one that deals with a subject about which most audiences are very familiar, the notorious Watergate break-in and the fall of President Richard Nixon, yet still manages to keep you guessing and on

Ted Tetzlaff's The Window *(1949).*   *Alfred Hitchcock's* Strangers on a Train *(1951).*

Alfred Hitchcock's Rear Window *(1954).*

Robert Aldrich's Kiss Me Deadly *(1955).*

John Boorman's Deliverance *(1972).*

Richard Sale's Abandon Ship! *(1957).*

Dustin Hoffman as Washington Post *reporter Carl Bernstein in Alan J. Pakula's* All the President's Men *(1976).*

Robert Aldrich's Twilight's Last Gleaming *(1977).*

the edge of your seat. There are psychological thrillers like *Night of the Hunter* and *Cape Fear*. There are espionage thrillers like *Orders to Kill* and *Operation Crossbow*. There are crime thrillers like *Rififi, Cash on Demand, Charley Varrick*, and *The Long Good Friday*. And there are thrillers that chillingly foreshadowed real life events such as *The Manchurian Candidate* and *Suddenly*, two super-tense dramas about political assassination.

The reader will quickly note the absence of such films, for example, as *Psycho* and *Jaws*. As tension-filled as these films undeniably are, I consider them as belonging more clearly to that other cinematic genre of tension and suspense: the horror film. I have also tried not to overload the book with Hitchcock films for a similar reason. The master of suspense is virtually a genre unto himself. His classic thrillers could easily fill this entire book, leaving very little space for the inclusion of others equally deserving of mention. Nevertheless, no book about screen thrillers could possibly be complete without acknowledging the work of Hitchcock, who is represented herein by the four I consider to be his best.

And now, on to the entire fifty. Enjoy!

Michael Anderson's Operation Crossbow *(1965).*

SPARROWS

(1926)

United Artists • B&W/87 Minutes

CREDITS

Director: William Beaudine; *Producer*: Mary Pickford; *Screenplay*: C. Gardner Sullivan; *Cinematographers*: Charles Rosher, Karl Struss, Hal Mohr; *Editor*: Harald McClernan; *Art Director*: Harry Oliver.

CAST

Mama Mollie: Mary Pickford; *Grimes*: Gustav von Seyffertitz; *Richard Wayne*: Roy Stewart; *Doris Wayne*: Mary Louise Miller; *Ambrose Grimes*: Spec O'Donnell; *Splutters*: Monty O'Grady; *The Children*: Muriel Mac-Cormac, Billy 'Red' Jones, Camilla Johnson, Mary McLane, Billy Butts, Jack Lavine, Florence Rogan, Sylvia Bernard, Seesel Ann Johnson.

* * *

William K. Everson calls it a horror film. Other film historians and contemporary critics call it a backwoods melodrama with Dickensian overtones, while reviewers and audiences of the day saw it as a heavy drama laced with moments of comic relief. *Sparrows* is, indeed, all of these things. But first and foremost, it is a taut and exciting tale of entrapment, escape and pursuit—in other words, a thriller.

Made for her own company during the latter days of her career, *Sparrows* was not a big box office success for the legendary Mary Pickford, the world's first international movie star. Pickford, or "Little Mary" and "America's Sweetheart" as she was called, specialized in comedies in which she played a rambunctious child or young girl, a role she succeeded in well into her thirties due to her diminutive stature, her youthful looks, and, of course, the lighting skills of her cameramen (she always hired the best). In *Sparrows,* she played a young girl also; otherwise, the film was unlike anything else she ever made. A stark and sometimes terrifying assault on the audience's nerve ends interrupted only occasionally by the bits of

Backwoods melodrama with Dickensian overtones and exciting tale of entrapment, escape and pursuit—Mary Pickford and Gustav von Seyffertitz in the silent thriller Sparrows.

Grimes (Gustav von Seyffertitz) tells Mama Mollie (Mary Pickford) to hand over the kidnapped Wayne baby.

Mollie (Mary Pickford) thwarts Grimes's plans by taking the baby and the children and fleeing with them into the treacherous swamp.

Grimes's obnoxious stepson, Ambrose (Spec O'Donnell), is always teasing Mollie (Mary Pickford) and her orphaned charges [a.k.a. ''sparrows.'']

Mollie (Mary Pickford) gets even with Ambrose (Spec O'Donnell), but Grimes catches her in the act and punishes her and the children by sending them to bed without supper.

Eventually, Mollie (Mary Pickford) and the children find their way to the safety of a launch, where they are rescued by police.

comic business Pickford's audiences expected from her, *Sparrows* did make money for her and United Artists. But it did not pack in the crowds her movies usually drew, and, as a result, she never attempted such a film again. To the end of her days, in fact, she considered *Sparrows* to be a "major miscalculation."

Though Pickford or her estate covetously held onto the rights of most of her films, *Sparrows* was allowed to fall into the public domain. As a result, it has become one of her most frequently screened efforts—even on television—and the one Pickford film with which audiences of today are most familiar. Largely because of this, its stature and popularity have deservedly grown over the years and *Sparrows* has become one of the silent cinema's most enduring films.

Pickford plays "Mama" Mollie, the eldest of several orphans held prisoner and strenuously overworked on a farm run by the grotesque, Dickensian figure of Mr. Grimes. Surrounded by quicksand and alligator infested swampland, the isolated farm is virtually impenetrable and seemingly escape-proof. As the film opens, Mollie and her charges have lofted a kite with a message scrawled on it requesting that someone come and rescue them. But the kite gets caught in the trees and is destroyed.

Another farmer arrives to trade with Grimes and a warning bell is rung signaling Mollie and the children to get out of sight and hide in the barn. Grimes's obnoxious stepson, Ambrose, teasingly prevents one of the children, Splutters, from hiding with the others, and the boy is discovered by the visiting farmer. Grimes glibly explains away the boy's presence, and the farmer, who needs an extra hand to dig potatoes, offers to buy the lad. As Splutters is taken away, he turns and sees the hands of the other children waving goodbye to him through the cracked boards of the barn.

Mollie gets even with Ambrose for what he did to Splutters, but Grimes catches her in the act and punishes her and the children by sending them to bed in the barn without supper. That night, the youngest of the children, a sickly toddler named Amy, dies in Mollie's arms. In addition to being its most moving scene, this sequence is also the film's most technically ingenious, being brought off in a single take with no obvious cuts or process work. As Mollie drifts off to sleep reading to the ailing child from the Bible, a wall of the barn miraculously fades away to a view of a field and the figure of Jesus, who steps into the barn, takes the child from Mollie. He then returns to the field as the wall rematerializes behind him. The camera then cuts to a close-up of Pickford's expressive face as she awakens, looks down, and realizes with sudden horror and grief that the offscreen baby in her arms is dead.

His financial situation desperate, Grimes falls in with a cutthroat named Bailey to kidnap the baby of a wealthy man named Wayne and hide the child at the farm until Bailey collects the ransom money. The details of the kidnapping scene eerily foreshadow the real-life Lindbergh case of some six years later as the camera cuts to the upstairs floor of Wayne's expensive home on a rainy night and the nurse finds an open window of the nursery with the top of a ladder sticking through and the baby's crib empty. A subsequent shot of a newspaper with the banner headline "Net Heightens in Wayne Baby Search" reveals a family photo of Wayne holding the blond, curly-haired toddler, who, although a baby girl and not a boy, is the spitting image of the Lindbergh child!

As the hunt for the baby widens, Grimes grows convinced that the ransom will not be paid and that the authorities will find their way to his doorstep—which they eventually do when their canvassing of the neighborhood turns up Splutters, who informs them about Grimes's illegal "baby farm." Grimes decides to kill the kidnapped girl and bury her body in quicksand. Mollie, however, thwarts his plans by taking the baby and the other children and fleeing with them into the treacherous swamp; Grimes, his bloodhound, and the kidnappers follow in pursuit. This perilous chase lasts approximately twenty minutes and contains one of the silent cinema's most famous sequences in which Mollie and her charges must crawl across an overhanging tree limb to get by a nest of alligators, the limb cracking and threatening to give way at any second. (The impact of this hair-raising scene is still considerable in that it was staged without recourse to special effects.)

Eventually, Mollie and the children find their way to the safety of a launch and stow away below, not realizing that the vessel belongs to the kidnappers, who arrive moments later and hastily disembark while being shot at by police in a pursuing launch. Scuttling their craft, the kidnappers try to sneak away in a lifeboat but are drowned when the police launch accidentally rams it in the dark. Mollie and her charges appear on deck and are rescued. But when the kidnapped baby is returned to her father, she longs for the caring arms of her "Mama" Mollie, and Wayne winds up taking in Mollie and all the other orphans, including Splutters.

Regardless of whatever reservations Mary Pickford may have had about the film, *Sparrows* remains a classic suspense thriller of the silent era and the high water mark in the career of its talented director, William Beaudine. Beaudine went on to become one of the talkies' most prolific directors of low budget grade "B" (and "Z") shlock, and never quite managed to fulfill the promise he showed here.

SUBMARINE

(1928)

Columbia Pictures • B&W/91 Minutes

CREDITS

Director: Frank R. Capra; *Producer*: Harry Cohn; *Writers*: Norman Springer and Dorothy Howell; *Cinematographer*: Joseph Walker; *Editor*: Ben Pivar; *Art Director*: Harrison Wiley.

CAST

Jack Dorgan: Jack Holt; *Bob Mason*: Ralph Graves; *"Snuggles"*: Dorothy Revier; *S-44 Captain*: Clarence Burton; *S-44 Crew Member*: Arthur Rankin.

* * *

Submarine put director Frank Capra (here billing himself as Frank *R.* Capra) on top in Hollywood. Prior to it, Capra wrote in his autobiography, "I had directed five cheapies for Columbia in seven months; a turkey called *For the Love of Mike*; and two [Harry] Langdon comedies, which Langdon clouded by telling the world he directed himself." It also pushed Harry Cohn's struggling "poverty row" studio Columbia into the big leagues alongside such established majors as MGM and Paramount.

According to Capra, the film cost $150,000 to make, a figure roughly five times that of the average Columbia picture. Every step of the way, Cohn held his breath (if not his tongue), fearing that his faith in Capra—whom Cohn had given free reign after dismissing the previous director, Irvin Willat, an established Hollywood professional with many "A" pictures to his credit—would prove ill-placed and that the final product would sink the studio's fortunes lower than the vehicle of the title.

Released in the closing days of the silents with an accompanying music and sound effects track on disc (a first for a Columbia picture), *Submarine* proved to be a megahit, boosting the fortunes of not only its studio and director but its two stars, Jack Holt and Ralph Graves, as well. They became major box office after this film and were frequently teamed on screen from then on.

Capra's silents and early talkies were markedly different from his later sound era films (*Mr. Smith Goes to Washington*, *It's a Wonderful Life*, et al.). Even the comedies were more cinematic, action-filled, and suspenseful, though, in many ways, no less "Capra-corny." It was a toss-up whether to include *Submarine* in this book or one of Capra's subsequent talkies with Holt and Graves, *Flight* (1929) and *Dirigible* (1931),

Navy divers Dorgan (Jack Holt, right) and Mason (Ralph Graves) play as hard as they work with Dorgan accusing his friend of always trying to steal his girl.

Swept off his feet by any girl who gives him the time of day, Dorgan (Jack Holt) marries the beautiful but faithless "Snuggles" (Dorothy Revier).

both of which are just as suspenseful (especially *Dirigible*) and in many ways slicker films. I opted for *Submarine* for two reasons: (1) I wanted some silents to be represented in this book about movie thrillers, and (2) the suspense in *Submarine* is a lot more concentrated than in *Flight* or *Dirigible*. Both of these later films conclude with tense and exciting rescue sequences, but they are relatively brief compared to the one in *Submarine*, which takes up more than a third of its running time and glued audiences of the day to their seats. This sequence and the overall film may not seem like much compared to something like the contemporary *Das Boot*. But for the moment, let's propel ourselves back in time and imagine that we're moviegoers in the age of innocence, a time when audiences were not accustomed to being put through the wringer quite as relentlessly as Capra does here.

Dorgan and Mason are navy men assigned to a sweeper in the Philippines. Their job is to pinpoint and destroy dangerous underwater wrecks. The film opens with some vivid underwater shots—many of them tight, claustrophobic close-ups—of Dorgan at-

taching a floating marker to a submerged wreck so that Mason's demolition team can accurately locate it and mine it from above. Back on board, Dorgan, who has a reputation for being able to dive deeper than any of his cohorts, strips off his bulky outfit and watches as Mason drops the mine. The rope attached to the mine tangles around Dorgan's foot and he is accidentally pulled overboard. Unable to free himself from the explosive's line, Dorgan is dragged precariously close to the wreck. But Mason jumps in after him and cuts him loose, and they return to the surface just as the mine explodes.

Back in port, Dorgan and Mason play as hard as they work, with Dorgan jokingly accusing his friend of always trying to steal his girls. Mason responds that he has to or Dorgan would wind up making a fool of himself by marrying one of them. The two ship out to San Diego where Dorgan continues his diving chores and Mason is transferred to S-44 submarine duty. On his own now, Dorgan meets an attractive dancehall dame at a local nightspot, the Palais Ballroom. He calls her Snuggles and she calls him Big Boy, her term

While Dorgan is away at sea, "Snuggles" (Dorothy Revier) launches into an affair with Mason (Ralph Graves), who has no idea she's married to his friend.

of endearment for all the guys. True to Mason's words, Dorgan is swept off his feet and weds her. Married life proves to be a bore for Snuggles, however, and when Dorgan ships out for a week on a diving job, she removes her wedding ring and heads back to the Palais Ballroom where she catches the eye of Mason, whose submarine has just returned to port. She and her new Big Boy engage in an affair (Capra nicely intercuts shots of the two of them frolicking in the surf with others of Dorgan going about his tense, solitary duty beneath the sea). Then, knowing that Dorgan is scheduled to return, Snuggles gives Mason the bum's rush.

Mason catches up with his old friend and suggests a night on the town. But Dorgan says he's married now and takes Mason home to meet the wife. Mason and Snuggles are shocked to see one another, but they play it cool until Dorgan is unexpectedly called away. Then Mason slaps her for two-timing his best friend and leading him on as well. As Snuggles begins to sob, Mason apologizes and tries to comfort her. Dorgan returns and sees them embracing. Encouraged by

Snuggles to believe that Mason had come on to her, Dorgan accuses his friend of once more trying to steal his girl and orders him out of the house and his life. Knowing that the truth would hurt Dorgan more, Mason keeps silent and leaves, their friendship permanently ruptured.

Back at sea, Mason's sub is struck by a destroyer during some smoke screen exercises. The control room is flooded and fills with battery gas, and the men are forced to seal themselves inside a small compartment as the sub sinks to the bottom, a depth of four-hundred feet. Unable to mount a rescue operation, the navy's only alternative is to send down a diver with an air hose, but the maximum depth their divers have ever managed to descend and live is two-hundred-fifty feet. One attempts the feat, and fails.

With only three oxygen tanks to sustain them, the sub's captain doles out the precious air to his crew every thirty minutes. Eventually, the generator lights flicker out and the terrified men are left in darkness. Now down to one oxygen tank, they begin to suffocate and hallucinate. The captain starts counting out

Mason (Ralph Graves) angrily confronts the two-timing "Snuggles" (Dorothy Revier).

Mason (Ralph Graves), the Captain (Clarence Burton), and crew await their doom in the sunken submarine.

bullets so that each man can commit suicide if he wishes.

Not unaware of the sub's plight, Dorgan struggles with his feelings about going to his former friend's aid, and with his conscience, of course; after all, the lives of many other men are at stake as well. Impatient with his indecision and their boring stay-at-home life together, Snuggles makes up his mind for him by dolling up for a night out at the Palais Ballroom and inadvertently revealing her former unfaithfulness to Dorgan in the process. Dorgan gives her the gate, flies to the wreck, succeeds in making the difficult dive,

and rescues the crew by attaching an air hose to the compartment with only minutes to spare.

The sub is raised and Dorgan and Mason resume their friendship sans Snuggles, who is last seen at the Palais Ballroom picking up another sucker in uniform. The film ends with Mason grinning at his pal as they arrive at another port and remarking facetiously, "Where do we go from here, *Big Boy*?"

Submarine was remade in 1937 by director Erle C. Kenton as *Devil's Playground*, with Richard Dix and Chester Morris fighting over Dolores Del Rio.

TERROR ABOARD

(1933)

Paramount Pictures • B&W/69 Minutes

CREDITS

Director: Paul Sloane; *Producer*: William LeBaron; *Screenplay*: Harvey Thew, Manuel Seff; *Cinematographer*: Harry Fischbeck; *Editor*: Eda Warren.

CAST

Blackie: Charlie Ruggles; *Maximillian Kreig*: John Halliday; *James Cowles*: Neil Hamilton; *Lili Kingston*: Shirley Grey; *Gregory Cordoff*: Jack LaRue; *Millicent Hazlitt*: Verree Teasdale; *Captain Swanson*: Stanley Fields; *Yacht Captain*: Thomas Jackson; *Radio Operator*: William Janney.

* * *

I'll admit that today's moviegoers are not likely to find the obscure 1933 thriller *Terror Aboard* as taut and gripping an experience as audiences of the time; in some respects, it's quite dated. At the same time, it's also remarkably modern, boasting a powerful sense of atmosphere with a plot that's unusual enough to keep even contemporary filmgoers hooked to the very end. It has, additionally, an urbane villain of almost contemporary sociopathic deviousness and viciousness, not to mention a scorecard of "creative deaths" that comes close to matching the mayhem on modern day screens.

The film's abundant mayhem, in fact, prompted many early thirties critics to cast aspersions on the integrity of the studio that produced the film, Paramount (which, forty-seven years later, would be similarly attacked for launching the high body count *Friday the 13th* series), and consign *Terror Aboard* to the cinematic dung heap. For example, here's what P.S. Harrison, publisher of a thirties film guide called *Harrison's Reports*, had to say about *Terror Aboard*: "It should sicken even the most morbid follower of horror melodramas, for there is one killing after another. One man is poisoned; another is shot; a woman is shoved into a refrigerator; a man is incited into killing another one and then himself; still another is stabbed; and as a final stroke of homicidal genius, a boatload of sailors are thrown into the sea and drowned."

In this scathing critique, Harrison neglects to catalog the film's most graphic moment of cinematic carnage when the villain plugs the boat's unsuspecting radio man and the camera lingers on the uncomprehending victim as he sags agonizingly into a chair to watch his life's blood seep from the bullet hole in his chest until the front of his coat is soaked. That scene must surely have wowed audiences of the time for it has a considerable impact even today.

As a result of all this ghoulishness, *Terror Aboard* is often considered to be a horror film—*Harrison's Reports* says as much—but it's really much more of a suspense thriller and mystery whose script looks forward to Agatha Christie's definitive body count suspenser *Ten Little Indians* (which was published in 1939 and made into the classic *And Then There Were None* in 1945) and borrows its mysterioso structure, bizarrely enough, from the ever-popular Foreign Legion adventure tale *Beau Geste* (filmed by Paramount in 1926 and again in 1939).

A brilliantly shot sequence of the freighter *City of Hope* cutting through a fog opens the film, the camera moving sinuously across the ship's bow and along its passageways, various crew members flitting in and out of the shadows like apparitions. A ship's bell announces another vessel, suddenly spotted off the bow, its cabin lights barely piercing the fog. Captain Swanson signals the ghostly vessel, whose engine is running, but there is no response. The superstitious crew speculates as to whether it might be the legendary *Flying Dutchman* (the equally legendary *Mary Celeste* is called to mind by this sequence as well), but as his freighter draws closer, Swanson sees that the vessel is actually a yacht named *Dulcina*. He keeps up with it all night, and in the morning, he, the freighter's doctor, and several crew members lower away to investigate.

Swanson sends one man aboard. When the crewman fails to reappear, the concerned captain and the others board the yacht as well. As they do, an unidentified man jumps overboard from the opposite side. They find their missing crew member on the deck with his head bashed in, and investigating further, they encounter the frozen body of a female passenger lying in a passageway and the corpse of yet

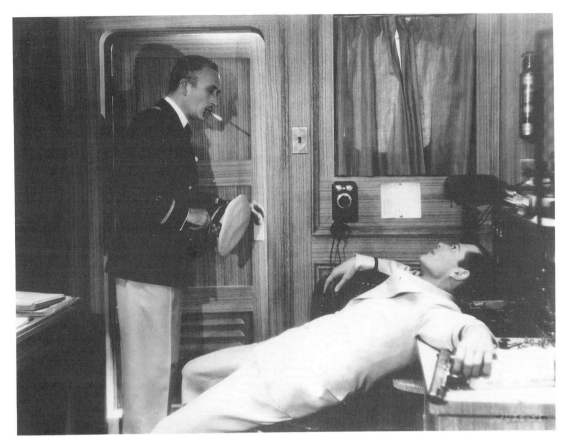

Informed that he is bankrupt and about to be indicted for larceny, Kreig (John Halliday) cooks up a plan to kill everyone on board his yacht, then scuttle the craft and disappear to an island paradise. His first victim is the radio operator (William Janney) who gave him the message.

Kreig's (John Halliday) ingenuity is unbounded. He kills the cook, who unknowingly holds the secret to who's committing the murders, by poisoning his bowl of soup, then asking that it be sampled because it "tastes funny." The cook does, dies, and everyone thinks the poisoned soup was meant for Kreig. From left: Neil Hamilton, Shirley Grey, Charlie Ruggles, Jack LaRue (back to camera), and Paul Porcasi as the chef.

Victims galore. Left to right: Jack LaRue, Thomas Jackson, and Verree Teasdale are all at the mercy of John Halliday in Terror Aboard.

another victim hanging in his stateroom. Smoke billows unexpectedly from the thundering engine room and they realize the yacht is doomed. Before abandoning it, however, Swanson and the doctor come upon a torn radiogram addressed to the yacht's wealthy owner, Maximillian Kreig. As they begin to read it, the camera cuts to a close-up of the message and then back to Kreig himself studying the same message as the radio operator who has just given it to him stands idly by. This revolutionary use of the "jump cut" (here flashing us back rather than forward in time) predates Orson Welles's celebrated "innovation" of the technique in *Citizen Kane* by a full eight years—and the French nouvelle vague directors' (Godard, et al.) touted experiments with it by decades!

In terms of cinematic inventiveness, the film's direction and editing become fairly routine after this—at least until the conclusion when, rather than jumping us forward again in time, the opening scenes are repeated (a la *Beau Geste*), though from a different perspective. But like *Beau Geste* also, the mystery as to how the yacht and its passengers got into their present state—and who the man was who jumped overboard—is compelling enough to keep us transfixed

without recourse to cinematic tricks.

The radiogram informs Kreig that he is now bankrupt and about to be indicted for larceny. This turn of events places the millionaire in immediate jeopardy and threatens his plans to entice one of his passengers, Lili Kingston—an apparent golddigger who has jilted her flyer fiancé, Jim Cowles, for Kreig—by promising her great wealth. So, he comes up with an alternate scheme: scuttle the craft and disappear to an island paradise with Lili. To do this, he must first get rid of everyone on board—captain, crew, and passengers alike. He starts out by shooting the radio operator who took the message. When the man's body is discovered, the devious Kreig spearheads the murder investigation himself, fomenting suspicion everywhere. He discovers that two of his passengers, Millicent Hazlitt and Gregory Cordoff, are having a flirtation; informs the jealous Mr. Hazlitt; suggests to Cordoff that the potentially violent Hazlitt may beat Millicent for her infidelity; then sits back to watch. Hazlitt and Cordoff come to blows and Hazlitt is killed. When Millicent confronts Kreig in private about having engineered the tragedy, he shoves her into a meat locker where she freezes to death, and later informs Cordoff that she committed suicide. His

Krieg's plans are interrupted by the unexpected arrival of Lily's jilted fiancé (Neil Hamilton) who is welcomed aboard by the cowardly steward (Charlie Ruggles).

Lili (Shirley Grey) and Cowles (Neil Hamilton) take refuge from the murderous Kreig in the yacht's boiler room.

lover now gone and he facing a jail term for the accidental murder of her husband, the despairing Cordoff hangs himself.

Kreig encounters a momentary inconvenience with the unexpected arrival of Lili's jilted fiancé, Cowles, who has been following the yacht in his plane, and crashed when he ran out of gas. Fishing Cowles out of the sea, Kreig promptly adds him to the death list. Kreig's ingenuity is unbounded. He kills the cook, who unknowingly holds the secret to who could have done in Millicent, by poisoning his own bowl of soup at dinner and telling the cook it tastes bad. The offended cook samples it, keels over dead, and everyone at the table assumes the deadly poison was meant for Kreig himself. When the maid discovers the vial of poison in Kreig's cabin, he pushes her overboard, unaware that the captain has witnessed the murder. The captain confronts him and, in a particularly grisly scene, is skewered on a sharp paper holder. The nervous crew decides to jump ship before the phantom killer gets to them. Anticipating this, Kreig has tampered with the lifeboat's ropes so that it crashes into the sea and the men are drowned. He also shoots one of them for good measure. Lili sees him do it and tells Cowles, and the two take refuge in the engine room as the fog rolls in and Kreig prowls the yacht in search of them.

Flash forward: The *City of Hope* encounters the ghostly vessel, and, come morning, Captain Swanson and his crew go to investigate. Kreig kills the man Swanson sends aboard, locates Lili and Cowles in the engine room, fires several shots into the machinery to start a blaze, then hops overboard to swim toward his island getaway. Lili, Cowles, and the yacht's steward, Blackie, are rescued as the vessel goes down, and Kreig gets his just desserts when he's eaten by a shark.

Terror Aboard is a good and sometimes surprising little thriller that moves along at a snappy pace and rivets the attention all the way. It does have some major deficiencies, however. Charlie Ruggles's comic relief bits as the cowardly steward are not very funny and grow quite tiresome after awhile—a liability suffered by Paramount's follow up to *Terror Aboard*, the equally ghoulish but less stylish *Murders in the Zoo*, which featured Ruggles in a similar role. And Neil Hamilton, who costarred in the silent *Beau Geste* and then went on to become one of the talkies' dreariest leading men, makes a very bland hero, delivering his lines with all the emotion of someone giving dictation. But John Halliday's urbane, witty, and almost-always-in-control Kreig more than makes up for them. His subtle shiver of cold and distaste after he shoves Millicent in the freezer is funnier than anything Ruggles does.

THE 39 STEPS

(1935)

Gaumont-British • B&W/81 Minutes

CREDITS

Director: Alfred Hitchcock; *Producer*: Michael Balcon; *Screenplay and Adaptation*: Charles Bennett and Alma Reville, based on the novel by John Buchan; *Cinematographer*: Bernard Knowles; *Editor*: Derek N. Twist; *Music*: Louis Levy; *Art Direction and Sets*: Otto Werndorff and Albert Jullion.

CAST

Richard Hannay: Robert Donat; *Pamela*: Madeleine Carroll; *Annabella Smith*: Lucie Mannheim; *Professor Jordan*: Godfrey Tearle; *Crofter's wife*: Peggy Ashcroft; *Crofter*: John Laurie; *Mrs. Jordan*: Helen Haye; *Mr. Memory*: Wylie Watson.

* * *

The classic forerunner of all modern day spy thrillers, John Buchan's 1915 tale of espionage on the eve of World War One, *The Thirty-Nine Steps,* is nevertheless a rather dull and lifeless work full of uninteresting characters—especially when compared to the fast-paced and delightfully performed film Alfred Hitchcock made from it. The probable reason the film version is so superior (even Buchan himself believed it to be an improvement) is that Hitchcock and his scenarists (one his wife) decided to retain only those aspects of the book which appealed to them strongly in terms of plot and cinematic possibilities. Obviously these aspects were few and far between for the film they turned out was practically a whole new work.

There's no point in cataloging all the differences between the book and the film, but the decision by the director to eliminate one major sequence from the book still surprises me because the sequence is so typically Hitchcockian. By choosing to scrap it, Hitchcock even altered the meaning of the title. In the film, the title refers to the code name of a nest of spies determined to deliver a vital British military secret into the hands of a foreign government. It works, as does the exciting substitute finale Hitchcock and his writers concocted to explain it. Nevertheless, the finale in the book where Buchan reveals *his* explanation of "the thirty-nine steps" is just as exciting, and, ironically, one that Hitchcock would borrow from and rework in future films. Indeed, he'd already used a similar idea for the suspenseful British Museum climax to his 1929 talkie *Blackmail,* and the Albert Hall sequence in his 1934 version of *The Man Who Knew Too Much* is in much the same vein.

In the book, "the thirty-nine steps" refers to the number of steps leading to the clock tower of Big Ben, where Prussian agents have planted a massive bomb timed to blow up the clock and nearby Parliament at a certain hour, thereby launching World War One. The job of foiling the scheme falls to visiting Canadian rancher Richard Hannay, who unwittingly learns some details of the conspiracy from a British agent who is later murdered in Hannay's apartment. Pursued by the police and foreign agents, Hannay flees to Scotland to unravel the mystery and clear his name. He winds up back in London atop the clock tower of Big Ben battling with enemy agents to defuse the bomb in the nick of time. In the end, he saves the day, is absolved of guilt, and the war is launched by other means. In Don Sharp's enjoyable 1980 version, the most faithful to Buchan's novel so far, the Big Ben finale is retained and suspensefully embellished by having various villains plunge to their deaths from the clock tower and hero Hannay (here played by Robert Powell) dangling from the clock's giant minute hand, its every tick threatening to send him hurtling to the street below. (Ralph Thomas's 1959 version starring Kenneth More is an outright remake—in color—of the Hitchcock classic instead, and is quite entertaining in its own right, though by no means on a par with the original.) This image of the hero fighting the bad guys for his life atop a familiar landmark is certainly Hitchcockian. It's something he could obviously have done great things with in his own version of *The 39 Steps,* and one can only wonder why he chose not to use it. Perhaps Hitchcock thought it might remind too many viewers of Harold Lloyd's silent comedy, *Safety Last,* and produce more giggles than gasps. Or perhaps he just decided to let the concept simmer in his mind over the years until he'd found a way to improve upon it, which he later did in

With his version of The 39 Steps, Hitchcock not only
reinvented John Buchan's dull spy novel, he revitalized the
almost as dull British cinema as well.

Handcuffed together, Pamela (Madeleine Carroll) and Hannay (Robert Donat) flee across the Scottish moors.

Critics and audiences loved—and continue to love—the film's sophisticated bantering between Robert Donat's urbane Hannay, the definitive Hitchcockian innocent-man-pursued, and Madeleine Carroll, the prototypical Hitchcock ice-cool blonde. Helen Haye is their host here.

Remarkably undated, Alfred Hitchcock's The 39 Steps *has lost none of its power to entertain. It remains the archetype of all such thrillers made by Hitchcock and everyone else ever since.*

such films as *Saboteur, Foreign Correspondent* and, especially, *North by Northwest,* all of them variations on *The 39 Steps.*

With *The 39 Steps,* Hitchcock not only reinvented Buchan's dull novel, but revitalized the almost-as-dull British cinema as well. Although he was already beginning to top a very short list of outstanding British filmmakers due to such successes as *The Lodger, Blackmail, Murder,* and *The Man Who Knew Too Much,* the film that pushed him over the top was *The 39 Steps.* In terms of style, wit, pacing, technical virtuosity, and, of course, thrills and suspense, it was miles ahead of anything he'd yet done. Even his most recent film and biggest critical and commercial hit so far, *The Man Who Knew Too Much,* seemed like a much earlier and creakier work by comparision—its justly celebrated and cinematically skillful Albert Hall sequence notwithstanding. And compared to the stodgy films being turned out by most of his British colleagues at the time, *The 39 Steps* sparkled like those then being made in Hollywood by people like Ernst Lubitsch and James Whale. Clearly, the master of suspense already had his sights set on Hollywood—if only to import its more zestful style of filmmaking to

his home turf.

The 39 Steps was a huge personal and professional success for Hitchcock. It cemented his reputation at home while firmly establishing it abroad as well. The film also crystalized many of the themes and techniques he'd been playing with hit-and-miss previously into a unified whole. Critics and audiences loved—and continue to love—its exhilarating mixture of intrigue and hair-breadth escapes, its large doses of suspense splashed with delightful bits of sly humor, and the sophisticated bantering between Robert Donat's urbane Hannay, the definitive Hitchcockian innocent man pursued, and Madeleine Carroll, the prototypical ice-cool Hitchcock blonde to whom Hannay is ceremoniously but inconveniently handcuffed for most of his adventure.

Compared to some of the equally classic Hitchcock thrillers of more recent vintage, *The 39 Steps* may have lost some of its power over the years to keep modern audiences on the edges of their seats, but it remains remarkably undated and has lost none of its power to entertain them. It's still a delicious romantic comedy thriller—and the archetype of all such thrillers made by Hitchcock and everyone else ever since.

FURY

(1936)

Metro-Goldwyn-Mayer • B&W/94 Minutes

CREDITS

Director: Fritz Lang; *Producer*: Joseph L. Mankiewicz; *Screenplay*: Fritz Lang and Bartlett Cormack, based on the story "Mob Rule" by Norman Krasna; *Cinematographer*: Joseph Ruttenberg; *Editor*: Frank Sullivan; *Music*: Franz Waxman; *Art Director*: Cedric Gibbons.

CAST

Joe Wilson: Spencer Tracy; *Katherine Grant*: Sylvia Sidney; *District Attorney*: Walter Abel; *Kirby Dawson*: Bruce Cabot; *Sheriff*: Edward Ellis; *Bugs Meyers*: Walter Brennan; *Charlie Wheeler*: Frank Albertson; *Tom Wheeler*: George Walcott.

* * *

Sit in on a conversation among film snobs long enough and it is inevitable you'll hear one (or all) of the following arguments fervently expressed: (1) That Orson Welles's *The Magnificent Ambersons*, even in its mutilated form, is a far better film than *Citizen Kane*; (2) that Alfred Hitchcock's Hollywood films are more patently commercial and less innovative and vital than his early British ones; and (3) that Hollywood ruined the career of director Fritz Lang. I've never agreed with any of these statements, but the last has always rankled me especially, for while I have the greatest regard for such highly expressive and personal Lang films as *Metropolis* and *M*, I believe his work in Hollywood, the bulk of his output, was, on the whole, just as expressive, personal, and cinematically skillful as his work in Germany, and considerably better acted (*M* being a notable exception.)

It is true that Lang's Hollywood films lack the epic sweep of much of his early work in Germany. But they are also devoid of the one quality which even Lang's strongest German film supporters agree gets in the way of appreciating much of his non-Hollywood work: namely, heavy-handedness. Because of their heavy-handedness, Lang's *Dr. Mabuse, Metropolis, Spione,* et al., as cinematically dazzling as they are, can be fairly rough sledding for audiences of today,

Everyman Joe Wilson (Spencer Tracy), whose belief in American justice and the ethic that hard work leads to safety, security, and success—The American Dream—will be put to the test in Fury.

particularly American ones. In contrast, Lang's Hollywood films are less fraught with overt symbolism, are acted with a lighter touch, and move along at the brisk pace audiences expect of American movies. The truth is that the filmmaking styles of the German and Hollywood studios were very different—unlike today where the influence of the American style of moviemaking has become somewhat all-pervasive. Lang simply adapted himself to both. Take a look at his post-Hollywood German films in the the sixties (*The 1,000 Eyes of Dr. Mabuse,* et al.). Despite his years of working in America, they seem not at all like Hollywood films, but resemble his German ones of the twenties and early thirties to a T.

In two respects, however, Lang's American films are no different at all from his German ones. One is thematic consistency (Lang may have had to adapt his style to suit Hollywood, but he continued to choose his themes to suit himself). The other is his choice of genre, for the bulk of Lang's German and American

Arrested by small-town deputy Bugs Mayers (Walter Brennan, left) as the man responsible for a sensational kidnapping in the area, Joe (Spencer Tracy) is locked up by the sheriff (Edward Ellis, seated) and held for questioning by the district attorney.

Spurred on by loudmouthed layabout Kirby Dawson (Bruce Cabot, right), the citizenry whips itself into a fury, breaks into the prison, and takes the law into its own hands.

films are thrillers. In fact, Lang allied himself with the thriller genre so strongly and directed so many of the best that as a result, his, like Hitchcock's, is the name most likely to spring to mind whenever the subject of the movie thriller is mentioned—even though these two filmmakers' contributions to the genre are not very similar.

After fleeing Hitler's Germany, Lang made one film in France, then came to America to work for MGM. He wrote several scripts for the studio but none of them was ever produced. On the verge of being dropped from his contract, he came up with a copy of a Norman Krasna story called "Mob Rule" and urged the studio to let him do it as his American film debut. Fortuitously, producer Joseph L. Mankiewicz was already developing the property, retitled *Fury*, and agreed that Lang was the ideal choice to direct. Released in June of 1936, the controversial film was a critical and box office success and launched Lang's Hollywood career. Despite this, however, studio chief Louis B. Mayer hated *Fury* and let Lang go. The director didn't make another film for MGM until *Moonfleet* in 1954, by which time Mayer had been ousted as head of the studio.

Although Lang shares credit for writing the film, there remains much disagreement as to how much he actually contributed. If it's true (per Mankiewicz and others) that he contributed almost nothing, *Fury* was surely written with him in mind for its story has much in common with his pre-Hollywood work, particularly the *Dr. Mabuse* films and *M*, and reflects similar concerns about the dangers of "mob rule," something that was fast becoming the order of the day in his native Germany.

The film's main character, Joe Wilson, is an Everyman with a strong belief system in American justice

Released in June 1936, the controversial Fury *launched the Hollywood career of the great German filmmaker—and expert thrillermaker—Fritz Lang.*

"They lynched what mattered to me ... my liking people and having faith in them." Spencer Tracy as Joe Wilson in Fury.

and the ethic that hard work leads to safety, security and success, the American Dream. Engaged to Katherine Grant, he postpones their wedding for a year so that he and his brothers can build up a gas station business and he can put enough money aside for him and Katherine to get married. He achieves his goals and sets out in his car to fetch her, only to be stopped along the way by a small-town deputy, Bugs Meyers, who is convinced by circumstantial evidence that Joe is the man responsible for a recent kidnapping in the area. The sheriff locks up Joe for questioning by the district attorney and rumors begin to fly around town that the kidnapper has finally been captured. Spurred on by a loudmouthed layabout named Kirby Dawson, the citizenry whips itself into a fury and decides to take the law into its own hands. The police station is besieged and, despite the sheriff's attempts to keep the unreasoning mob at bay, the place is overrun and set afire. Alerted to the story, the newsreel boys arrive on the scene to film the carnage. Katherine, who has set out to locate her missing fiancé, passes through town at the same time, sees her beau in the window of the jail cell, and faints as the trapped man is presumably killed in the blaze.

Joe manages to escape, however, keeping the fact that he's still alive a secret from everyone, including the grief-stricken Katherine. His once trusting and naïve character now takes on diabolical shadings of Lang's manipulative Dr. Mabuse as he begins orchestrating a plan to bring the mobs' ringleaders to trial for murder—a crime which, like the one he'd been accused of, they actually did not commit. The townspeople, including the sheriff, stonewall the D.A.'s attempts to expose what happened that night by covering up for one another. Without a corpse—concrete evidence that Joe was even in the jail at the time—the D.A.'s case seems lost until the telltale newsreel is permitted to be shown in the courtroom and the eyewitness Katherine is persuaded to testify by Joe's brothers, who know that he is actually alive. Afterward, Katherine discovers this herself and confronts Joe with the fact that his hatred and desire for revenge have transformed him into something worse than the unreasoning mob itself, a cold and calculating murderer—a man she no longer knows or is able to love. Her words penetrate his shell of bitterness and hate, and after some soul-searching, he reveals himself to the court, letting the defendants off the hook—though not by much, for they have been made to sweat for their lives (as he had done) and will have to live the rest of their days with the guilt and shame of their deeds.

Critics of Lang's Hollywood career consider *Fury's* "happy ending" to be inconsistent with the "dire outlook" expressed in the director's pre-Hollywood work, believe it was probably forced upon him by the MGM dream merchants in order to boost the film's chances at the box office, and feel that it spoiled what was otherwise a tense, absorbing, and realistic film. (The same accusation would be leveled at Lang's ending for *The Woman in the Window,* see separate chapter.) In other words, the ending was a cheat. The truth is that the outlook expressed in Lang's German films was never all that dire (could there be a happier ending than the one he gives us in *Metropolis*?) and that Lang completely endorsed the conclusion of *Fury* (except the hokey final clinch between Joe and Katherine) because Joe's turnabout due to a crisis of conscience is precisely the film's point. Mobs don't think and reason, but individuals do—and *must* in order to rise above the mob. As Joe says to the court, "I came to save them, yes. But not for their sakes. Men or women who lynch another human being are a disgrace to humanity. They who pretend to be humans showed themselves at the first smell of blood to be beasts."

Fury's conclusion is not a phony Hollywood "happy ending" but the only possible one if the film is to have any meaning. Nor in one sense is it all that "happy," for while Joe has retained his decency, he is still a changed man. As he tells the court: "They lynched what mattered to me...my liking people and having faith in them."

MAN HUNT

(1941)

Twentieth Century-Fox • B&W/105 Minutes

CREDITS

Director: Fritz Lang; *Producer*: Darryl F. Zanuck; *Screenplay*: Dudley Nichols, based on the novel *Rogue Male* by Geoffrey Household; *Cinematographer*: Arthur Miller; *Editor*: Allen McNeil; *Music*: Alfred Newman; *Art Directors*: Richard Day and Wiard B. Ihnen.

CAST

Captain Alan Thorndike: Walter Pidgeon; *Jerry Stokes*: Joan Bennett; *Major Quive-Smith*: George Sanders; *Mr. Jones*: John Carradine; *Vaner*: Roddy McDowall; *Doctor*: Ludwig Stossel; *Lord Risborough*: Frederick Worlock; *Lady Risborough*: Heather Thatcher; *Captain Jensen*: Roger Imhof.

* * *

Irrespective of its aesthetic values, *Man Hunt* deserves a top spot in the thriller hall of fame because, at the time, it was an unusual and politically courageous film to have been made in Hollywood, a place not usually known for political courage due to its overriding concern with the Almighty Buck.

America had not yet entered the war and much of the public, from men on the street to their representatives in Congress, remained staunchly isolationist. This attitude would change overnight when the Japanese attacked Pearl Harbor on December 7, but at the time of *Man Hunt's* production (early 1941) and release (June 1941), it was unusual for a commercial film from a major studio to chance alienating half its potential audience by taking sides as fervently as this one does. Largely due to the efforts of director Fritz Lang, who had fled Nazi Germany, *Man Hunt* denounced the European dictator with unbridled fury and forthrightly insisted that Hitler had to be stopped at all costs. That the film was set in England (then at war with Hitler and suffering mightily) and that the fictional mouthpiece for its impassioned message was a British subject mattered not at all. The film was made in America by an American company and featured an American actor, Walter Pidgeon (Canadian actually, but one of Hollywood's most popular leading men at the time), in the starring role of the apolitical British sportsman who comes to the decision not only that Hitler must be executed, but also that he himself must be the executioner.

Published in Britain in 1939 just prior to Britain's involvement in the war, Geoffrey Household's source novel, *Rogue Male* (which Lang and writer Dudley Nichols adapted fairly faithfully), played things a bit coy by not mentioning Hitler, the Nazis, or Germany by name, although there was very little doubt in the reader's mind about Household's references. Interestingly, the film doesn't mention Hitler by name either—he's referred to as the "Führer." But Fritz Lang left even less doubt in the viewer's mind as to the object of his wrath because the actor playing the dictator was made up to look exactly like Hitler. And unlike Household, Lang was not coy at all about referring to Germany, the Nazis—or even Hitler's personal mountaintop aerie, Berchtesgarten—by name in the film. This is something even Charlie Chaplin hadn't done in his anti-Hitler satire, *The Great Dictator*, released the year before (though admittedly Chaplin left very little visual doubt about the targets of his vitriol either).

Rogue Male is basically a novel-length reworking of Richard Connell's classic short tale of suspense, *The Most Dangerous Game*, which has also been filmed several times. In both, a world famous professional big game hunter falls into the clutches of a diabolical amateur sportsman, escapes, then has to match his skill and cunning against his former captor in a protracted, cross-country game of survival of the fittest. In *The Most Dangerous Game*, the hunted is an American, Bob Rainsford, and the hunter is the deranged Count Zaroff, an expatriate Russian nobleman with a passion for guns and human trophies. *Rogue Male's* hunted is Captain Alan Thorndike, the adventurous brother of a stodgy, Neville Chamberlain-like member of Britain's House of Lords, and the hunter is a fastidious Nazi major, Quive-Smith, a top Hitler aide. (Interestingly, in the most recent screen version of *The Most Dangerous Game*, 1956's *Run for the Sun*, Connell's Count Zaroff was finally transformed into a Nazi too—and the demise of one of his

Thorndike is presented for questioning to Major Quive-Smith (George Sanders), a Nazi officer who fashions himself a crack amateur sportsman.

Nazi goons at the hands of the film's hunted Rainsford character [played by Richard Widmark] was lifted almost whole cloth from *Rogue Male* and *Man Hunt.*)

In *Man Hunt,* Thorndike enters Germany surreptitiously and stalks Hitler to his closely guarded mountaintop lair. As the dictator strolls about the balcony, Thorndike sights him in the crosshairs of his telescopic rifle and pulls the trigger. But there is only a *click,* for Thorndike, a sportsman not an assassin, has intentionally left the rifle unloaded. About to leave, Thorndike abruptly changes his mind, slips a live round into the chamber, and takes aim at Hitler again. Does he intend to shoot? Or is he just making the game more authentic by playing it with a loaded gun this time? We don't know the answer because we have no insights into Thorndike's character as yet.

Thorndike (Walter Pidgeon) insists he had no intention to shoot Hitler—that he was engaged in a "sporting stalk" and nothing more. But Quive-Smith (George Sanders) is unconvinced.

Thorndike (Walter Pidgeon) makes it back to England with Quive-Smith and several other disguised Nazis in hot pursuit.

*Jerry (Joan Bennett) and Thorndike's (Walter Pidgeon)
relationship serves to illuminate Thorndike's complex character.*

Thorndike doesn't know the answer either, for his motivations are equally unclear to himself at this point. A guard spots Thorndike, jumps him, and makes the gun discharge prematurely. Thorndike is presented for questioning to Major Quive-Smith, a Nazi officer who fashions himself a crack amateur sportsman and is familiar with Thorndike's name and reputation. Thorndike insists that he had no intention to shoot Hitler—that he was engaging in a "sporting stalk" and nothing more. Quive-Smith is unconvinced and seizes the opportunity to create an international incident by demanding that Thorndike sign a confession that he's a spy and assassin in the service of the British government. Despite several beatings, Thorndike refuses. Quive-Smith decides he can accomplish the same propaganda goal without a signed confession by killing Thorndike, making his death look like an accident, "discovering" the man's armed corpse near Hitler's estate, and raising a storm of controversy by announcing this discovery to the world. Thorndike is taken back to the spot where he was captured and pushed off a cliff. But he survives and makes it back to England with Quive-Smith and several other disguised Nazis in hot pursuit.

Unable to turn for help to the British government, which must remain disassociated from him for political reasons, Thorndike finds himself a hunted man on the streets of London. Aided by Jerry Stokes, a young Cockney prostitute who falls hopelessly in love with him, Thorndike survives several close calls (including a superbly executed chase through the London underground) with his Nazi hunters and escapes to the

*Aided by Jerry Stokes (Joan Bennett), a young Cockney
prostitute, Thorndike (Walter Pidgeon) survives several close
calls with his pursuers.*

Thorndike (Walter Pidgeon) escapes his Nazi pursuers by fleeing to the countryside, where he literally holes up in a cave.

countryside where he literally holes up in a cave, hoping that Quive-Smith will give up and the situation will blow over. But Quive-Smith learns of his whereabouts from a slip of paper found in Jerry's apartment and tracks him down. In the film's penultimate scene, Quive-Smith informs Thorndike that Jerry has been killed, and, as evidence, produces the tam-o'-shanter with the arrow-shaped hatpin Thorndike bought for her and pushes it through a hole to the trapped man. In a bid for time, the enraged Thorndike agrees to look over Quive-Smith's false confession and sign it. Meanwhile, he hastily fashions a bow and arrow from a piece of wood, his belt, and Jerry's hatpin. He returns the signed confession and while Quive-Smith is examining it, he fires the arrow through the hole and kills his hated adversary. The war having started as the film ends, Thorndike, now knowing his true mission and purpose, parachutes back into Germany to take that second shot at Hitler and this time follow through.

Though heavily propagandistic, *Man Hunt*'s primary focus—and source of its considerable suspense and power to grab—is character. The title actually refers to Thorndike's search for himself—and the reason why he really did put a live round in his gun if it was just a "sporting stalk." And it is Quive-Smith, a three-dimensional character in his own right, who finally provides the answer.

Similarly, Jerry Stokes is not just dropped into the plot to provide the film with some "love interest," but to illuminate Thorndike's character as well. And their scenes together, particularly their moving final leave-taking on a London bridge (a scene that almost didn't make it into the final film) are warmly intimate, insightful, and endearing.

Shot entirely on a Hollywood sound stage where Lang and company vividly recreated everything from a lush Bavarian forest to an authentic replica of the London Underground system, *Man Hunt* is a superior piece of suspense filmmaking and movie magic. Like many of the classic thrillers in this book, it has also been remade. But though not without its virtues, Clive Donner's 1976 version, which retained the title *Rogue Male* and starred Peter O'Toole as Thorndike and John Standing as Quive-Smith, still doesn't come close to Fritz Lang's 1941 production.

DOUBLE INDEMNITY
(1944)

Paramount • B&W/107 Minutes

CREDITS

Director: Billy Wilder; *Producer*: Joseph Sistrom; *Screenplay*: Billy Wilder and Raymond Chandler, based on the novel by James M. Cain; *Cinematographer*: John F. Seitz; *Editor*: Doane Harrison; *Music*: Miklos Rozsa; *Art Directors*: Hans Dreier and Hal Pereira.

CAST

Walter Neff: Fred MacMurray; *Phyllis Dietrichson*: Barbara Stanwyck; *Barton Keyes*: Edward G. Robinson; *Mr. Jackson*: Porter Hall; *Lola Dietrichson*: Jean Heather; *Mr. Dietrichson*: Tom Powers; *Nino Zachette*: Byron Barr; *Mr. Norton*: Richard Gaines; *Sam Gorlopis*: Fortunio Bonanova; *Joe Pete*: John Philliber.

* * *

James M. Cain based his novel of greed and passion on the real life Ruth Snyder/Judd Grey case.

Although James M. Cain's memorable novel of crime and passion, *The Postman Always Rings Twice*, predated his equally noted one on the same theme, *Double Indemnity*, by almost a decade, it's *Indemnity* that has proven to be the more influential—largely due to the uncompromising and suspenseful film writer-director Billy Wilder made from it. Wilder's work has become the model for just about every thriller of this type (*Born to Kill, The Prowler, Pushover, Body Heat*, et al.) that's come our way since.

Unlike Tay Garnett's 1946 screen version of *Postman*, a superb *film noir* despite its watering down of some of the racier elements in Cain's novel, *Double Indemnity* came to the screen with the full force of the author's ugly tale of lust, greed, and murder wholly intact. In many ways, Wilder's film is even tougher and more uncompromising than Cain's novel. In fact, it was the iconoclastic Wilder's intention to make it so that prompted his partner, writer-producer Charles Brackett, to back off the project even though he and Wilder were then one of Hollywood's most critically and commercially successful teams. (They would resume their successful if stormy relationship on the subsequent *The Lost Weekend* and several others before finally going their separate ways for good in 1951.) Brackett found Cain's book distasteful, felt the film

Wilder had in mind would be little more than a "dirty movie," and told him to get another collaborator. Wilder tried to get Cain himself. But Cain was working on another film project, so Wilder opted for Raymond Chandler instead. Despite the excellence of his work on the script, however, Chandler detested working with Wilder and disliked the final film. Cain on the other hand totally approved of what Wilder did to his book and even considered the film to be an improvement over it.

Whether the film does improve upon Cain's novel is debatable, of course. The two works are certainly different. In addition to changing the names of Cain's main characters (the book's Walter Huff and Phyllis Nirdlinger became Walter Neff and Phyllis Dietrichson on the screen), Wilder gave his film an

"Closer than that, Walter." Insurance fraud investigator Barton Keyes (Edward G. Robinson) and close friend, top salesman Walter Neff (Fred MacMurray), in Billy Wilder's classic Double Indemnity.

Neff (Fred MacMurray) meets Phyllis Dietrichson (Barbara Stanwyck), the blonde bombshell wife of a wealthy oil man, and falls victim to what Cain called "the love rack."

The lovers (Fred MacMurray and Barbara Stanwyck) devise a scheme to murder her husband and collect $100,000 in double indemnity insurance.

Dietrichson (Barbara Stanwyck) and Neff (Fred MacMurray) dump the body of her husband (Tom Powers) on the railroad tracks. The police and the insurance company will conclude the man's death was an accident.

entirely different ending, which he shot but subsequently scrapped and substituted with another that is also very different from the novel's, and altered the structure of the story as well. Whereas Cain tells his tale in linear fashion, Wilder, who is similar to Hitchcock in that he prefers stories of suspense rather than surprise, lets the audience know the fate of his main character, Walter Neff, right off the bat—then has Neff reveal in flashback the web of circumstances that led to his current situation. This structure would serve Wilder equally well later on in *Sunset Boulevard,* whose story unfolds in the same fashion—although the narrator this time is not dying at the beginning of the film, but is actually dead!

A mortally wounded Neff arrives at his office one night and confesses into the dictaphone of his friend and mentor, fraud investigator Barton Keyes, the details of a murder plot and insurance scam that has gone fatally awry. Wilder cuts back to the dying Neff several times, but for the most part the film unfolds via a series of lengthy flashbacks accompanied by Neff's caustic voice-over narrative of how it all happened.

A top insurance salesman with a spotless record, Neff meets Phyllis Dietrichson, the blond bombshell wife of a wealthy California oilman, while trying to renew her husband's automobile policy, and becomes a victim of what James M. Cain called the "love rack." Neff and the unhappily married Phyllis become infatuated and soon devise a scheme to murder her husband, make it look like an accident, and collect $100,000 in double indemnity insurance so they can run off together. Knowing the wily Keyes will be able to see through any plan that isn't completely foolproof, Neff uses all his skill and cunning to make sure that doesn't happen. With Phyllis's help, Neff gets Dietrichson to unknowingly sign the fateful policy, then sets up an airtight alibi for the night of the murder.

Phyllis persuades her husband to go through with a scheduled college reunion even though he has broken his leg and is wearing a cast. She drives him to the train station with Neff hiding in the back seat. Neff kills Dietrichson on the way, then boards the train himself, sporting the dead man's cast and crutches. The plan is for Neff to jump unseen from the rear platform of the train at a prearranged spot where he and Phyllis will then dump the corpse on the tracks. When the body is found, the police and Keyes will conclude that the unfortunate man stumbled and fell from the slow moving train while getting a breath of air and will rule the death an accident—requiring the insurance company to pay up.

Posing as Dietrichson, Neff hobbles to the rear of the train as it leaves the station, but gets the first hint that all may not work out as planned when he unexpectedly finds the open platform occupied by a talkative gent named Jackson who is smoking a cigar. As the train nears the spot where Phyllis is waiting, Neff asks Jackson to fetch a cigarette case for him. As soon as the man leaves, Neff tosses the crutches over the side and jumps from the train. He and Phyllis place the body on the tracks, but then, in one of the film's most gripping (and Hitchcockian) scenes, their car refuses to start. As the motor sputters and groans but fails to catch, Wilder involves us as accomplices in the crime, not just witnesses, by making us squirm and hold our breath as much as the worried lovers. When the motor finally does turn over, we breathe as much of a sign of relief as they do.

The couple keeps a low profile while the insurance investigation proceeds. As Neff planned, Dietrichson's death is ruled an accident. Even the redoubtable Keyes is convinced—until he starts wondering why Dietrichson didn't file an accident claim when he broke his leg. As Keyes gets closer and closer to the truth that Dietrichson was, in fact, murdered, the lovers' scheme begins to unravel, their relationship falls apart, and they wind up shooting each other. (In the novel, the lovers get away with the crime because Keyes has no proof, but they are clearly doomed anyway due to their growing guilt and mistrust of one another.)

His lover dead, Neff has staggered back to his office and confesses the crime into Keyes's dictaphone. When he finishes, he looks up and sees the grim-faced Keyes standing in the doorway. Neff asks his friend to give him a head start for Mexico, but Keyes tells the mortally wounded man he'll never make it to the elevator. As Neff slumps to the floor, he reveals why the dogged investigator couldn't finger Phyllis's accomplice. "Because the guy you were looking for was too close, Keyes. Right across the desk from you." "Closer than that, Walter," the heartbroken older man responds as the film fades to black.

Cain loosely based his novel on the real-life case of Ruth Snyder and Judd Gray who conspired to murder Snyder's husband for $100,000 in insurance money during the late twenties. Unlike Cain's fictional couple, however, Snyder and Gray were caught and sent to the electric chair. An enterprising newspaper reporter smuggled a camera into the execution chamber and snapped a shot of Snyder moments before the juice was turned on. One of the most famous (and infamous) photos in the history of yellow journalism, the ghoulish shot caused a furor when the newspaper put it on the front page of its next edition.

Wilder's cinematic roman à clef about the Snyder/ Gray case was to have ended with a similarly horrific scene showing Neff's execution in California's gas

Double Indemnity *came to the screen with the full force of Cain's ugly tale of lust, greed, and murder wholly intact.*

chamber. But Wilder felt the scene to be too strong, and anticlimatic as well, so he replaced it with the trenchantly written and beautifully performed confrontation scene between the self-destructive Neff and the fatherly Keyes that movingly concludes this exceptionally fine and biting thriller.*

*Double Indemnity was remade twice for television. In 1954, there was an hour-long "vest pocket" version with Frank Lovejoy and Laraine Day, and in 1973, a humdrum made-for-TV movie by director Jack Smight starring Richard Crenna, Samantha Eggar, and Lee J. Cobb that was virtually scene-for-scene with Wilder's classic.

THE WOMAN IN THE WINDOW

(1944)

RKO Pictures • B&W/99 Minutes

CREDITS

Director: Fritz Lang; *Producer*: Nunnally Johnson; *Screenplay*: Nunnally Johnson, based on the novel *Once Off Guard* by J. H. Wallis; *Cinematographer*: Milton Krasner; *Editor*: Marjorie Johnson; *Music*: Arthur Lange; *Art Director*: Duncan Cramer.

CAST

Professor Richard Wanley: Edward G. Robinson; *Alice Reed*: Joan Bennett; *District Attorney*: Raymond Massey; *Heidt*: Dan Duryea; *Dr. Barkstone*: Edmond Breon; *Inspector Jackson*: Thomas E. Jackson; *Mrs. Wanley*: Dorothy Peterson; *Mazard*: Arthur Loft; *Steward*: Frank Dawson; *Dickie*: Bobby Blake.

* * *

Most critics are in agreement that *The Woman in the Window* is one of Fritz Lang's most accomplished Hollywood melodramas, a consistently enthralling and relentlessly suspenseful thriller right up to the very end—at which point, most also tend to agree, Lang sabotaged his film by tacking on a "phony Hollywood happy ending." Worse still, they insist, the happy ending he tacked on was one of the hoariest of all melodramatic cliches: the dire circumstances in which the film's main character finds himself turn out to be in his imagination. In other words, it's all a dream. The fact that the novel on which the film is based did not end this way and that screenwriter-producer Nunnally Johnson was himself opposed to such a conclusion just added more fuel to the critics' overriding belief that Hollywood had crippled the career of the once great German director, who was no longer interested in pursuing Artistic Truth but just catering to box office tastes.

The same accusation had been leveled at Lang's first Hollywood film, *Fury* (see separate chapter). In both cases, Lang defended his "happy endings" because they were consistent with his own personal outlook and because the material demanded them in order to have any meaning.

In an impassioned article written for the *Penquin Film Review* four years after the later film's release,

Professor Richard Wanley (Edward G. Robinson) enjoys a quiet dinner at his club with pals Dr. Barkstone (Edmond Breon, left) and the District Attorney (Raymond Massey) shortly before being lured by "the siren call of adventure." (Frank Dawson is the steward.)

Lang openly declared, "My choice [of ending *The Woman in the Window* as a dream] was conscious. If I had continued the story to its logical conclusion, the logical ending [would have] seemed to me a defeatist ending, a tragedy for nothing, brought about by an implacable Fate—a negative ending to a problem which is not universal, a futile dreariness which an audience would reject." Clearly this statement of Lang's artistic purpose—which is consistent with the non-defeatist attitudes expressed in his work as a whole—defuses the argument that he was just pandering to commercial tastes. In fact, close examina-

Wanley (Edward G. Robinson) strikes up a conversation with the woman (Joan Bennett) who posed for the portrait that so fascinates him, and she invites him back to her apartment to see more of the artist's work.

Mazard (Arthur Loft), Alice's (Joan Bennett) "sugar daddy," slaps her around when he finds her with Wanley.

After killing Mazard in self-defense, Wanley (Edward G. Robinson) cleans off the weapon and he and Alice (Joan Bennett) make plans to dispose of the body.

Wanley (Edward G. Robinson) accepts the D.A.'s (Raymond Massey) offer to go along and observe Inspector Jackson's (Thomas E. Jackson) investigation into Mazard's murder.

tion of the film reveals that his choice of ending is not only appropriate to the material but also entirely consistent with another Lang motif from film to film—the rite of passage which allows a character to explore and finally come to terms with his own belief system, one way or the other.

As *The Woman in The Window* begins, the focal character, Richard Wanley, an assistant professor of psychology at Gotham College, is lecturing his stu-dents on degrees of criminal behavior and respon-sibility, guilt, and merited punishment. A person who kills in a moment of passion or self defense, he insists, is not as criminally responsible as a person who kills premeditatedly—and his guilt and punishment should fit the crime. Director Lang subsequently puts Wanley in a situation where he (and we) will exam-ine his theories in intimate terms—with Wanley himself acting as a litmus test.

The guilt-ridden Wanley (Edward G. Robinson) inadvertently keeps calling attention to his involvement in the murder by blurting out details of the crime before the D.A. (Raymond Massey) and Inspector Jackson (Thomas E. Jackson) make them known.

When his wife and children leave town for an extended family visit, Wanley finds himself unexpectedly lonely. On his way to a dinner engagement with his friends, the District Attorney and Dr. Barkstone, he spots a painting in the window of an art gallery and is drawn to the beautiful, raven-haired woman in the portrait. His friends later tease him about being lured by the "siren call of adventure" while his wife's away, but Wanley jokingly dismisses such a suggestion because of his age and stolidity.

After dinner, Wanley retires to his club's reading room for some bookish relaxation, instructing the steward to rouse him at 10:30 so that he can get home in time to prepare for his next lecture and get a good night's sleep. After later leaving the club, however, Wanley is drawn once more to the portrait of the woman in the gallery window—and as he studies it fondly, the subject of the portrait suddenly appears in the flesh beside him. Her name is Alice Reed. They strike up a friendly conversation and she invites him back to her apartment to see more of the artist's work.

As they chit-chat over a drink, a man enters the apartment, flies into a jealous rage, slaps Alice around, then attempts to strangle Wanley, who defends himself by killing the man with a pair of scissors. The victim turns out to be a married financier named Mazard who under an assumed name has been carrying on a clandestine romance with Alice. As the three of them cannot be connected, Wanley sees a way out of the unfortunate mess—which would likely tarnish Alice's reputation and lead to his professional ruin if they called in the police—by disposing of the dead man's body in the woods out of town, then agreeing never to see or communicate with each other again.

Mazard's body is found and identified and Wanley's D.A. friend is called into the case. The likely suspect appears to be Mazard's personal bodyguard, a man named Heidt, who has since vanished, but the D.A. intends to leave no stone unturned. Wanley accepts the D.A.'s offer to go along on the investigation, but he inadvertently keeps calling attention to his own involvement in the murder by blurting out details of the crime before the police make them public. The D.A. jokingly (yet also with a hint of suspicion) attributes the professor's insights as good amateur guesswork. Nevertheless, Wanley realizes if he isn't more careful he'll succeed in putting a noose around his own neck.

Mazard's vanished bodyguard turns up at Alice's apartment. Having dropped the financier off there on several occasions, he knows Alice is somehow involved and demands $5,000 for his silence. Unable to come up with the cash herself, Alice rings up Wanley for help. Wanley knows that the blackmailer will continue to bleed them dry and sees no other alternative but to commit another murder—this time a premeditated one. Wanley gives Alice some powders Dr. Barkstone had prescribed for his nerves—an overdose of which will cause a lethal heart attack but be untraceable as poison. As Wanley waits nervously by the phone for news, Alice carries out their plan by poisoning Heidt's drink, but he grows wise to her, smashes the glass, and demands even more hush money, which she must come up with in twenty-four hours. After Heidt leaves, Alice calls Wanley and tells the distressed man of her failure. As neither of them can come up with the necessary cash in time, Wanley realizes the game is up. Wracked by guilt and shame, he hangs up the phone, takes an overdose of the deadly powders himself, and sits in an easy chair to await his death.

Outside Alice's apartment, Heidt is killed in a shootout with police, who find a substantial amount of cash on his body as well as some other incriminating evidence suggesting that Heidt was, indeed, Mazard's murderer. Knowing they're now off the hook entirely, Alice rushes back to her apartment and phones Wanley, but by this time the powders have started to take effect and the hapless professor's phone just keeps ringing. Lang's camera closes in on the unconscious professor, then, in an amazing effect brought off without a single dissolve or cutaway, pulls back to reveal Wanley (who is even dressed in a different set of clothes!) sleeping in his chair at the club. The steward wakes him promptly at 10:30 and Wanley realizes he's been experiencing a terrible dream—an illustration of his own theories which he has now subjectively confirmed. As he leaves the club, he pauses once more before the gallery window. In a replay of the scene that launched his nightmare, a woman appears and asks for a light. But this time, the wary professor turns her down flat and beats a hasty retreat.

One of the cleverest things about *The Woman in the Window* is that upon viewing the film a second time, the clues that it's a dream are all there for us to see. Events are telescoped in the manner of dreams and the story is filled with convenient implausibilities (for example, the doctor's giving Wanley a potentially lethal poison and handy method for murder), which, in dream logic, wouldn't strike us as implausible at all. The fact that these clues escape our attention the first time around is due to Lang's relentless build-up of suspense—he barely gives us time to breathe, let alone time to question.

The success of *The Woman in the Window* occasioned Lang and the film's three leads (Robinson, Bennett, and Duryea) to reteam not long afterward for the similarly-plotted but less effective *Scarlet Street*.

57

SORRY, WRONG NUMBER

(1948)

Paramount Pictures • B&W/89 Minutes

CREDITS

Director: Anatole Litvak; *Producers*: Hal Wallis and
Anatole Litvak; *Screenplay*: Lucille Fletcher, based on
her radio play; *Cinematographer*: Sol Polito; *Editor*:
Warren Low; *Music*: Franz Waxman; *Art Directors*:
Hans Dreier and Earl Hedrick.

CAST

Leona Stevenson: Barbara Stanwyck; *Henry Stevenson*:
Burt Lancaster; *Sally Hunt Lord*: Ann Richards; *Dr.
Alexander*: Wendell Corey; *Waldo Evans*: Harold Ver-
milyea; *J. B. Cotterell*: Ed Begley; *Fred Lord*: Leif
Erickson; *Morano*: William Conrad; *Joe*: John
Bromfield.

* * *

Sorry, Wrong Number was one of the high water marks
of the classic radio drama series, *Suspense*. Initially
broadcast May 25, 1943, with Agnes Moorehead in
the lead role of the bedridden heroine, Leona Stevenson, who overhears a murder being planned on the
telephone and gradually comes to realize the intended
victim is herself, it glued listeners to their chairs from
coast to coast. It was a perfect vehicle for the medium
of radio because its story—told via a series of phone
conversations and interior monologues—unfolded
quite naturally and realistically through the use of
sound alone. This presented director Anatole Litvak
and writer Lucille Fletcher with quite a challenge
when they came to adapt and expand Fletcher's
sensational radio play for the visual medium of the
movies some five years later. They were more than up
to that challenge though, and the film they made
emerged a classic thriller in its own right, which
played just as effectively on the screen as it had over
the air. It even earned Barbara Stanwyck a Best
Actress nomination for her all-stops-out performance
as the invalided heroine whose panic builds when she
realizes not only that she's the one targeted for death
but also that her own husband is behind the murder
plot.

The film version unfolds in much the same way as
the radio play. The telephone remains the primary

Leona (Barbara Stanwyck) begins the process of stealing Henry
(Burt Lancaster), a poor boy from the other side of the tracks,
from her closest college friend, Sally Hunt (Ann Richards).

instrument through which Leona puts the pieces of
the murder plot together and attempts to seek help.
Befitting the requirements of the screen, however,
director Litvak opens things up by taking us out of
Leona's bedroom and showing us all the characters on
the other end of the line—the police, a college friend,
a doctor—as the evidence is developed and the clock
ticks toward the hour of doom. As a substitute for
Leona's expository interior monologues and to avoid
the monotony of just intercutting between characters
talking on the phone, Litvak makes frequent use of
flashbacks and flashbacks within flashbacks to keep
the story rolling and visually alive. And in the best
tradition of *film noir*—of which this is a fine example—atmospheric lighting, tortuous camera angles,

Leona (Barbara Stanwyck) and Henry (Burt Lancaster) during happier days. Director Anatole Litvak makes frequent use of flashbacks and flashbacks within flashbacks to keep the story rolling and visually alive.

The beginning of the end for Leona (Barbara Stanwyck) and Henry (Burt Lancaster) in Anatole Litvak's Sorry, Wrong Number, based on the radio play by Lucille Fletcher.

The ill-fated bride and groom. Leona (Barbara Stanwyck) is a spoilt rich girl doomed by her insecurities and her need to always get her own way. Henry (Burt Lancaster) is doomed by his pride and ambition.

Leona (Barbara Stanwyck) may not deserve the fate Henry (Burt Lancaster) has planned for her. But she's played no small part in pushing him in his murderous direction.

Leona (Barbara Stanwyck) overhears a murder being planned on the telephone and gradually comes to realize she's the intended victim.

and sinuous camera movements are employed with considerable effectiveness to build excitement and suspense. Despite its radio origins, *Sorry, Wrong Number* is a visual showstopper—and probably the best film Anatole Litvak ever directed—that keeps you on edge without pause right up to its surprising and ironic finish. (To see how easily it could have been botched by lesser talents, just compare it to the visually dull and hopelessly inflated 1989 made-for-television version starring a miscast Loni Anderson.)

In some respects, the film is also an improvement over the radio version, particularly in the characterization of its two principal leads, Leona and her murderous husband Henry, both of whom are equally "trapped" by their situation and earn our sympathies as well as our distaste in equal measure. Leona is not all heroine, and Henry is not all villain.

Leona is a spoiled rich girl trapped by her insecurities and used to always getting her way. She is vituperative, jealous, demanding, manipulative, thoughtless of her husband's (or anyone else's) feelings, and neurotically tied to her possessive father, J. B. Cotterell. She may not deserve the fate her husband has planned for her, but she's played no small part in

pushing him in his murderous direction.

Having stolen Henry from the arms of her closest college friend, Sally Hunt, Leona persuades her father to give her new husband a do-nothing executive position in the old man's multimillion dollar pharmaceutical firm. Henry, a poor boy from "the other side of the tracks," is quickly trapped by his newfound wealth and position. But he also has a conscience and a commendable degree of pride. Frustrated by his dead-end job and being under the financial thumb of both Leona and her father, he interviews for a job with a competitive firm so that he can strike out on his own, support Leona with his own money, and move out of Cotterell's mansion into an apartment of their own. When he announces his plans to Leona, however, she throws a fit and suffers a mild heart attack that lands her in bed. In reprisal, Cotterell scotches Henry's aspirations and threatens to break him if he doesn't start playing to Cotterell and Leona's tune.

Cornered, Henry sees a way to build a secret nest egg of his own that will allow him to break free of his bonds (with or without Leona) while getting even with Cotterell in the bargain. With the help of a chemist named Evans who works in one of Cotterell's manufacturing plants, he begins stealing drugs and sets up a distribution operation with a syndicate boss named Morano. But then Henry gets greedy and starts skimming off the top.

Morano demands exorbitant restitution in exchange for Henry's life and blackmails the in-over-his head young man into paying the money out of his wife's life insurance policy. As Leona's heart condition has gotten progressively worse and she is now totally bedridden, her death seems imminent. All Henry has to do is wait. But then he is shocked to learn from Leona's doctor that the woman's condition (an emotional bid for sympathy and attention developed when she was a child) is entirely psychosomatic.

With no other way out now, Henry hatches his murder plan, a few scant details of which Leona accidentally overhears when she places a call to her husband's office and believes she's gotten a wrong number. As the clock ticks toward the hour of death, she and Henry learn that Morano and his men have been arrested and that Henry is now off the hook. But Leona isn't. As she talks to Henry on the phone, she can hear the killer approaching up the stairs of her deserted penthouse.

In a surprise twist worthy of Hitchcock, Henry makes an eleventh hour attempt to rouse her from her imaginary illness and save her life. But for these two star-crossed lovers, it may just be too late.

As both compelling character study and nail-biting thriller, *Sorry, Wrong Number* is first class all the way.

WHITE HEAT

(1949)

Warner Bros. • B&W/114 Minutes

CREDITS

Director: Raoul Walsh; *Producer*: Louis F. Edelman; *Screenplay*: Ivan Goff and Ben Roberts, based on a story by Virginia Kellogg; *Cinematographer*: Sid Hickox; *Editor*: Owen Marks; *Music*: Max Steiner; *Art Director*: Edward Carrere.

CAST

Cody Jarrett: James Cagney; *Verna Jarrett*: Virginia Mayo; *Hank Fallon (Vic Pardo)*: Edmond O'Brien; *Ma Jarrett*: Margaret Wycherly; *Big Ed*: Steve Cochran; *Evans*: John Archer; *Cotton Valetti*: Wally Cassell; *Het Kohler*: Mickey Knox; *The Trader*: Fred Clark; *Roy Parker*: Paul Guilfoyle; *Bo Creel*: Ian MacDonald.

* * *

If *The Godfather* series is the *Gone With the Wind* of gangster movies, then Raoul Walsh's *White Heat* is surely *The Origin of the Species*. Released on the eve of the talkies' third decade, the film is both a throwback to the thirties style of gangster thriller that made its star and studio's reputations and a stage-setter for the apocalyptic visions of such future thrillers as Robert Aldrich's *Kiss Me Deadly* (see separate chapter) and several others included in this book.

As its main character, Cody Jarrett, evolves from being an out-of-date, Depression-spawned desperado who robs trains in the manner of his Old West forebears to an up-to-date, conscienceless killer with grandiose dreams, *White Heat* treats us to a cinematic history of the crime thriller's own evolution. It moves from being a straightforward, rat-a-tat thirties-style gangster film, to a late thirties/early forties-style prison picture, to an urban heist movie, to a *film noir*ish exercise in post-war disillusionment, amorality, and duplicity, to a contemporary psychological thriller about a new type of killer—the pathological nobody who really doesn't care if he's caught, or even if he dies, so long as he makes a name for himself. And who does so by conjuring up an image of Armageddon.

White Heat marked James Cagney's return to Warners after years of making films for other studios and going it alone with his own independent Cagney Productions, whose offerings had flopped with critics and the public. He needed a hit, professionally and financially, and although he'd never been fond of the gangster roles that had made him famous, the part of Cody Jarrett, "the mug to end all mugs" as he viewed the role, in *White Heat* seemed a good bet. He threw himself into it with a fervor that astonished everyone, and the film became his biggest critical and commercial success in years. Ironically, Cagney himself never particularly liked *White Heat*, calling it "just another cheapjack job" and his electric performance in it just "a cheapie one-two-three-four kind of thing." To the end of his days, the onetime song-and-dance man who had won his only Oscar (though not his only nomination) for playing a song-and-dance man, the kind of role he preferred, regretted that the public preferred to see him brandishing a gun on screen rather than tap dancing.

Cagney's Cody Jarrett is not just your average screen tough guy; he's a psychopath whose dreams of making it "to the top of the world" take on an apocalyptic meaning by the end of the film. Cody knows his old-fashioned desperado methods don't stand a chance in the postwar world of sophisticated detection devices that enable the police to track his every move—where undercover cops act with the cunning, efficiency, and cool duplicity of the cleverest superspies. But he presses on anyway because, unlike the screen gangsters of the thirties, winning out over the law isn't his primary aim.

During a railroad heist at the beginning of the film, Jarrett cold-bloodedly plugs the train's engineers because they overheard his name and can identify him to police. At this point, he's still acting the part of the traditional gangster who seeks to keep his identity unknown in order to evade capture. By the end of the film, however, his psychosis has progressed to the point where such concerns no longer matter to him.

To throw the police off his trail, Jarrett confesses to a robbery committed in another state at the same time as the railroad job and gets a minor two-year sentence. Convinced that Jarrett is guilty of the railroad heist and killing the engineers (among others) and intent on getting the goods on him, the police place undercover cop Hank Fallon in Jarrett's cell with instructions to befriend him and encourage him

Cody (James Cagney) and Verna (Virginia Mayo) make plans following a successful train robbery in White Heat.

James Cagney as Cody Jarrett, the "mug to end all mugs," in White Heat, *with Virginia Mayo as his two-timing moll, Verna.*

The police place undercover cop Hank Fallon (Edmond O'Brien) in Jarrett's (James Cagney) cell with instructions to befriend the criminal and encourage him to escape.

The breakout. Cody (James Cagney) takes Parker (Paul Guilfoyle) along for the ride for having tried to drop a steel beam on him in prison.

Edmond O'Brien, James Cagney and Virginia Mayo in Raoul Walsh's blistering crime thriller, White Heat.

"Made it, Ma! Top o' the world!"

to escape. Posing as a convicted felon named Vic Pardo, Fallon carries out his assignment with such unscrupulousness that it is ultimately the dangerous but pathetically sick Jarrett who gains our sympathy.

Having lost his mother (and only confidante) and having allowed Fallon to fill her role, Cody is sent completely around the bend on discovering Fallon's duplicity. For the repugnant Fallon, however, it's not enough to have successfully carried out his assignment; it is he who volunteers to shoot Jarrett down.

Wounded, Jarrett triumphantly shouts, "Made it, Ma! Top of the world!" as he suicidally pumps bullets into the petroleum tanks atop which he has been trapped, and is subsequently blown to eternity—an undying cinematic moment that also stands as an unsettling metaphor of the derangement of our nuclear age and its frightening potential to enable some future name-seeking Cody Jarrett to go out in a real "blaze of glory." And take most of us with him.

Cagney's powerful performance blisters the screen in such memorable, Oscar-worthy moments as the scene where he goes berserk in prison upon hearing of his mother's death and starts slugging guards right and left until he's finally subjugated and carried away to be straight-jacketed, screaming like some wounded animal stricken to the depth of its soul. But he's equally powerful and convincing in subtler scenes like the one where he learns that Fallon, the only person other than his mother the mistrustful, paranoid Jarrett has ever allowed to get close to him, is an undercover cop. The fleeting expression of astonishment, pain, then despair that crosses Cagney's face before he flies into a vengeful rage and launches himself on his final, self-destructive path is a truly memorable piece of screen acting.

But Edmond O'Brien's performance as Fallon is no less remarkable. Even though we know that Fallon is a cop assigned to get close to Jarrett in order to bring him down, there are times when his friendliness toward Jarrett and seemingly genuine concern for the man convinces even us. We actually forget now and then that Fallon's every word and gesture is calculated—and are almost as surprised as Jarrett ultimately is whenever Fallon drops the masquerade. And we're angered too. For while Jarrett is by no means an admirable character, it's clear from the beginning that he's a desperately sick man who's getting sicker—that his homicidal paranoia probably stems from his psychological inability to get close to people combined with a deep craving for such contact at the same time. Fallon's ability to so coldly and efficiently pierce the sick man's armor and destroy him may make Fallon a terrific undercover cop. But it also makes him thoroughly despicable as a human being.

THE WINDOW

(1949)

RKO Pictures • B&W/73 Minutes

CREDITS

Director: Ted Tetzlaff; *Producer*: Frederick Ullman, Jr.; *Screenplay*: Mel Dinelli, based on *The Boy Who Cried Murder* by Cornell Woolrich; *Cinematographer*: William Steiner; *Editor*: Frederic Knudtson; *Music*: Roy Webb; *Art Directors*: Walter E. Keller and Sam Corso.

CAST

Mrs. Woodry: Barbara Hale; *Mr. Woodry*: Arthur Kennedy; *Tommy Woodry*: Bobby Driscoll; *Mr. Kellerson*: Paul Stewart; *Mrs. Kellerson*: Ruth Roman; *Murdered Man*: Richard Benedict.

* * *

When I see *The Window* now, the first thing that strikes me is how Hitchcockian cinematographer-turned-filmmaker Ted Tetzlaff's (he shot Hitchcock's *Notorious*) palm-sweating direction is. And how much the film looks forward to Hitchcock's masterpiece on a similar theme, *Rear Window* (see separate chapter). In both films, a vulnerable protagonist witnesses a murder through an open window on a hot, steamy summer night, fails to get anyone to believe him except the killer, becomes the killer's prey himself, and winds up clinging from a precarious height to escape the killer's clutches before falling to safety. *The Window*'s eyewitness is vulnerable to the killer because he's a little boy, and disbelieved because he's prone to spinning fanciful tales. Whereas *Rear Window*'s bachelor hero L.B. Jefferies (James Stewart) is vulnerable to the killer because he's confined to his apartment, alone, with a broken leg—and disbelieved at first because he doesn't have any tangible proof, and because he's probably letting his imagination run away with him due to the boredom of his confinement. Completing the link, both films were derived from short stories written by the same author, Cornell Woolrich.

When I saw *The Window* for the first time, however, I did not approach it with such an objective and analytical eye. I was five years old, and though I had been taken to a number of movies before this one, *The*

Window was the first to stay with me as I grew older. While I forgot most other films I'd seen as a youngster, I continued to recall *The Window* in very vivid detail. This is not surprising, I suppose, since its threatened protagonist was someone I could totally identify with—a small boy with a fertile imagination not unlike the one with which I was plaguing my own parents. *The Window* scared the bejeezus out of me. But I was certainly not alone. Adults were driven to the edges of their seats as well by this expertly crafted, low-budget thriller which became RKO's "sleeper" hit of 1949, scoring big box office and critical accolades wherever it played, earning a surprise Academy Award nomination (for best film editing), and winning a special Oscar for its superlative twelve-year-old star, the ill-fated Bobby Driscoll. It had such an impact that it has been borrowed from by countless other thrillers since (including *Rear Window*) and has even been remade twice—as *The Boy Who Cried Murder*, an obscure 1966 British thriller starring "Fizz" MacIntosh in the title role, and as *Cloak and Dagger*, Australian director Richard Franklin's free-wheeling and vastly overblown 1984 version starring *E.T.*'s Henry Thomas as the imaginative young hero who this time around gets inadvertently involved in an espionage plot. I haven't seen the British film, but *Cloak and Dagger* completely lacks the superbly realized child's perspective and emphasis on claustrophobic tension that made the original so nail-bitingly effective back in 1949—and make it work just as effectively today.

Unable to sleep one suffocatingly hot summer night, Tommy Woodry grabs his pillow and climbs onto the firescape of his parents' fourth floor tenement apartment to cool off. But it's just as hot there, so he climbs one more level and falls asleep outside the window of the apartment belonging to his upstairs neighbors, the Kellersons.

Awakened by a shaft of light from the apartment, he peers through the window, which is open just a crack with the shade pulled down, and sees the Kellersons robbing a man they've apparently drugged. The man revives and in the struggle that follows, Mr. Kellerson kills him with a pair of scissors. As the

Bobby Driscoll as Tommy Woodry, the "boy who cried murder," in The Window.

Tommy (Bobby Driscoll) tries to convince the police that he saw his upstairs neighbors, the Kellersons, commit murder.

Grounded to his room by his father to avoid getting into any more mischief, Tommy (Bobby Driscoll) tries unlocking the door with a coathanger unaware that the murderous Mr. Kellerson is awaiting for him on the other side.

Kellerson (Paul Stewart) tracks the terrified boy (Bobby Driscoll) to the abandoned tenement building next door.

Tommy (Bobby Driscoll) crawls onto a rafter to escape Kellerson (Paul Stewart) and finds himself trapped, the timber threatening to give way any second.

Kellersons dispose of the corpse in the abandoned building next door, Tommy scurries back to his apartment and wakes his mother to tell her what happened. But she says he was just dreaming and orders him to go back to sleep. When his father returns home from working the night shift, Tommy reveals his story a second time, but as the boy has a habit of making things up, neither parent believes him.

Tommy turns to the police, who send a man over to investigate posing as a building inspector. But the policeman finds nothing. Upset with the boy, Mrs. Woodry takes Tommy upstairs to apologize to the Kellersons, inadvertently cluing them into the fact that he saw the murder.

Mrs. Woodry is called away overnight to take care of her ailing sister. Forced to leave the boy alone while he's at work and worried that his young son will get into more mischief, Mr. Woodry grounds Tommy to his room, then seals the window and locks the door for good measure. While Woodry is gone, Kellerson gets into the Woodry apartment and Tommy falls into his clutches. But the boy escapes and leads Kellerson and his wife on a suspenseful chase before they catch him again. Kellerson knocks Tommy unconscious and returns him to the apartment, where he intends to let the youngster fall from the fire escape so that his death will look like an accident. Mrs. Kellerson balks at this, however, and as the two argue, Tommy, who has awakened, flees to the abandoned building next

door.

In the exciting sequence that follows, the murderous Kellerson relentlessly pursues the terrified boy through the building's bombed-out rooms and narrow, unlit corridors, and up the stairs, which collapse just as they pass (a truly amazing setpiece that Tetzlaff shoots from below so that the wreckage falls into the camera lens—and the viewer's face).

Tommy crawls onto a rafter to escape, but finds himself trapped, the rotting timber threatening to give way any second. Kellerson tries to reach for him, but falls to his death when the structure supporting him collapses. Coming home and finding his son gone, Woodry has called in the police. Hearing the boy's screams coming from the abandoned building, they rush in and rescue him by having the boy jump into a safety net. As the film ends, the Woodrys promise to believe the boy from now on—and Tommy promises not to make up stories ever again.

Though Ted Tetzlaff directed several other effective thrillers after this, *The Window* remains his crowning achievement—and the crowning achievement of his talented young star, and Disney stalwart of the era, Bobby Driscoll, whose career went into decline not long after. Never recovering from the fame heaped upon him at such a young age, Driscoll died of a drug overdose twenty years later, his needle-marked body discovered in a dilapidated tenement building eerily similar to the one from which he'd been rescued in *The Window.* He was thirty-two.

STRANGERS ON A TRAIN
(1951)

A Warner Bros. Release • B&W/101 Minutes

CREDITS

Director: Alfred Hitchcock; *Producer*: Alfred Hitchcock; *Screenplay*: Raymond Chandler and Czenzi Ormonde, based on the novel by Patricia Highsmith; *Cinematographer*: Robert Burks; *Editor*: William H. Ziegler; *Music*: Dimitri Tiomkin; *Art Directors*: Ted Haworth and George James Hopkins.

CAST

Guy Haines: Farley Granger; *Bruno Antony*: Robert Walker; *Anne Morton*: Ruth Roman; *Senator Morton*: Leo G. Carroll; *Barbara Morton*: Patricia Hitchcock; *Miriam Haines*: Laura Elliott; *Mrs. Antony*: Marion Lorne; *Mr. Antony*: Jonathan Hale.

* * *

It is safe to say that at one point in all of Hitchcock's films, the protagonist comes to assume a Kafkaesque (or Catholic?) guilt for a crime that he (or she) did not commit. And so it is with *Strangers on a Train,* one of the master's most enjoyable and consistently suspenseful thrillers.

Tennis pro Guy meets twisted rich boy Bruno and suddenly finds himself up to his ears in guilt. As strangers on a train, the two casually agree to "exchange murders." Bruno will kill Guy's estranged wife, Miriam, who refuses to grant Guy a divorce so that he can marry Senator Morton's daughter, Anne. In return, Guy will slay Bruno's disapproving father. The trouble is, Bruno is serious and goes through with his end of the bargain. But Guy incurs Bruno's wrath when he fails to reciprocate. So, Bruno nastily pins the dead wife's murder on Guy and with such skill that both the police and Anne are convinced of Guy's guilt. More to the Hitchcockian point, Guy begins to feel guilty himself, for he not only benefited from the crime but also subconsciously may have wished it done. This is tellingly revealed in one of the film's famous scenes.

Tennis pro Guy (Farley Granger) meets twisted rich boy Bruno (Robert Walker) and the two of them agree to "exchange murders" in Alfred Hitchcock's classic suspense thriller Strangers on a Train.

Bruno (Robert Walker) casually picks up Guy's (Farley Granger) lighter, which will play a key part in the film's suspenseful conclusion.

*Guy (Farley Granger) is tempted to break his wife's (Laura
Elliott) neck when she refuses to give him a divorce. But Bruno
will do the deed for him.*

Bruno (Robert Walker) and his dotty mother (Marion Lorne).

Guy (Farley Granger) incurs Bruno's (Robert Walker) wrath when he fails to meet his end of the "bargain."

Guy has just returned home by taxi. He suddenly hears a disembodied voice calling out his name. He crosses the street to find Bruno waiting for him behind an iron fence. Suddenly a police car pulls up in front of the apartment and Guy ducks automatically out of sight next to Bruno, the fence's shadows falling across the two of them and making them look as if they're both behind bars. Not only does this scene symbolically illustrate Guy's growing feelings of complicity, but also Guy himself affirms this when he remarks to Bruno, "Now you've got me acting guilty."

The pressures of guilt build so against Guy that he realizes he must do something or perish. He must *act*, to not only clear himself but absolve himself of his "sins" as well. And this decision triggers the exciting climax, one of the most suspenseful in the entire Hitchcock canon.

Bruno intends to seal Guy's doom by planting the innocent man's lighter at the amusement park where the dead woman's body was found. Realizing this, Guy must catch him in the act. To do so, he must quickly wrap up a tennis match in three sets, slip away from the police, and get to the park before Bruno does. The match begins slowly as Guy launches into the first set. He wins it and Hitchcock cuts to Bruno leaving the house. Back at the tennis match, the pace quickens as Guy wins a second set. Then he

starts to lose. But he unknowingly gets a breather when Hitchcock cuts back to Bruno, who accidentally drops the all-important lighter in a storm drain. As Guy plays hard to regain the precious time he thinks he's lost, Bruno squeezes his arm through the grate, his fingers inches from the lighter. When he finally touches it, the lighter slips away and drops to a lower level. Bruno manages to recapture it just as Guy wins the third and final set. The race shifts to the amusement park where Guy finally confronts his nemesis, who jumps onto a merry-go-round with Guy still in pursuit. The police see them struggling and fire a shot which accidentally strikes the man operating the ride and the merry-go-round speeds out of control. Another park employee crawls precariously beneath the whirling machine and brings it to a screeching halt, collapsing the structure in the process and trapping the mortally wounded Bruno in its wreckage. As the police cluster around, Guy tries to make Bruno confess, but Bruno sticks to his story that it was Guy who murdered Miriam and that the man's incriminating lighter is somewhere near the murder scene. As he dies, however, everyone sees the telltale lighter slip from Bruno's grasp. The truth is revealed, Guy is absolved, and he (not to mention the audience) is finally let off the tension-filled hook.

Unrelentingly suspenseful though it is, *Strangers on*

On his way to plant the incriminating lighter at the scene of the crime, Bruno (Robert Walker) accidentally drops it into a storm drain.

a Train is not a hard-edged thriller. It is full of Hitchcockian humor, the most notable example of which is the running joke about Bruno's relationship with his mother, a somewhat scatterbrained lady who giggles and mumbles to herself and gets off on painting weird pictures. When Anne Morton visits the woman and tries to talk her into persuading Bruno to give himself up, Mrs. Antony dismisses Anne's plea with a non sequitur: "Bruno sometimes goes a little too far," she giggles as she exits up the stairs. Then Bruno comes on the scene. After cleverly manipulating Anne's on-again-off-again suspicions about Guy's guilt, he departs up the stairs as well, offering Anne a bizarre little wave of the hand so reminiscent of his doting mother's gestures that we begin to understand where Bruno's "idiosyncrasies" may have come from.

The amusement park murder of Miriam also contains a fair amount of Hitchcock's impish and sardonic humor. As Bruno begins to stalk Miriam there, he is suddenly brought up short by a little boy carrying a balloon who pulls a gun on him. The gun is a toy. Nevertheless, in a fit of pique at being "threatened," Bruno pops the kid's balloon. He then follows Miriam to the tunnel of love, where she hops on board one of the boats, her two suitors in tow. Bruno follows in the boat behind. As the boats disappear into the tunnel, we suddenly hear Miriam scream and wonder if

Bruno has struck. But as the boats emerge from the tunnel, we see that Miriam is very much alive. She screams again and we see one of her boyfriends tickling her.

The actual murder itself is treated as a grisly and disturbing affair, however, although Hitchcock distances us from that grisliness a bit by showing the murder to us as a distorted reflection in Miriam's fallen eyeglasses. After killing her, Bruno exits the amusement park and, on the way out, helps a blind man across a busy street.

The overall wit of the piece is best exemplified, however, by Robert Walker's sophisticated performance as the sociopathic Bruno, whose engaging manner and high style make him one of the most multifaceted (and perversely appealing) villains in Hitchcockian cinema. He is, as Guy himself remarks, "a very clever fellow"—a cunning "God of the Underworld" (Pluto is the name of the boat that transports Bruno through the tunnel of love to his date with murder). There are times when we almost wish that he'll get away with it.*

*The bland 1969 remake of the film, now called *Once You Kiss a Stranger,* altered the characters to have one a golf pro and the other (in the Robert Walker part) a woman—played by Carol Lynley. The 1987 Danny DeVito black comedy, *Throw Momma From the Train,* was made as an obvious tip-of-the-hat to Hitchcock by spoofing the original.

RAWHIDE

(1951)

[a.k.a. *Desperate Siege*]
Twentieth Century-Fox • B&W/86 Minutes

CREDITS

Director: enry Hathaway; *Producer*: Samuel G. Engel; *Screenplay*: Dudley Nichols; *Cinematographer*: Milton Krasner; *Editor*: Robert Simpson; *Music*: Sol Kaplan; *Art Directors*: Lyle Wheeler and George W. Davis.

CAST

Tom Owens: Tyrone Power; *Miss Vinnie Holt*: Susan Hayward; *Rafe Zimmerman*: Hugh Marlowe; *Yancy*: Dean Jagger; *Sam Todd*: Edgar Buchanan; *Tevis*: Jack Elam; *Gratz*: George Tobias; *Luke*: Jeff Corey; *Tex*: Louis Jean Heydt.

* * *

In addition to doing outright remakes of many of their past successes, the major studios had a practice of dusting off some of their more obscure properties, reshaping the storylines, and setting them in different milieus, then reshooting them as "new" films. Such is the case with *Rawhide,* which saw its first screen incarnation as a lively 1935 Fox gangster film called *Show Them No Mercy.*

In *Show Them No Mercy,* a married couple with a baby (Rochelle Hudson and the wimpish Edward Norris) seek refuge from a storm in a seemingly deserted old house that turns out to be the lair of kidnappers. As the Feds close in on the gang, the couple struggle to save their own lives and that of their baby by outwitting the intelligent and somewhat refined, though still dangerous, gang leader (Cesar Romero) and his more brutish sidekick (Bruce Cabot).

Frequent John Ford collaborator Dudley Nichols and director Henry Hathaway, a genre specialist equally at home on the range as with suspense films, were charged fifteen years later with turning the script of the 1935 movie into a tense Western. They accomplished this relatively easily by retaining the earlier film's basic storyline and pouring on the suspense by making their couple fend for themselves. What emerged was a much tenser tale (though the 1935 film did have its nail-biting moments) as well as

The news arrives at Rawhide Station that a dangerous criminal named Zimmerman has escaped from Huntsville Prison and is headed this way in director Henry Hathaway's Hitchcockian suspense thriller decked out in cowboy garb.

a very unusual hybrid: a Hitchcockian suspense thriller decked out in cowboy garb.

Tyrone Power and Susan Hayward play the couple, here named Tom Owens and Vinnie Holt, although in *Rawhide* they aren't married. Owens is the son of an East Coast magnate who has been sent West to learn the family business from the bottom up by working as "mule boy" at Rawhide Station, one of his father's overland mail stagecoach stops between San Francisco and St. Louis. Holt's a former saloon singer who's delivering her dead sister's baby girl to relatives in San Francisco, where she hopes to take a job. When soldiers stop by the station to warn Owens and his

Tom Owns (Tyrone Power) forces Vinnie Holt (Susan Hayward) and her baby to remain at the stage stop for their protection until the prisoners are recaptured.

Assuming that Owens (Tyrone Power) and Holt (Susan Hayward) are married, Zimmerman (Hugh Marlowe) threatens the lives of the man's wife and child if Owens fails to cooperate with Zimmerman's plan, which is to rob the next morning's eastbound stage of a gold shipment.

Though they eventually overcome their mutual hostility in order to survive, Owens (Tyrone Power) and Vinnie (Susan Hayward) never develop any real affection for one another.

The captives (Tyrone Power and Susan Hayward) take turns beneath one of the beds digging a hole through the adobe wall so that they can escape.

Hathaway stages the movie more like a claustrophobic film noir *thriller than a Western, using tight close-ups to heighten the tension and suspense.*

boss, Sam Todd, that some dangerous prisoners led by a man named Zimmerman have escaped from Huntsville jail, Holt and her baby are forced to remain at the station for their protection until the prisoners are recaptured. Posing as a sheriff in pursuit of the gang, Zimmerman arrives, smooth talks his way inside, and he and his gang take everyone hostage. Todd is killed when he attempts to go for his gun. Assuming that Owens and Holt are married, Zimmerman threatens the lives of the man's wife and child if Owens fails to cooperate with his plan, which is to rob the next morning's eastbound stage of a gold shipment. Another stage is due in beforehand, however, and Owens is charged with making everything at the station look relaxed and normal to the driver and his passengers so that the stage will depart on schedule and no suspicions will be aroused. Though he agrees to play along, Owens scribbles a message about the gang's presence and plans which he intends to slip to the stage driver. While he's unharnessing the coach's horses for feeding, however, the note slips from his pocket and is buffeted by the wind next to Zimmerman's feet. Zimmerman fails to see the piece of paper, however, and Owens manages to retrieve it, but by this time his opportunity to slip it to the driver has passed.

Later, at dinner, Owens gets hold of a gun and conceals it beneath a newspaper for use after the stage is gone. But the wily Zimmerman is on to him and as soon as the stage departs, he confiscates the pistol. Eventually, Owens manages to steal a knife from the kitchen, and when he and Holt are locked in their room, they take turns beneath one of the beds digging a hole through the adobe wall so that Owens can crawl outside and get his own pistol, which Holt had mislaid earlier behind the water trough. But their efforts are slowed considerably when the knife blade snaps in two. Working exhaustively through the night, they break through to the outside, but the hole still isn't large enough for either of them to crawl through.

Zimmerman rousts them to get things ready for the arrival of the stage. The ongoing tension between the intelligent Zimmerman and his chief henchman, the animalistic Tevis, finally erupts during the preparations, however, and Tevis shoots Zimmerman in the back. During the excitement, Owens gets to the gun behind the water trough and pins Tevis down. But Tevis sees his chance to escape when Holt's toddler, having crawled out the hole in the bedroom wall,

suddenly appears in the line of fire. He orders Owens to surrender the gun or he'll kill the child. And to show he means business, he fires several shots that explode in the dirt precariously close to the frightened baby's feet. In the exciting denouement, the duo rescues the baby and kills Tevis, though Owens is wounded in the process. When the stage arrives, the astonished driver asks the bloodied "mule boy" what the hell he's been up to and the weary Owens responds, "Just learning the business."

In addition to these highlights, Nichols and Hathaway sprinkle numerous other nerve-racking moments throughout the film, which Hathaway has staged in a style more akin to a claustrophobic *film noir* thriller than a typical Western. Even most of the outdoor scenes are shot in tight close-ups—of faces, objects, gestures—rather than wide shots in order to heighten the tension and suspense.

Character tension is not lacking either. Though they eventually come to terms in order to survive, Owens and Holt never develop any real liking for one another, and there is no indication whatsoever that they might become lovers after the final fade-out. Demanding, bitchy, and generally mistrustful of men, she constantly blames him for getting her into this mess by forcing her off the stage. At best, he tolerates her in order to pull off the charade that they're married, which is the only hold they have over their captor.

Civilized, intelligent, and occasionally compassionate, though still quite capable of brutal violence, Zimmerman views his fellow gang members, particularly Tevis, as neanderthals whom he rebukes and orders about as if they literally were subhuman. He gets on with no one, except the Eastern raised and educated Owens, whom he seems to consider more of an equal and tries to engage in some friendly conversation now and then. To add to his character's inscrutability, there even appears to be a hint of latent homosexuality in Zimmerman's attitude toward Owens. Tevis suggests as much when he scorns Zimmerman for having "sworn off women" while in prison. We subsequently learn that Zimmerman was sent to jail for murdering his two-timing girlfriend's lover and that's why he is so bitter toward and mistrustful of the opposite sex (in this respect, he's a lot like Vinnie Holt), but that explanation doesn't necessarily dispel our suspicions entirely. He makes a most fascinating and engaging villain, which is something else *Rawhide* has in common with Hitchcock's thrillers.

THE TALL TARGET

(1951)

Metro-Goldwyn-Mayer • B&W/78 Minutes

CREDITS

Director: Anthony Mann; *Producer*: Richard Gold-stone; *Screenplay*: George Worthington Yates and Art Cohn; *Cinematographer*: Paul C. Vogel; *Editor*: Newell P. Kimlin; *Art Directors*: Cedric Gibbons and Eddie Imazu.

CAST

John Kennedy: Dick Powell; *Ginny Beaufort*: Paula Raymond; *Caleb Jeffers*: Adolphe Menjou; *Lance Beaufort*: Marshall Thompson; *Rachel*: Ruby Dee; *Lieutenant Colter*: Richard Rober; *Homer Crowley*: Will Geer; *Mrs. Alsop*: Florence Bates; *Abraham Lincoln*: Leslie Kimmell.

* * *

Detective John Kennedy (Dick Powell, seen here with Adolphe Menjou, Ruby Dee, Paula Raymond, and Marshall Thompson) finds himself in a hotbed of secessionsists, spies, and assassins in Anthony Mann's thriller about the "Baltimore Plot" to kill newly elected President Abraham Lincoln, the title character of The Tall Target.

The title refers to Abraham Lincoln, who was marked for assassination by Southern radicals on several occasions before the fatal bullet fired by John Wilkes Booth on April 14, 1865, finally struck him down. The film is a fictionalized account of a failed first attempt on Lincoln's life that occurred while the President-elect was traveling from Harrisburg, Pennsylvania, through Baltimore on his way to his 1861 inauguration in Washington.

Referred to by historians as "The Baltimore Plot," the plan was to shoot Lincoln in Baltimore, a hotbed of anti-Union and anti-Lincoln extremism, while he was delivering a preinaugural address there. One of the chief conspirators was a Baltimore barber named Cypriano Ferrandino, and it was through him that Allan Pinkerton, founder of the famous detective agency, learned of the conspiracy and foiled it. He did so by disguising the President-elect in a broad-brimmed hat and secreting him on board a late-night commercial sleeper rather than the highly visible inauguration train, then cutting the telegraph wires out of Harrisburg so that no one in Baltimore could be alerted. The sleeper proceeded through Baltimore on into Washington unnoticed, prompting Lincoln to solemnly remark, "Did any President come to his inauguration so like a thief in the night?"

One of the more intriguing aspects to this incident was the brief involvement of a New York City Chief of Detectives named John Kennedy, who, like Pinkerton, also got wind of the Baltimore Plot, sent some operatives to the city to investigate, but supposedly dismissed the plot as a hoax when they failed to uncover any substantive information. Historians continue to disagree as to who actually cracked the case, Kennedy or Pinkerton, but Anthony Mann's Hitchcockian thriller about the affair shows no such indecision. It places Kennedy squarely in the thick of things, working frantically alone and seemingly unheeded by anyone in authority until the film's closing minutes when he unmasks the primary assassin, heaves him from the train, then learns from one of Pinkerton's disguised on-board operatives that his (Kennedy's) reports of the conspiracy had come to Lincoln and Pinkerton's attention early on and been taken quite seriously all along.

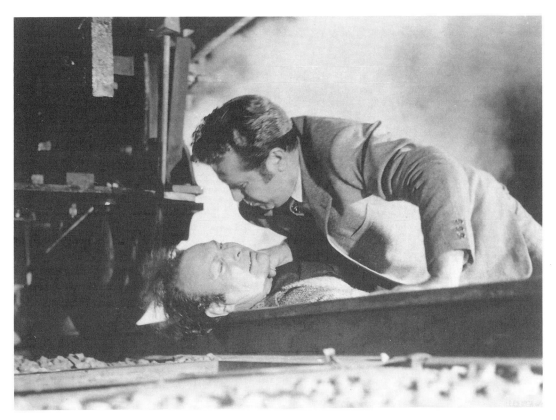

Kennedy (Dick Powell) struggles with one of the conspirators (Leif Erickson), who has stolen Kennedy's gun and identity papers.

Ruby Dee, Marshall Thompson, Paula Raymond, and Dick Powell in The Tall Target.

To achieve tension and suspense, The Tall Target *takes many of its cues from Hitchcock, particularly the master's* The Lady Vanishes, *which Mann's film closely resembles.*

Kennedy's strongest ally, a grandfatherly New York State Zouave played by Adolphe Menjou, turns out to be a ringleader in the conspiracy to assassinate President Lincoln.

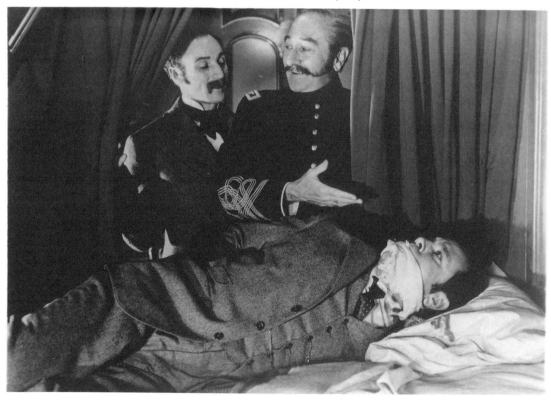

Kennedy (Dick Powell) escapes, and the hunt is on.

Apart from placing Kennedy on board the midnight train and having him play a fictional game of cat and mouse with several of the conspirators, the script quite accurately explores the details of the Baltimore Plot and how it was brought down. The script and director Mann also do a good job of illustrating the extremely volatile political atmosphere in which the incident took place. We tend to forget that the now-deified Lincoln was not so well loved at the time by many Americans, who viewed him as a potential destroyer and "Satan," and who, as one of the secessionist characters in the film states quite openly, "would willingly shake the hand of the man who shoots him." The film's authentic portrait of the period's political extremism and public approval of shooting a President still echoes disquietingly when we realize that our nation hasn't changed much in a hundred years. For just over a decade after the film's release, another President who was similarly vilified (and loved) would be gunned down for political reasons as well. That this President shared the name of the film's real life protagonist,

John Kennedy, adds even eerier resonances to *The Tall Target.*

Making the less well known detective the protagonist rather than Pinkerton also allowed the filmmakers to have it both ways. It enabled them to adhere to the facts of the case with regard to Pinkerton yet left them free to speculate as to what might have occurred had Kennedy become more intimately involved as well. This was an important decision in terms of creating tension and suspense, for as with Fred Zinnemann's *The Day of the Jackal,* Frederick Forsyth's account of a failed attempt on the life of French President Charles de Gaulle, we know from the beginning what the outcome will be. De Gaulle wasn't killed, and neither was Lincoln, at least not this time around. So, Kennedy's fate becomes our primary concern. Will *he* survive this nest of spies?

To achieve tension and suspense, *The Tall Target* takes many of its cues from Hitchcock, particularly the master's *The Lady Vanishes,* which Mann's film closely resembles. The bulk of the film's action is confined to the claustrophobic interior of a fast-moving train. Characters disappear and/or pose as others; even Kennedy's identity is called into question early on when one of the conspirators takes his place. The train is stopped to take on an ill passenger (Lincoln in disguise) who is installed in a private compartment and looked over by a woman who may or may not be what she seems. And like Paul Lukas's helpful doctor in the Hitchcock film, the character in *The Tall Target* who appears to be Kennedy's strongest ally, a grandfatherly New York State Zouave played by Adolphe Menjou, turns out to be a ringleader in the conspiracy. There is also a scene involving a message scrawled on a train window that parallels a similar one in *The Lady Vanishes.* In Hitchcock fashion also, Kennedy becomes a hunted man by the authorities and must resort to playing hide-and-seek with them as well the conspirators.

The Tall Target was a transitional film for director Anthony Mann, one of America's most accomplished though often unsung genre filmmakers (he died in 1968). It fell between his innovative *film noir* crime melodramas of the forties and his colorful series of classic Westerns with James Stewart in the fifties. A *noir* film itself, it is not a major Mann work thematically, though it does rank in skillfulness with his more thematically personal transitional films of the period, *Devil's Doorway* and *Winchester '73.* The unusual plot rolls along as swiftly and with as many twists and turns as the train itself, the tension and suspense seldom slackening. And in a very atypical move for a Hollywood thrillmaker, Mann sought no aid from a composer in keeping his audience on edge. The film has no music score.

THE NARROW MARGIN

(1952)

RKO Pictures • B&W/70 Minutes

CREDITS

Director: Richard Fleischer; *Producer*: Stanley Rubin; *Screenplay*: Stanley Rubin, from a story by Martin Goldsmith and Jack Leonard; *Cinematographer*: George E. Diskant; *Editor*: Robert Swink; *Art Directors*: Albert S. D'Agostino and Jack Okey.

CAST

Brown: Charles McGraw; *Mrs. Neall*: Marie Windsor; *Mrs. Sinclair*: Jacqueline White; *Forbes*: Don Beddoe; *Tommy Sinclair*: Gordon Gebert; *Kemp*: David Clarke; *Densel*: Peter Virgo; *Sam Jennings*: Paul Maxey; *Train Conductor*: Harry Harvey; *Tommy's Nursemaid*: Queenie Leonard; *Vincent Yost*: Peter Brocco.

* * *

Brown (Charles McGraw) takes an instant dislike to the sharp-tongued gangster's moll (Marie Windsor) he's been assigned to protect.

Like *The Window* (see separate chapter), RKO's *The Narrow Margin* was a "sleeper" that surprisingly out-performed many of the studio's more prestigious, big-budget films and won the hearts and minds of many critics as well. It even copped an Oscar nomination (for best motion picture story), which was even more unexpected since the film was little more than a "B" movie thriller, one of many that RKO—and *every* studio—ground out each year. That it has endured while so many "A" films of the period have long since faded into obscurity is a tribute to the "B" movie concept itself—a concept that may have denied film-makers decent budgets, but, at the same time, allowed them to exercise their skills and imaginations without studio interference and sometimes come up with artful results—maybe even a classic.

The Narrow Margin is not a great film by any means, but it *is* a classic example of this type of movie success story: a marvelously written, crisply acted, cinematically inventive, and tautly directed little thriller that still puts many of its "A" budget brethren to shame—including Peter Hyams's multimillion dollar 1990 remake, retitled *Narrow Margin*, starring Gene Hackman and Anne Archer.

In fact, comparing the two versions is quite illuminating, for the main difference between them goes straight to the heart of what this book is all about: what separates the *bona fide* thriller—the film that strives to create and sustain audience tension—from the film that strives mainly to wow audiences with a series of thrills.

Though the plots of the two are roughly the same and both take place on a fast-moving train, the 1990 version sacrifices audience tension by repeatedly taking us outside the train and having the principals run and fight atop it and cling precariously to its sides in a series of hair-raising set pieces. Whereas the 1952 version allows the principals—and us—virtually no escape. The bulk of the action is confined to the claustrophobic corridors and compartments of the train itself, sweeping up the characters and the audience in a taut guessing game of who's who and what's what. In other words, Hyams's film concentrates on stunts—and is exciting mostly when the stunt men and women go into action. The original film concentrates on tension and suspense, and, as a result, grabs us all the way through.

In a rare moment of relaxation aboard the train, Brown (Charles McGraw) befriends an attractive blonde, Mrs. Sinclair (Jacqueline White), and her little boy (Gordon Gebert).

Brown (Charles McGraw) cleverly gets Mrs. Neall (Marie Windsor) on board the train without her being seen, and hides her in a spare compartment next to his own.

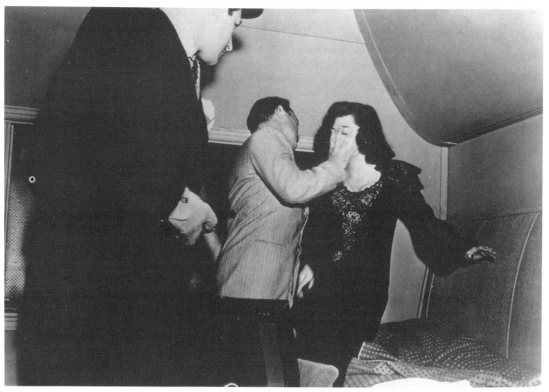

Mob hit men Densel (Peter Virgo) and Kemp (David Clarke) discover where Brown has hidden Mrs. Neall (Marie Windsor). They kill her, but, in a susprise twist, she turns out to have been a policewoman in disguise.

Sinclair (Jacqueline White) is the real Mrs. Neall. And as the train rushes westward and the film speeds to its exciting climax, Brown (Charles McGraw) realizes he has inadvertently led the mobsters straight to her.

Peter Virgo, Jacqueline White, and Charles McGraw in Richard Fleischer's low budget but impressive The Narrow Margin, *RKO's "sleeper" of 1952.*

Policeman Forbes and his younger partner, Brown, are sent to Chicago to pick up a key witness, Mrs. Neall, the ex-wife of a dead mobster, in a grand jury probe of mob payoffs to government officials and transport her to Los Angeles to testify. In possession of the secret payoff list, she is targeted for assassination by hit men. Not knowing what the woman looks like, they keep close tabs on the cops instead, who lead them straight to her door. Forbes is killed protecting Mrs. Neall, a sharp-tongued "cheap and flashy" type to whom Brown takes an instant dislike, feeling the life of such a woman a poor exchange for his partner's, who has left behind a wife and two young daughters.

Forced to go it alone now, Brown cleverly gets her on board the train without her being seen and hides her in a spare compartment next to his own. As the train leaves the station, one of the hit men makes his presence known to Brown right away; the others are initially less conspicuous. Brown's suspicions fall on a number of people and he grows increasingly edgy and prone to making mistakes as he tries to cover his back from several directions at once.

Unable to find the woman and growing impatient, the mobsters come out into the open and try to bribe Brown to hand over the woman and the payoff list. Brown refuses, but as the war of nerves escalates and he nears the breaking point, one begins to wonder if he might not take them up on their offer after all.

In a rare moment of relaxation, Brown befriends an attractive blonde named Mrs. Sinclair, who is traveling to Los Angeles with her little boy, Tommy, and the boy's nursemaid. As Brown spends more and more time with her, he unwittingly arouses the mobsters' suspicions that *she* may be Mrs. Neall. Already stressed to the maximum, Brown now finds himself charged with protecting both women, and doing a poor job of it. The mobsters discover where he's hidden Mrs. Neall and kill her. But in a surprise twist, she turns out to be a police woman from Internal Affairs Division who has been posing as Mrs. Neall in the event that Brown might succumb to bribery and turn the witness over. Sinclair is the real Mrs. Neall, and as the train rushes westward and the film speeds to its exciting climax, Brown realizes he has inadvertently led the mobsters right to her.

Like *The Tall Target* (see separate chapter), *The Narrow Margin* uses the cacophony of sounds of the train itself, rather than a music score, to build atmosphere. And director Richard Fleischer sustains this atmosphere visually with some very inventive camerawork and marvelous trick photography; it's hard to believe the film was shot on a studio sound stage and not on a real train. Technically, the film is a real tour de force.

Largely because of *The Narrow Margin,* Fleischer (son of veteran animator Max Fleischer) quickly graduated to "A" films and went on to direct a number of other impressive thrillers, including *Violent Saturday* and *See No Evil,* and a string of vivid "docudramas" based on real life crimes, the best of which is *10 Rillington Place,* a realistic and disturbing look at the the notorious John Reginald Christie/ Timothy Evans case of the late 1940s which had resulted in the abolition of capital punishment in England.

THE HITCH-HIKER

(1953)

RKO Pictures • B&W/71 Minutes

CREDITS

Director: Ida Lupino; *Producer*: Collier Young; *Screenplay*: Collier Young and Ida Lupino; *Cinematographer*: Nicholas Musuraca; *Editor*: Douglas Stewart; *Music*: Leith Stevens; *Art Directors*: Albert S. D'Agostino, Walter E. Keller.

CAST

Roy Collins: Edmond O'Brien; *Gilbert Bowen*: Frank Lovejoy; *Emmett Myers*: William Talman; *Captain Alvarado*: José Torvay; *Themselves (Newscasters)*: Sam Hayes, Wendel Niles; *Inspector General*: Jean Del Val; *Government Agent*: Clark Howat; *José*: Natividad Vacio.

*   *   *

Though far from abundant, there are more women directors at work in the film industry today than ever before in motion picture history. Prior to the eighties and nineties, however, few women had been able to crack this traditionally male dominated society, particularly in Hollywood.

During the silent era, Lois Weber had established a presence in Hollywood as actress, writer, and director of a number of controversial "social problem" films made for her own production company, but her career faded with the coming of the talkies. Dorothy Arzner,

The campfire scenes where Bowen and Collins can't figure out whether Myers (William Talman) is asleep or watching them are especially chilling and tense.

*Myers (William Talman) threatens Bowen (Frank Lovejoy, left)
and Collins (Edmond O'Brien) with death if they fail to carry
out his every instruction.*

*Collins (Edmond O'Brien, left) and Bowen (Frank Lovejoy)
plan to make a break from Myers (William Talman) when they
stop at a country store in Mexico. But the plan fails.*

a former scriptwriter for Paramount, took up the banner in the closing days of the silents with a series of low budget comedies and emotional dramas not unlike Weber's films in that they tended to feature women as the central characters of their plots. Because of their popularity with female audiences, such films were dubbed "women's pictures," and male directors were urged to crank out similar ones to meet the profitable demand. The phrase stuck until the feminist sixties and seventies when it finally went the way of the dinosaur.

Arzner made a more successful transition to the talkies, however, and continued directing until 1943 when her career in Hollywood abruptly came to an end (she died in 1979). Her most famous and successful credits as a director include *Christopher Strong* (1933) with Katharine Hepburn and *Craig's Wife* (1936) with Rosalind Russell—"women's pictures" both. True, other women directors succeeded in making a film or two in Hollywood during this same period, but their names are largely forgotten today. Weber and Arzner, though not exactly household names, remain the most well known to us because they were more prolific and managed to hang on

longer than the rest—with one exception: Ida Lupino, the only one of her minority number to be found in critic Andrew Sarris's auteurist study of the Hollywood directorial landscape, *The American Cinema* (E.P. Dutton, 1968).

More famous as an actress—indeed, from the mid-thirties through the mid-fifties, she was a major star—Ida Lupino used her clout in the industry to move behind the cameras in the early fifties by forming an independent production outfit called The Filmmakers Company with then husband, writer-producer Collier Young (later the co-creator of the television series *One Step Beyond*). She directed her last film, the comedy *The Trouble With Angels*, in 1965. During these years, she held the field virtually all by herself.

To use the antiquated term of the studio heads, most of Ms. Lupino's directorial efforts can be classified as "women's pictures" too—emotional dramas featuring women in central roles. *Never Fear* (1950) was about a dancer (Sally Forrest) who struggles to overcome polio, a disease that has shattered her life and career. *The Outrage* (1950) dealt with the social problem of violence against women by focusing on the

Trapped! Edmond O'Brien and Frank Lovejoy find themselves at the mercy of escaped convict Emmett Myers (William Talman) in Ida Lupino's The Hitch-Hiker.

William Talman's performance as the icily soft-spoken title character, a remorseless killer with a bum eye, steals the show.

psychological ordeal of a single rape victim (Mala Powers). *Hard, Fast and Beautiful* (1951) was about a young woman (Sally Forrest again) who is pushed into a tennis career by her ambitious mother (Claire Trevor), achieving great fame but little happiness until she finally decides to stand on her own. *The Bigamist* (1953) was a low key drama with a sensational theme that focused as much sympathetic attention on the two women in his life (Joan Fontaine and Lupino herself) as it did on the title character (Edmond O'Brien).

The Hitch-Hiker (1953) broke the mold—or the stereotype, as it were—for it was not only an anomaly in Lupino's directorial career but also that of every other female director up to this time as well. It was a flat-out action and suspense thriller that not only didn't feature a central female character, but also had a virtually all-male cast.

The plot of the film is straightforward and starts building suspense and tension from the opening shot: a gun is pointed at the viewer and the words *The Hitch-Hiker* fill the screen. The title character is Emmett Myers, a violent ex-con thumbing his way to Mexico so that he can jump over to Central America and disappear. He robs, kills, and steals the cars of various people along the way and a manhunt is launched to capture him. When the car of his latest victim, a traveling salesman, runs out of gas, Myers is picked up by Gil Bowen and Roy Collins, two ex-Army buddies bound for a hunting and fishing trip to Mexico. Myers pulls his gun and threatens the two men with death if they fail to carry out his every instruction. Knowing the mass killer has nothing to lose and will shoot them anyway as soon as he gets to his destination, the desperate men make plans to escape during one of several overnight rest stops. When this fails and Collins is wounded, they must rely on their wits—and a good deal of luck—to outfox the wily killer. With their car running low on fuel, Myers forces them at gunpoint to break open a pump at a closed gas station and Bowen leaves his inscribed wedding ring behind. The police discover it, pick up the trail, and track the killer and his two hostages to the Santa Rosalia jumping off point where Bowen finally succeeds in overcoming the criminal just as the authorities arrive. The film ends as the enraged Myers, struggling in the arms of the police, spits in the face of the man he once accused of being "soft" and is then led away.

As the trio heads deep into Mexico, Lupino alternates tight close-ups of the men inside the claustrophobic car with long shots of the wide open spaces to offer a constant visual reminder of Bowen and Collins's desperate feelings of being trapped while freedom beckons just beyond their grasp. She also offers numerous suspenseful set pieces along the way, including an especially tense—and, finally, quite emotional—scene at a Mexican country store where the three stop for supplies. Bowen and Collins load up a box with canned goods as Myers watches them from a few feet away, his hand poised on the gun concealed in his pocket. Collins's intention—skillfully implied by Lupino via looks and gestures between the two men rather than words—is to overcome Myers by tossing the heavy box at him as they are leaving. But the plan is foiled when the store owner's child tugs at Myers's sleeve to show him her doll just at the wrong moment and Collins passes by them in frustration, compelled to abandon the scheme for fear the child might get hurt. As Collins goes out the door, Myers grumbles at the child and Bowen (he and Collins both are married but only Bowen has children) scoops her up, embraces her in a manner that is not only protective but also clinging, and tells her, in Spanish, to "Go with God"—as if, not knowing whether he'll come out of this alive, he's bidding his own children an emotional farewell through her.

O'Brien and Lovejoy are effective and convincing as the continually frustrated hostages, but it is Talman's performance as the icily soft-spoken Myers, a remorseless killer with a bum eye that won't stay closed, that steals the show. The campfire scenes where Bowen and Collins try to decide whether he's actually asleep and if they should make their break as Myers sits with his gun poised at them, his one eye shut and the other still cracked open, are especially chilling and tense.

Although a critical and financial success, *The Hitch-Hiker* failed to open doors immediately for Lupino and others of her sex who sought to take on genres heretofore exclusively identified with male directors. But it eventually did open them by proving conclusively that there was no valid reason for those doors' remaining shut. *The Hitch-Hiker* was, and remains, a taut, gritty, and cinematically skillful low budget thriller with a firm grip and a crackling pace. It's a shame that, for whatever reason, Ida Lupino didn't get the opportunity to do more of them.

THE WAGES OF FEAR

(1953)

International Affiliates • B&W/149 Minutes

CREDITS

Director: Henri-Georges Clouzot; *Producer*: Henri-Georges Clouzot; *Screenplay*: Henri-Georges Clouzot and Jerome Geronimi, based on the novel *La Salaire de la Peur* by Georges Arnaud; *Cinematographer*: Armand Thirard; *Editors*: Henri Rust, Madeleine Gug, and Etiennette Muse; *Music*: Georges Auric; *Production Designer*: Rene Renoux.

CAST

Mario: Yves Montand; *Jo*: Charles Vanel; *Luigi*: Folco Lulli; *Bimba*: Peter Van Eyck; *Bill O'Brien*: William Tubbs; *Linda*: Vera Clouzot; *Hernandez*: Dario Moreno; *Smerloff*: Jo Dest.

* * *

Dubbed "the French Hitchcock," director Henri-Georges Clouzot (1907–77) was responsible for two of the best remembered and most widely imitated suspense movies of the fifties: the mystery-cum-horror film *Les Diaboliques* (1955) and the hugely successful thriller that preceded it and lauched Clouzot's international reputation, *The Wages of Fear*.

Interestingly, both projects were initially offered to the master himself. Hitchcock turned *Les Diaboliques* down for not being his cup of tea. Even so, it must have connected with him in some way, for Hitchcock would recall many of its elements—the oppressive atmosphere of grand guignol gloom transposed to a modern setting, its chilling surprise ending, and, most notably, the bathroom murder of its heroine—in his classic *Psycho*. Pierre Boileau and Thomas Narcejac, the authors of the novel upon which Clouzot's film was based, didn't give up though and wrote a subsequent novel, *D'entre les morts,* with Hitchcock expressly in mind. Their perseverance paid off for the master obviously found this one more to his tastes and transformed the book into his masterpiece, *Vertigo* (see separate chapter).

In the case of *The Wages of Fear*, Hitchcock actually did want to make the film and attempted to buy the rights, but negotiations with the novel's author,

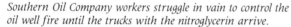

Southern Oil Company workers struggle in vain to control the oil well fire until the trucks with the nitroglycerin arrive.

Mario (Yves Montand) surveys the precarious situation facing him as he single-handedly backs his nitro-loaded truck onto a rickety bridge. His partner, the cowardly Jo, having accidentally fallen from the bridge while guiding him, has meanwhile scurried out of sight to avoid the danger if it collapses and the truck falls.

Georges Arnaud, and publisher reached some sort of nationalistic impasse and Clouzot jumped in and secured the rights to the book for himself. His film went on to win the grand prize at Cannes and several other international awards and become one of the most financially successful movies the French film industry ever exported.

It's not hard to imagine Hitchcock making a glossier, faster-paced, and, perhaps, less faithful "entertainment" (in the Graham Greene sense) out of Arnaud's book than Clouzot's gritty, existentialist nightmare. Perhaps this is why negotiations with Arnaud broke down, for Clouzot's film follows the book quite scrupulously—although for U.S. release almost twenty minutes were cut to speed up the action and make the film more appealing to American audiences. (The eliminated scenes have since been replaced in the restored 149-minute American version now extant on laserdisc via the Voyager Company's Criterion Collection.) But with all respect to Hitchcock, it's hard to imagine his having made a more thrilling and suspenseful film than Clouzot did. *The Wages of Fear* may get off to a slow start, but once it quite literally gets rolling, it's one of the most nail-biting thrillers ever made.

Though it was shot in France, the film is convincingly set in an unnamed, oil-rich but otherwise impoverished Central American country dominated by the Southern Oil Company, an American petroleum giant. One of the company's wells has caught fire and is raging out of control. The only way to put out the fire is to blow the wells with nitroglycerin.

95

*Encountering a rock slide. Mario (Yves Montand) and Jo
(Charles Vanel) help rig some nitro to clear the way, then pull
their truck safely back to await the blast.*

Mario (Yves Montand) navigates the crater filled with oil from a ruptured pipeline created by the explosion of Bimba and Luigi's truck.

When the truck gets hung up on a tree branch, Mario (Yves Montand) wades into the oil-filled crater to remove the obstacle.

From the company's headquarters in a small, dirt-poor village hundreds of miles away, the company's boss, Bill O'Brien, solicits four volunteers to drive two trucks loaded with nitro (in the hopes that at least one will make it) across the treacherous mountain roads leading to the site of the blaze. The job, which will pay $2,000 to whomever gets through, falls to four down-and-out European expatriates looking for enough money to bankroll an escape from their desperate situation and an opportunity to regain some self-respect.

One truck is driven by Mario, a young, fun-loving, irresponsible Corsican looking to finance his return ticket home, and Jo, a flashy, seemingly fearless French gangster who has used up all his money fleeing from the law. The other truck is driven by

Luigi, a rotund Italian with a terminal illness (and therefore nothing to lose) who wants to bequeath the money to his family back home, and Bimba, a Dutch refugee. As the hair-raising trip progresses, we gain insights into each man's character, but Clouzot tends to concentrate on the relationship between Mario, who proves to be more determined and resourceful than expected, and Jo, whom Mario initially hero-worships because of his fearless, tough guy image. But that image quickly crumbles under the strain of the nerve-racking journey and Jo reveals himself to be a coward underneath.

As if the narrow, winding, rut-filled jungle road weren't enough of a challenge, the drivers encounter several major obstacles along the way that test their skills and nerve even more. In order to negotiate a

The truck safely across, Mario (Yves Montand) pulls Jo (Charles Vanel), whose leg has been crushed by the truck's wheels, from the morass of oil.

sharp uphill turn, for example, they must back their trucks onto a dilapidated wooden bridge that juts out from the face of a cliff. The lead truck driven by Luigi and Bimba makes the swing fairly easily but puts a severe strain on the already dangerous structure in the process. With Jo guiding him, Mario backs the second truck onto the bridge whose supports are now in danger of giving way entirely. Jo accidentally falls from the bridge and disappears from view. Thinking his partner has been killed, Mario is faced with completing the treacherous maneuver on his own. As the structure sways precariously and its rotting boards start to crumble, the truck's tires lose traction and one of the bridge's support cables gets caught on the truck's rigging. But Mario manages to pull the truck safely onto the road just as the bridge collapses. He then finds Jo hiding among the rocks to escape the blast if the truck had fallen, and realizes his tough guy partner is a coward at heart. Needing the man's help, however, Mario gives Jo a second chance, but Jo reveals his cowardly streak again when the drivers encounter their next major obstacle—a rockslide that has blocked the road with a huge boulder. As Bimba and the others cleverly plan to remove the boulder with some of the explosive nitro, the fearful Jo refuses to help them and scurries away to safety. Once the road is cleared, Mario finds him and threatens to kill him if he doesn't shape up, which Jo eventually does in the film's grisliest and most harrowing scene.

Luigi and Bimba's truck explodes and the hole created by the blast fills with oil from a ruptured pipeline. Mario and Jo rig a winch to pull their truck across, but its wheels get hung up on a submerged tree branch and its progress is temporarily stalled. Jo wades into the slick morass to remove the obstacle, but when the truck regains traction, his leg is trapped beneath one of the wheels, and Mario, who can't afford to stop, is compelled to run over him. As soon as the truck is across, Mario pulls his mortally wounded partner to safety and loads him back onto the truck to complete the last lap of their journey. His leg hideously mangled, Jo expires from his wounds just short of their destination, and the sole-surviving Mario delivers the nitro on his own—only to be accidentally killed himself in the film's bitter and ironic conclusion.

A classic screen thriller on all counts, *The Wages of Fear* spawned numerous imitations—most notably the 1958 Warner Bros. rip-off, *The Violent Road*—and one outright remake, William Friedkin's *Sorcerer* (1977), which the director dedicated to Clouzot himself. Though boasting a substantially larger budget than Clouzot's film and some truly amazing special effects, *Sorcerer* failed to generate much empathy for its characters and not much tension either because Friedkin places such spectacular obstacles in the way of his four heroes that the viewer ultimately grows weary and says, "Forget it, guys. Turn around and go home."

REAR WINDOW

(1954)

Paramount Pictures • Color/113 Minutes

CREDITS

Director: Alfred Hitchcock; *Producer*: Alfred Hitchcock; *Screenplay*: John Michael Hayes, based on the short story by Cornell Woolrich; *Cinematographer*: Robert Burks; *Editor*: George Tomasini; *Music*: Franz Waxman; *Art Directors*: Hal Pereira and Joseph McMillan Johnson.

CAST

L. B. Jefferies: James Stewart; *Lisa Fremont*: Grace Kelly; *Detective Thomas J. Doyle*: Wendell Corey; *Stella*: Thelma Ritter; *Lars Thorwald*: Raymond Burr; *Miss Lonelyhearts*: Judith Evelyn; *The Composer*: Ross Bagdasarian; *Miss Torso*: Georgine Darcy; *The Lady Sculptor*: Jesslyn Fax; *Mrs. Thorwald*: Irene Winston.

* * *

Alfred Hitchcock tended to dismiss his entertaining 1954 thriller *Dial M for Murder* as just a "run for cover" effort. "I just did my job, using cinematic means to narrate a story taken from a stage play," he told François Truffaut. "Many filmmakers take a stage play and begin to 'open it up.' Whereas in *Dial M,* I did my best to avoid going outside. In other words, what I did was to emphasize the theatrical aspects. All the action takes place in a living room."

In light of this statement, *Dial M* emerges not as some impersonal assignment in which the director was "coasting, playing it safe" (as Hitchcock insisted to Truffaut), but as a dress rehearsal for his next film, *Rear Window,* one of his most technically ingenious and popular thrillers in which he "emphasized the theatrical aspects" even more strongly than he had in *Dial M.* Although the action in *Rear Window* isn't restricted to a single room, the protagonist, L. B. Jefferies, is—and, for most of the film, so is the camera that shares with us every facet of Jefferies's confined point of view.

A globe-trotting magazine photographer who suffered a broken leg on his last assignment, Jefferies is confined to a wheelchair in his New York City apartment with his leg in a cast. It's the dog days of summer and the city is experiencing a record heat

The view from L. B. Jefferies's rear window.

wave. Bored out of his skull and anxious to get back to work (his cast is to be removed in a week's time), Jefferies passes the hours by watching his neighbors in the apartments across the way go about their private business—a pastime that isn't really all that different from his occupation, which is to observe and record the lives and actions of others. In effect, Jefferies is a professional Peeping Tom. Now, thanks to his broken leg and confinement, he's doing the same thing at home. In the film's ironic conclusion, this secondary occupation leads to double trouble and he winds up with *two* broken legs.

Jefferies also is spelled from boredom by frequent visits from his high society girlfriend, Lisa Fremont, who is pushing him toward marriage. Though they obviously care for each other, the subject of marriage is the cause of much tension between them for it is Jefferies's belief that they come from two different worlds, and he could no more adapt to Lisa's lifestyle that she could to his. As the film unfolds, aspects of their rocky relationship, their opposing points of view on compatibility and marriage, their hopes and their fears—real *and* imagined—are intriguingly mirrored

In addition to passing the time looking at his neighbors, the convalescent Jefferies (James Stewart) also is spelled from boredom by frequent visits from his high society girlfriend, Lisa Fremont (Grace Kelly).

Aided by his nurse, Stella (Thelma Ritter), and Lisa (Grace Kelly), Jefferies (James Stewart) sets about getting the proof that Thorwald is a murderer.

"But what did the murderous Thorwald do with his late wife's head?" The armchair sleuths (Thelma Ritter, Grace Kelly, James Stewart) keep asking themselves. A slide Jefferies took weeks ago may yield an important clue.

The window of the Thorwalds' apartment now flung wide open, Jefferies sees the suspicious Thorwald (Raymond Burr) stripping the bed and bundling up his wife's belongings.

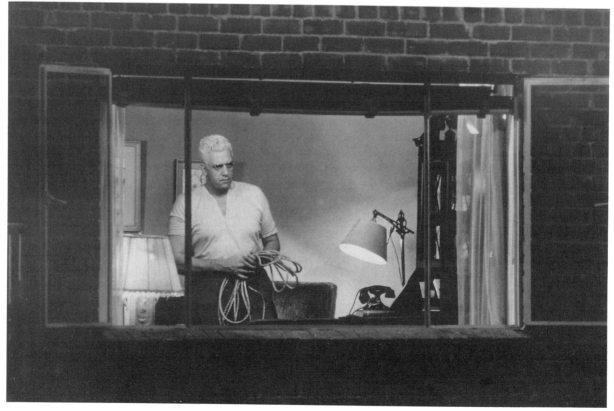

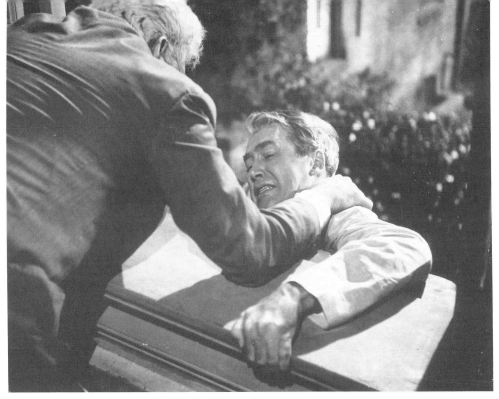

Thorwald (Raymond Burr) pays a deadly call on Jefferies (James Stewart) in the memorable finale.

by the different people Jefferies observes from his rear window perch. (*Rear Window*'s superlative, Oscar-nominated John Michael Hayes screenplay is uncommonly well thought out and rich with nuances and subtle revelations of character even by Hitchcock standards.)

Two of the "performers" in Jefferies's rear window "theatre" are a hefty, gray-haired salesman named Lars Thorwald and Thorwald's nagging, invalided wife. In the wee hours of the morning, Jefferies is awakened by a scream and the sound of breaking glass from one of the darkened apartments. Shortly after, Jefferies observes Thorwald leaving his apartment several times with his sample case tucked under his arm—and later sees him cleaning and wrapping a saw and a knife. In the morning, the window of the Thorwalds' bedroom now flung wide open, Jefferies sees Thorwald stripping the bed and bundling up his wife's belongings, and he comes to the conclusion that Thorwald did away with the woman during the night.

Jefferies calls in a detective friend, Tom Doyle, to look into the matter. But Thorwald either has covered his tracks too well or is completely innocent. With no proof that Thorwald is a murderer, Doyle is forced to drop the case. So Jefferies, aided by his nurse, Stella, and Lisa, both of whom are as convinced as he that Thorwald killed his wife, sets about getting the proof Doyle needs. And as Lisa gets progressively more turned on by the challenge of solving the crime—and

takes more and more chances to do so (including entering Thorwald's apartment in one of the film's most suspenseful scenes), Jefferies sees they're more compatible than he'd thought and their romance blossoms.

While searching Thorwald's apartment, Lisa finds the proof they need (the late Mrs. Thorwald's stashed wedding ring), but Thorwald catches her in the act. Jefferies calls the police in a panic, and they arrive in time to prevent Lisa from being harmed. They arrest her for breaking and entering, but before she's led away, she flashes Jefferies a sign that she's got the wedding ring.

Thorwald sees her do this and realizes at last that he's being watched from the apartment across the way, triggering the tension-filled finale in which he pays a deadly call on the trapped, wheelchair-bound Jefferies, who defends himself by popping off flash-bulbs to briefly blind Thorwald and keep him at bay until help arrives. It does, but not before Thorwald manages to push Jefferies out the window, and Jefferies breaks his other leg.

Hitchcock's delightful romantic comedy thriller ends with Jefferies once again confined to a wheelchair with both legs in casts, as Lisa keeps an eye on him while reading a book about adventuring on far away places. When she sees Jefferies has fallen asleep, she quickly puts the book down and picks up something more to her liking: *Harper's Bazaar.*

SUDDENLY

(1954)

United Artists • B&W/77 Minutes

CREDITS

Director: Lewis Allen; *Producer*: Robert Bassler; *Screenplay*: Richard Sale; *Cinematographer*: Charles G. Clarke; *Editor*: John F. Schreyer; *Music*: David Raksin; *Art Director*: Frank Sylos.

CAST

John Baron: Frank Sinatra; *Tod Shaw*: Sterling Hayden; *Pop Benson*: James Gleason; *Ellen Benson*: Nancy Gates; *Benny*: Paul Frees; *Bart*: Christopher Dark; *Dan Carney*: Willis Bouchey; *Slim Adams*: Paul Wexler; *Jud*: Jim Lilburn; *Pidge*: Kim Charney.

* * *

Frank Sinatra has been a superstar for so long and is such a show business institution that it seems impossible to believe that his career could ever have been on the skids. And yet by the early fifties, Sinatra's days as a popular singer and teen heartthrob seemed to be over and he was struggling to make a comeback. His Oscar win for his high profile supporting performance as the doomed Maggio in the hit 1953 war film, *From Here to Eternity*, gave his career the shot in the arm it needed and by 1955 he was back on top of the music world again.

To show that his powerful performance in *Eternity* was no fluke and to further demonstrate his range, Sinatra cannily decided to follow it with an even more high profile dramatic role—a starring one this time— that was as different from the devil-may-care Maggio as possible. Possibly taking his cue from James Cagney, onetime hoofer turned screen tough guy, Sinatra went completely hard-boiled with his next outing by playing the cold-blooded, sociopathic John Baron in *Suddenly*, a gritty low budget thriller about a plot to assassinate the President of the United States. Though *Suddenly* was a box office success, it was not the sort of prestigious production that attracted Academy voters and it failed to garner Sinatra a second Oscar nomination. Nevertheless, his lacerating performance in it did the trick for him and cemented his reputation as a serious and versatile dramatic actor. "Who would have dreamed when Frank Sinatra was

the fascination of the bobbysox brigade that he would ever be cast ... to play [so] repulsive [a] role," wrote the *New York Times*. "But we think that Mr. Sinatra deserves a special chunk of praise for playing the lead gunman with an easy, cold, vicious sort of gleam. His memorable playing of Maggio in *From Here to Eternity* served fair notice that the singer could act a dramatic role. In *Suddenly*, he proves it in a melodramatic *tour de force*."

Following the assassination of John F. Kennedy, whose presidential campaign Sinatra had actively supported, United Artists, at Sinatra's insistence, withdrew *Suddenly* (along with his other UA-released assassination-themed film, *The Manchurian Candidate*) from circulation, and both films sat on the shelf for years. The often repeated explanation for Sinatra's pulling both films from public view is that the star was concerned his films may have inspired JFK's alleged assassin, Lee Harvey Oswald, and Sinatra didn't want them to inspire any other sickos out there. That Oswald was rumored to have viewed *Suddenly* on television just days before the assassination would seem to lend a certain credence to this explanation. There's no way of knowing if Oswald actually did see the film that week—although its actual airing could easily be substantiated by checking the local Dallas-Fort Worth television listings. Even if Oswald had seen *Suddenly*, though, I'm not sure how significant it would be since it is widely believed by criminologists that assassins tend to be inspired by the real-life deeds of others, not the cinematic exploits of fictional ones like *Suddenly*'s John Baron. In fact, the film raises this very point when Baron, a self-confessed loner with little formal education and a desperate need to *be somebody*, gets into a discussion with his hostage, Sheriff Tod Shaw, about previous presidential assassination attempts and reveals a remarkable degree of knowledge about the motives and methods of the killers of Lincoln, Garfield, McKinley, and even FDR's failed assassin, Joseph Zangara, whose deeds Baron is determined not only to emulate but also to surpass.

We now know that Sinatra pulled *The Manchurian Candidate* (see separate chapter) from distribution due

Sterling Hayden as small-town sheriff Tod Shaw and Frank Sinatra as loathsome presidential assassin John Baron in Suddenly, *Sinatra's first film after winning the Oscar in* From Here to Eternity.

Baron (Frank Sinatra) poses as an FBI agent to convince Ellen (Nancy Gates) and her father-in-law (James Gleason) to let him and his men secure their house, which overlooks the train station where the President of the United States is scheduled to arrive in a few short hours.

Sterling Hayden, Frank Sinatra, Kim Charney, James Gleason, and Nancy Gates in Suddenly.

The psychopathic Baron (Frank Sinatra) straightens out the
sheriff's (Sterling Hayden) broken arm with a gleeful twist.
James Gleason, a horrified Nancy Gates, and young Kim
Charney look on.

Baron (Frank Sinatra) tells Ellen (Nancy Gates) that, unlike
him, she doesn't have what it takes to kill a man. In the end,
she will prove him quite wrong.

"Without the gun, you would never have spit at me. You would have never even noticed me. But because of the gun, you'll remember me as long as you live." Frank Sinatra, Sterling Hayden, and Nancy Gates in Suddenly.

to a dispute with United Artists over profits. It is likely that the less well known and much older *Suddenly*, potentially a hot UA property again because of its similar theme and sudden topicality, was held back by Sinatra due to his anger with the company as well. That Sinatra and United Artists finally rereleased the more acclaimed *The Manchurian Candidate* and allowed the more obscure *Suddenly* to fall into the public domain, at which point it was widely distributed on television and videocassette by a variety of companies, suggests that *Suddenly*'s absence from the screen for so many years had little to do with concern over social responsibility either.

The title refers to the town where the assassination plot is to be carried out, a small California way-stop for road agents, gamblers, and gunslingers during the roaring days of the Old West where nothing much happens anymore. Sheriff Tod Shaw receives a wire that a special train carrying the President and his entourage will be stopping in Suddenly at 5:00 PM and that he is to cooperate with the Secret Service, who will arrive on an earlier train, in arranging security and transportation for the President's safe transfer upstate. The Secret Service men show up on schedule and inform Shaw of a tip that an assassination attempt is in the works. With Shaw's help the area surrounding the train station is thoroughly searched and secured. Only one spot remains to be checked out: a hilltop house overlooking the train station where Shaw's girlfriend, Ellen Benson, a war widow, lives with her little boy, Pidge, and her father-in-law, a retired ex-Secret Service man.

Shaw checks out the house himself, accompanied by Dan Carney, the agent in charge of the operation and an old friend of Benson's. Unaware that John Baron and two other men have gained entrance to the house posing as FBI men, Shaw and Carney walk into

a trap. Carney is killed and Shaw is wounded. Baron holds Shaw and the three other occupants of the house at gunpoint while his henchmen set up a table and sharpshooter's rifle at a living room window overlooking the train station. As the clock ticks toward the hour of the President's arrival, the captives try to figure a way to foil Baron's seemingly foolproof plan without losing their own lives in the bargain. They succeed by electrocuting one of the assassins, who causes the rifle to go off prematurely, alerting the Secret Service below to their whereabouts. No longer caring about getting away, Baron takes aim with the rifle as the President's train pulls into the station. Instead of stopping, however, the train goes on through, and as Baron whimpers "It didn't stop! It didn't stop!" he's shot down by Ellen and finished off by Shaw.

Although Richard Sale's suspenseful screenplay and Lewis Allen's claustrophobic direction (most of the film's action is confined to a single room) keep the viewer on edge straight through, there are some lapses in credibility. For example, the plan to kill Baron by attaching a cable from the TV set to one of the legs of the metal table holding the gun and spilling a glass of water on the spot where Baron will have to stand to fire the rifle is patently obvious, and yet neither Baron nor his cohort catch on at all. It is unlikely that two professional hit men would have so little knowledge of even the basics of electricity that they would fail to see through such a plan immediately.

The glue that really holds *Suddenly* together and makes it such a top-notch thriller is Sinatra's galvanizing performance as John Baron. The film has often been criticized for not providing enough motive to Baron's madness, but this is hardly the case. We're never told who the conspirators were who hired Baron, or what *their* motives are, but considering the fact that almost thirty years after the Kennedy assassination many Americans are still wondering who was really behind that monstrous act and why, *Suddenly*'s deliberate vagueness on these points seems more prophetic than a weakness.

Even Baron doesn't know who hired him, nor does he care, for he has his own agenda. And that agenda is clearly revealed in his gleaming eyes, in his twisted grin, even in his words. "Without the gun, I'm nothing, and I never had anything before I got one," he tells Shaw. "First time I got one in my hands and killed a man, I got some self-respect. I *was* somebody. Without the gun, you would never have spit at me. You would have never even noticed me. But because of the gun, you'll remember me as long as you live." John Baron's motives are very clear. And as performed by Frank Sinatra, his character chillingly believable indeed.

RIFIFI

(1954)

Miracle Films
A United Motion Picture Organization Release • B&W/117 Minutes

CREDITS

Director: Jules Dassin; *Producer*: Rene G. Vuattoux; *Screenplay*: Jules Dassin, Rene Wheeler, Auguste le Breton, based on the novel *Du Rififi chez les Hommes* by Auguste le Breton; *Cinematographer*: Philippe Agostini; *Editor*: Roger Dwyre; *Music*: Georges Auric; *Art Director*: Trauner.

CAST

Tony Stephanois: Carl Mohner; *Jo Stephanois*: Jean Servais; *Mario*: Robert Manuel; *Cesar*: Perlo Vita (Jules Dassin); *Mado*: Marie Sabouret; *Pierre Grutter*: Marcel Lupovici; *Louis Grutter*: Pierre Grasset; *Remi Grutter*: Robert Hossein; *Louise*: Janine Darcey.

* * *

In his *TV Movies and Video Guide,* critic Leonard Maltin calls Jules Dassin's taut crime melodrama *Rififi* "the granddaddy of all caper/heist movies" and bestows upon it his highest rating of four stars. While I have no argument with Maltin's rating of the film, I do question his calling it "granddaddy," for that honorary title really belongs to John Huston's *The Asphalt Jungle*, which preceded *Rififi* by four years and obviously served as a model for the later film—not to mention every other caper/heist movie made since.

The plots of both films are roughly the same. A disparate group of professional crooks pools its talents and resources to pull off an elaborate jewel robbery which is staged in intricate and suspenseful detail. The heist's a success, but then the caper goes sour. Both films conclude with the ostensible "hero" setting things right by shooting down the "bad guys" and making off with the loot. But because he's taken several bullets in return, he expires before his ill-gotten gains can do him much good.

Rififi director Dassin began his career in Hollywood in the forties making crime thrillers (*Brute Force, The Naked City, Night and the City*), in the realistic, urban vein of *The Asphalt Jungle*. Then he shifted his filmmaking activities to Europe after being blacklisted during the McCarthy witchhunt era

Carl Mohner and Marie Sabouret in Jules Dassin's classic caper/heist movie, Rififi.

and was surely not unaware of the Huston film and the tremendous impact it had, particularly in France where Huston's work was virtually lionized by critics and audiences alike. Neither was the author of the French novel upon which *Rififi* was based, Auguste le Breton, a specialist in European crime thrillers who wrote in the same hard-nosed style as such American counterparts as James M. Cain and W.R. Burnett (the author of the novel *Asphalt Jungle* and Huston's collaborator on the film's script).

But *Rififi* is far more than just an accomplished clone of *The Asphalt Jungle*, for while there are many striking similarities between the two films, there are

The gift of one of the stolen jewels to a singer (Marie Sabouret) in rival gangster Pierre Grutter's (Marcel Lupovici) cabaret blows the robbery apart.

Using the pseudonym Perlo Vita, director Jules Dassin plays the role of the nattily dressed, womanizing safecracker Cesar, shown here with cabaret singer Mado (Marie Sabouret).

The ill-fated robbers in Rififi: *Left to right, Robert Manuel, Perlo Vita [Jules Dassin], Carl Mohner, and Jean Servais.*

A full half hour of the film's 117-minute running time is devoted to the palm-sweating robbery sequence, which is rendered without dialogue and in almost complete silence.

Tony (Carl Mohner) arrives at the Grutters' hideout to exchange the stolen loot for his kidnapped nephew.

substantial differences as well. For one thing, *Rififi's* underworld milieu is a lot sleazier and more convincing than Huston's film, whose MGM gloss and employment of familiar Hollywood actors at times work counter to the director's attempts at achieving documentary-like realism. Huston's accomplished cast is certainly persuasive, but Dassin's cast of virtual unknowns (to American audiences anyway) led by Carl Mohner—a sort of dissolute version of Paul Henreid—really *look* the part. (Using the pseudonym Perlo Vita, Dassin himself plays the role of the nattily dressed, womanizing safecracker Cesar whose gift of one of the stolen jewels to a singer in rival gangster Pierre Grutter's cabaret blows the successful operation apart. To audiences familiar with Dassin for his costarring role in his big international success *Never on Sunday*—in which he appeared under his own name—he is practically unrecognizable as Cesar.)

Another element separating the two films is that *Rififi's* caper, unlike *Jungle's*, goes sour not due to a falling out among the co-conspirators but because a rival gang tries to horn in on their take. From a character point of view, this brings about an important difference in motivation between the films' two leads as they try to recoup their losses. When *Jungle's* caper goes sour, Dix Handley's (Sterling Hayden) luckless attempt to right things springs from a misguided hope for personal salvation, whereas *Rififi's* Tony Stephanois (Carl Mohner)—like the Dustin Hoffman character in Ulu Grosbard's probing study of the criminal psyche, *Straight Time* (1978)—shifts into high gear over this unexpected yet challenging turn of events because he's hopelessly addicted to his nefarious lifestyle. As a result, both men doom themselves, but for very different reasons—low level crook Handley, a mere strong-arm functionary in *Jungle's* heist, tries vainly to claw his way out of the pit his personal failings have placed him in (a favorite Huston theme) whereas master thief Tony, who orchestrates *Rififi's* heist, fatally opts to dig himself in even further. The fact that Tony is also trying to save the life of his kidnapped nephew (Grutter's gang is holding the boy hostage as ransom for the stolen loot) is beside the point; Tony is actually *exhilarated* by what he feels he now has to do.

These differences in style and content don't necessarily add up to one film's being superior to the other, of course. That's up to the individual viewer to decide. (Personally, I think Huston the greater filmmaker overall, but in this case I believe *Rififi* to be more effective and biting than Huston's similar treatment of the subject.)

In one specific area, however, there is no question but that Dassin's film outshines Huston's, and that area is the robbery sequence. Huston's prototype heist is certainly suspenseful, although he devotes much less screen time both to its planning and execution than Dassin does. Typically, Huston is more concerned with what happens to his foibled characters *after* they grab the loot. Dassin is no less concerned with the fate of his characters, but he also spends a lot more screen time detailing the robbery's various planning stages so that we're able to see each step of the way what elements could go wrong and what the ingenious robbers come up with to surmount these obstacles. After which, he devotes a full half hour of the film's 117 minute running time to the robbery sequence itself, a bravura piece of moviemaking which, except for the occasional sound of the men's tools, is rendered without dialogue and in almost complete silence.

To get inside the jewelry shop, which is protected by a super alarm system designed to go off at the slightest sound, the thieves must cut through the floor of an apartment just above the store. Having practiced with a similar alarm system, they've calculated just how light a blow they must make with their hammers and chisels, even at such a distance, to avoid triggering the alarm below. No system is exactly the same, however, so they never really know when they might strike a blow that will prove too loud. After making a small hole in the ceiling—a time-consuming, sweat-inducing process for them and the viewer—they must then chip out a much larger opening through which they can lower themselves by means of a rope. The problem is, if any debris strikes the floor below, the alarm will likely go off. To overcome this obstacle, they insert a closed umbrella through the mini-hole they've made, then open the umbrella once it's through. The chipped debris falls silently into it and as it fills up, they empty the umbrella by hand.

Once the larger hole is created, the rope is dropped through and Tony descends into the shop with a fire extinguisher. He pads over to the alarm system and painstakingly sprays enough foam through the grate to immobilize the bell. The tension doesn't let up even at this point, however, for Dassin has several other suspenseful cards up his sleeve. But there's no point in detailing them all here. Suffice to say that the robbery sequence in *Rififi* is a real showpiece which has not been surpassed, though many filmmakers have tried, including Dassin himself, whose light-hearted caper/heist thriller *Topkapi* (1964) contains an even more elaborately staged robbery sequence that's unarguably suspenseful, but for sheer white-knuckle tension, it still doesn't match the one in his classic *Rififi*.

THE DESPERATE HOURS

(1955)

Paramount Pictures • B&W/112 Minutes

CREDITS

Director: William Wyler; *Producer*: William Wyler; *Screenplay*: Joseph Hayes, based on his novel and play; *Cinematographer*: Lee Garmes; *Editor*: Robert Swink; *Music*: Gail Kubik; *Art Directors*: Hal Pereira and Joseph MacMillan Johnson.

CAST

Glenn Griffin: Humphrey Bogart; *Dan Hilliard*: Fredric March; *Jesse Bard*: Arthur Kennedy; *Eleanor Hilliard*: Martha Scott; *Hal Griffin*: Dewey Martin; *Chuck*: Gig Young; *Cindy Hilliard*: Mary Murphy; *Kobish*: Robert Middleton; *Ralphie Hilliard*: Richard Eyer.

* * *

William Wyler's *The Desperate Hours* remains the definitive treatment of the people-held-hostage-by-a-gang-of-dangerous-thugs type of thriller. The plot of *The Desperate Hours* was by no means new when Joseph Hayes tackled it in his novel of the same name upon which the film is partly based, but Hayes orchestrated the traditional elements of this well-worn theme so skillfully in his book that he succeeded in breathing new life into them, and his book went on to become *the* model for this tense type of drama, a status it enjoys to this day.

The book shot immediately to the top of the bestseller lists and was adapted (by Hayes himself) into an equally popular 1954 Broadway play. It starred Paul Newman—an up-and-coming, twenty-nine-year-old New York actor at the time with to his credit but one movie role (in the dreadful *The Silver Chalice*)—as Glen Griffin, the violent leader of the escaped gang. William Wyler purchased the movie rights and hired Hayes, for whom *The Desperate Hours* was turning into a not-so-minor cottage industry, to write the screenplay based on his novel and play. Though Newman had scored a bullseye on Broadway in the role of the youthful Griffin, his name as yet meant nothing to filmgoers, so Wyler aged the character twenty-plus years and gave the part to veteran Hollywood "bad guy" Humphrey Bogart. Griffin turned out to be Bogart's second-to-last movie

role (he died in 1957 after making one more film, *The Harder They Fall*), a role that ironically brought his movie career almost full circle. For the central plot of *The Desperate Hours* is strikingly similar to *The Petrified Forest*, the 1936 gangster movie (also based on a successful Broadway play) that launched Bogart's Hollywood career in which Bogart played Duke Mantee, a hostage-taking escaped prisoner not unlike Glenn Griffin.

For the pivotal role of Griffin's chief adversary, Dan Hilliard, the resourceful family man whose suburban home is invaded by the thugs, Wyler wanted Spencer Tracy, but Bogart (who years earlier had made *Dead End* with Wyler) squabbled with Tracy over billing, and Tracy finally bowed out. The part went instead to Fredric March, who had won an Oscar under Wyler's direction for *The Best Years of Our Lives* playing a family man in turmoil like Dan Hilliard in *The Desperate Hours* with a very different set of problems. Though March's role in *Hours* is less flashy than Bogart's, his is the more interesting character and March's performance ultimately steals the show. The climactic scene where the humiliated and vengeful but decent and moral Hilliard gets the drop on Griffin, clearly wants to kill him but overcomes these feelings and says with grim-faced determination, *"Get out of my house!"* is brought off by March with stinging conviction—although it's not a finale likely to satisfy many proponents of vigilante justice.

Griffin, his younger brother, Hal, and a loutish convict named Kobish escape from an Indiana penitentiary, but instead of hightailing it out of state, they head for Indianapolis to rendezvous with Griffin's girlfriend, who is scheduled to arrive at midnight with cash to aid them in their getaway. Needing a place to hide out for a few desperate hours, they randomly pick the suburban home of the Hilliards, break in, and hold the family hostage at gunpoint while Griffin relays their location to his girlfriend by coded telephone message. Alerted to the breakout, the police and the FBI set up roadblocks and put a tail on Griffin's girlfriend instructing that she not be picked up until she leads them to Griffin's hideout. But a

The Hilliards (Martha Scott, Richard Eyer, Fredric March, and Mary Murphy) shortly before their peaceful suburban home is invaded by three dangerous escaped convicts in The Desperate Hours.

Kobish (Robert Middleton) orders Mrs. Hilliard (Martha Scott) and her daughter Cindy (Mary Murphy) to go about their daily routine, including answering the phone, as if all was normal.

Though March's role in The Desperate Hours *is less flashy than Bogart's, his is the more interesting character and his performance steals the show.*

Strained nerves and exploding tempers. The put-upon Hilliard (Fredric March) orders his son (Richard Eyer) to tow the line.

Chuck (Gig Young) gets Cindy (Mary Murphy) out of the house on a pretense as the police close in on Kobish (Robert Middleton) and the others.

zealous state policeman blows the operation by hauling her in on a traffic violation. She manages to escape, however, ditching her car in the process, and calls Griffin with the bad news. He instructs her to put the cash in an envelope and mail it to Hilliard's office.

Forced to hole up in the house longer than he'd planned, Griffin avoids arousing attention by having the Hilliards go about their normal daily routine. Their little boy is kept home from school, but Hilliard himself is permitted to go to his office so that he can be there when the mail arrives, and his daughter, Cindy, is allowed to go to work and keep a scheduled date with her boyfriend, Chuck. Neither of them reveals what's happening for fear the other members of the family will be killed, but the hell they're going through shows in their strained nerves and shortness of temper, arousing Chuck's suspicion that something is very wrong.

As the police, who still have no idea where the gang is holed up, tightens its net around the area, the gang members begin to argue among themselves, and Hal decides to forget the money and get away while he still can. During a coincidental run-in with the police, Hal panics, is killed in a shoot-out and freak accident, and the cops find Hilliard's address in his pocket. They cordon off the neighborhood. Chuck manages to

get Cindy out of the house on a pretense. As Hilliard returns home with the envelope full of cash, some plainclothes cops pick him up and he is told that the police plan to mount an assault to recapture Griffin. Realizing what might happen to his hostaged family, Hilliard pleads for time to get Griffin out of the house on his own. The FBI man in charge gives him ten minutes and Hilliard, whose nerves are now stretched to the breaking point, goes back into the house to play his final hand, cleverly using an unloaded gun as his trump card.

Though tautly directed by Wyler, who makes excellent use of depth-of-focus photography to allow the viewer to take in the suspenseful action going on in several rooms and on different floors of the Hilliard home in a single frame, *The Desperate Hours* may strike today's audiences as dated and a bit too restrained, making it an obvious candidate for remake treatment. In fact, it was updated and remade in 1990 by director Michael Cimino as *Desperate Hours* and starred Mickey Rourke as a youthful, more vicious but equally ill-kempt version of the Glenn Griffin character and Anthony Hopkins as the Hilliard character. Scripted by several writers, including Joseph Hayes himself, the remake, to put it kindly, failed to best or even equal the original in acting, direction, or suspense—and fared poorly at the box office as well.

BAD DAY AT BLACK ROCK

(1955)

Metro-Goldwyn-Mayer • Color/81 Minutes

CREDITS

Director: John Sturges; *Producer*: Dore Schary; *Screenplay*: Millard Kaufman, based on a story by Howard Breslin; *Cinematographer*: William C. Mellor; *Editor*: Newell P. Kimlin; *Music*: Andre Previn; *Art Directors*: Cedric Gibbons and Malcolm Brown.

CAST

John J. Macreedy: Spencer Tracy; *Reno Smith*: Robert Ryan; *Hector David*: Lee Marvin; *Coley Trimble*: Ernest Borgnine; *Liz Wirth*: Anne Francis; *Sheriff Tim Horn*: Dean Jagger; *Doc Velie*: Walter Brennan; *Pete Wirth*: John Ericson; *Hastings*: Russell Collins; *Sam*: Walter Sande.

* * *

A train makes an unscheduled stop in a one-horse desert town. A man gets off looking for information and is greeted with hostility by the suspicious townsfolk who come to needle and finally threaten to kill the mysterious stranger if he doesn't get out of town.

Sound like the standard plot ingredients of a score of typical Westerns? Well, essentially that's what *Bad Day at Black Rock* is. But writer Millard Kaufman and director John Sturges added several twists to this oft-told take that lifted *Bad Day at Black Rock* above its generic roots and transformed it into one of the classic suspense films of the fifties.

For one thing, they set their story not in the American West of the 1880s, but of 1945, the year of the Japanese surrender that ended World War Two, a shift that made their Western more immediate to contemporary audiences. And for another, they pinned their tense tale on the theme of racial prejudice against Japanese Americans, which was not only a first for a Western, but a first for the postwar American cinema as well. That the film was made for MGM, a studio that had generally tended to avoid controversial subject matter, was also unusual, and probably wouldn't have occurred were it not for the fact that by this time, MGM's ultra-conservative "mom and apple pie" boss, Louis B. Mayer, had been ousted by the more social-minded Dore Schary, who not only gave

the project the go-ahead but also personally oversaw the production of *Bad Day at Black Rock*.

The film opens with a series of spectacular panoramic shots of the Southern Pacific hurtling across the vast, barren desert. The train pulls into the station at Black Rock, a dirtwater town consisting of a gas station, a few stores, a jail, and a hotel. The arrival of the train, which hasn't stopped at Black Rock in four years, sparks immediate interest among the town's few residents, most of them layabouts, who are thrown into further turmoil when a middle-aged stranger in a dark business suit gets off and asks for directions to a place called Adobe Flat. The stranger's name is John J. Macreedy and he has a crippled left arm. Macreedy's easygoing but authoritative manner and style of dress suggest that he is a "big shot" of some kind. Two cowboy toughs, Hector David and Coley Trimble, alert their boss, Reno Smith, to the fact that Macreedy is asking questions about Adobe Flat, and Smith wires a private detective agency in Los Angeles to find out who Macreedy is. But the agency comes up with nothing.

Smith demands to know why Macreedy is interested in Adobe Flat. The tight-lipped Macreedy replies that he's looking for a Japanese farmer named Komoko who lives there, but doesn't explain why. Smith says Komoko was shipped off to a relocation center during the war and never returned. Macreedy seems to accept this, but rents a jeep from the local garage owner, Liz Wirth, to visit Komoko's old place anyway. He finds nothing but a burned out rubble and what looks to be a grave. On his way back to town, Macreedy is run off the road by the troublemaking Coley Trimble. Trimble threatens him again later, but the seemingly docile and easily intimidated stranger surprises everyone by flattening the bully with some professionally executed karate chops.

From the conscience-stricken hotel clerk, Pete Wirth, Macreedy learns that Komoko was killed by Smith, David, and Trimble who, along with Wirth, got "patriotic drunk" after Pearl Harbor and paid a visit to Komoko's farm for some taunting "fun." This got violently out of hand when they set the farm on

Reno Smith (Robert Ryan) demands to know why the mysterious stranger, John J. Macreedy (Spencer Tracy), is so interested in Adobe Flat.

Macreedy (Spencer Tracy) rents a jeep from garage owner Liz Wirth (Anne Francis) so that he can visit the farm where Komoko lived before being shipped off to a relocation center, never to return.

Trimble (Ernest Borgnine) threatens Macreedy (Spencer Tracy) again. But the seemingly docile and easily intimidated stranger will soon surprise everyone by flattening the ruffian. (Walter Sande is the bartender.).

Macreedy (Spencer Tracy) tries to get a telegram to the state police requesting help, but Hastings (Russell Collins) never sends it.

Walter Brennan, Spencer Tracy, and John Erickson in John Sturges's Bad Day at Black Rock, *one of the classic suspense films of the fifties.*

The conscience-stricken Wirth (John Erickson) finally reveals the truth about what happened to Komoko and agrees to help Macreedy (Spencer Tracy) get out of town alive.

fire and Komoko burned to death. Knowing that Smith and the others can't afford to let their murderous secret become known and that they will not allow him to leave the town alive, Macreedy tries to send a wire to the state police requesting help, but the message is never delivered. Stuck in town overnight as Smith and the others plan an "accident" for him, Macreedy assumes the Gary Cooper *High Noon* role and tries to get those in town who were not directly involved in Komoko's death (but had kept silent about it) to ease their guilty consciences by helping him slip away to avoid death and inform the authorities.

As night falls and the conspirators close in, Pete Wirth persuades his sister, Liz, to drive Macreedy out of town in her jeep while the doctor and the sheriff, who have also agreed to help, keep the toughs occupied. She agrees, but double-crosses Macreedy by leading him into a trap so that her lover, Reno Smith, can shoot him. As Smith can't afford to leave any witnesses, he kills Liz first, then turns on Macreedy, a resourceful ex-Army man, who ducks for cover beneath the jeep and defends himself by draining gas from the carburetor to make a Molotov cocktail. As the gunman emerges from cover, Macreedy hurls the explosive and the villainous Smith is burned to death just as Komoko had been.

As the law takes away the others who were involved in Komoko's death and Macreedy waits for his train the next morning, he explains to the doctor why he had come to Black Rock to seek out Komoko in the first place. Komoko's son had been killed saving Macreedy's life during the war and earned a posthumous medal for his heroics. Having lost the use of his arm in the incident, Macreedy had come to believe the life the boy had saved was no longer worth much of anything, but felt delivering the medal to the dead boy's parents was the least he could do. By bringing Smith and the others to justice, however, Macreedy had gained back his self-respect. The doctor admits that thanks to Macreedy's efforts the town too has gotten back its self-respect and he asks for the medal as a memento "to build on." Macreedy gives it to him, climbs aboard the Southern Pacific, and the departing train disappears over the barren desert horizon.

The whole thing was loosely remade by MGM five years later as the Mickey Rooney movie, *Platinum High School,* relocated to the "urban jungle."

KISS ME DEADLY

(1955)

United Artists • B&W/105 Minutes

CREDITS

Director: Robert Aldrich; *Producer*: Robert Aldrich; *Screenplay*: A.I. Bezzerides, based on the novel by Mickey Spillane; *Cinematographer*: Ernest Laszlo; *Editor*: Michael Luciano; *Music*: Frank DeVol; *Art Director*: William Glasgow.

CAST

Mike Hammer: Ralph Meeker; *Carl Evello*: Paul Stewart; *Dr. Soberin*: Albert Dekker; *Eddie Yeager*: Juano Hernandez; *Pat Chambers*: Wesley Addy; *Friday*: Marian Carr; *Velda*: Maxine Cooper; *Christina Bailey*: Cloris Leachman; *Lily Carver*: Gaby Rodgers; *Nick*: Nick Dennis; *Sugar Smallhouse*: Jack Lambert; *Charlie Max*: Jack Elam; *Ray Diker*: Mort Marshall; *Harvey Wallace*: Strother Martin.

* * *

One of the things I most enjoy about writing film books is the opportunity it affords me to familiarize younger movie fans with the work of an unsung filmmaker whose work I find special—and to jump start the memories of older fans familiar with his work so that his name stays alive. The late Robert Aldrich is such a filmmaker.

Aldrich holds a unique position in the American cinema because he's the only mainstream Hollywood director I can point to whose work was so genuinely, consistently, and entertainingly subversive. I don't mean subversive in the political sense that the late, unlamented House Un-American Activities Committee applied the word—although Aldrich's films were often *very* political indeed. For example, his *Twilight's Last Gleaming* (see separate chapter) is one of the strongest indictments of our government's way of doing business that the screen has ever presented. And in other films, Aldrich boldly satirized or outright slew many another sacred American cow as well.

Aldrich was a subversive in the creative sense. He didn't try to redo or outdo other filmmakers' past contributions to whatever genre he was currently working in—he tried to *undo* them. (In fact, the title of Aldrich's subversive 1956 war film *Attack!* could al-

most stand as his artistic credo.) While the iconoclastic and acerbic Billy Wilder may have bitten the hand that fed him in films like *Sunset Boulevard* and *Fedora*, those were romantically straight as an arrow compared to Aldrich's virulent undermining of the Hollywood myth (and movies about that myth) in *The Big Knife* and *Whatever Happened to Baby Jane?*—wherein Aldrich not only bit the same hand but also practically chewed it off.

Aldrich's artistically subversive qualities ranged from boldly casting against type on occasion (James Stewart in *The Flight of the Phoenix*, for example; see separate chapter) to bringing books to the screen that he didn't particularly like. Joseph Wambaugh's *The Choirboys*, a *Catch-22*-ish chronicle of the hard life and fast times of the Los Angeles police, is a case in point. Aldrich didn't just undermine the book's hard-edged but ultimately pro-police stance in his 1977 film version, he thoroughly undid it by making a film that was so willfully and offensively trashy that it effectively destroyed the book on the screen—which was clearly Aldrich's intention since he obviously disliked and bitterly disagreed with its point of view.

Kiss Me Deadly is another good example of Aldrich's subversive qualities—maybe even the best example. Not so much a thriller as an anti-thriller, the film not only undermines the chauvinistic, fascist-minded point of view of Mickey Spillane's potboiler but has all the conventions of the traditional movie detective yarn as well. Made in the artistically and politically conservative 1950s, the film startlingly offered a hero, Mike Hammer, who is a pimpish, violent sleazeball as the film begins and gets even worse as it unfolds (following an interrogation of the unsavory Hammer, a policeman disdainfully remarks, "Open a window!"); a heroine, Hammer's secretary, Velda, who is little more than a prostitute for her money-grubbing boss; a convoluted and confusing mystery that refuses to unravel itself even as the film concludes; and an explosive finale that leaves us guessing whether the "hero" and "heroine" survived—not that we really care since neither they nor anyone else in the film is particularly likable. And yet the film holds our atten-

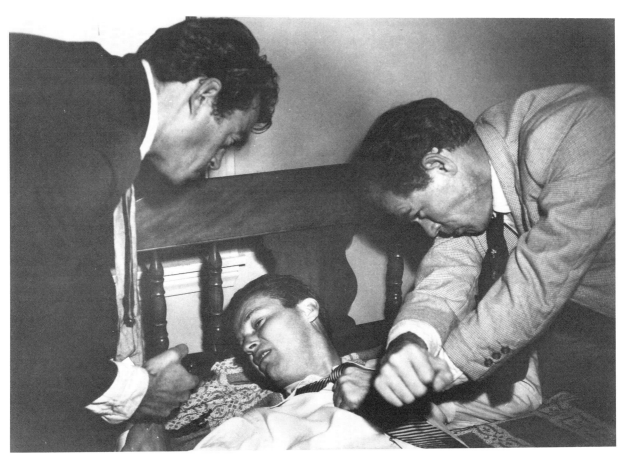

The violent Hammer (Ralph Meeker) gets some of this own treatment from thugs Charlie Max (Jack Elam, left) and Sugar Smallhouse (Jack Lambert).

The police request a meeting with Hammer (Ralph Meeker) as his loyal "secretary," Velda (Maxine Cooper), looks on.

Hammer (Ralph Meeker), a pimpish, violent sleazeball, and his "secretary," Velda (Maxine Cooper), who is little more than a prostitute for her money-grubbing boss.

Hammer (Ralph Meeker) and the duplicitous Lily (Gaby Rodgers) look for a clue in a book of poems owned by the late Christina Bailey.

This still of Hammer (Ralph Meeker) and Velda (Maxine Cooper) locking arms in the sand reveals that a scene showing that they safely escaped the exploding beach house was shot.

But the scene was cut so that their fate would be left open to question.

tion and keeps us entertained all the way. It's no wonder French *nouvelle vague* directors like Godard looked to this oddball gem as a "bible" when they began challenging the enshrined traditions of their own cinema in the late fifties and early sixties.

According to Aldrich, he and screenwriter A.I. Bezzerides kept little of Spillane's book but the title and some of the characters. The plot of the film, which is basically a reworking of *The Maltese Falcon,* turns on a group of conniving, unscrupulous characters who use the gumshoe "hero" to locate a missing object that is so valuable it is worth killing for. Unlike *Falcon,* the nature of the object is withheld from us and the "hero" until the film is almost over. Rather than being the "stuff that dreams are made of," however, it proves to be the stuff of nightmares—a genuine Pandora's box.

Hammer picks up a half-naked hitchhiker named Christina Bailey who has just escaped from a lunatic asylum where she was being held against her will. They're caught by Christina's shadowy pursuers, Hammer is knocked out, and the terrified woman is tortured for information as to the object's location, but she stubbornly takes the secret to her grave. The dead woman and the unconscious Hammer are placed in his car, which is shoved off a cliff. Hammer survives, however. When his cop pal, Pat Chambers, tells him the FBI is interested in the Bailey case and to keep out of it, Hammer realizes he's onto something bigger and potentially more lucrative than his penny ante peeper activities and goes against Chambers's advice to pur-

sue the case on his own. The violent trail leads to a group of racketeers, a mysterious doctor named Soberin, and a seemingly vulnerable but ultimately duplicitous dame, Lily Carver, who manipulates the money-hungry Hammer the way Brigid O'Shaughnessy manipulated *Falcon's* Sam Spade. Unlike Spade, however, Hammer has no moral fiber whatsoever. He's just as morally bankrupt as Lily and uses people—particularly his secretary, Velda—in the same shabby fashion.

Hammer and Lily locate the elusive prize—a black box containing an unidentified radioactive substance that scorches Hammer's hand when he briefly opens the lid to peek inside. The conniving Lily makes off with the box and joins her accomplice, the Kaspar Gutman-like Dr. Soberin, at a beachhouse where Velda is being held captive. Although Soberin won't tell Lily the market value of the box's mysterious contents (or even what the market is to be), she concludes that 100 percent is better than a fifty-fifty split and kills him. Hammer shows up to save Velda and retrieve the box—though not necessarily in that order, knowing him—and Lily plugs him too.

Lily, the film's modern Pandora, opens the box to see what's inside and is gruesomely enveloped in flame by the radioactive surge. As Hammer and Velda scramble out the door, the place explodes in a manner suggesting a nuclear blast. Aldrich's distinctly offbeat thriller ends with this apocalyptic image—which still has audiences and critics debating whether Hammer and Velda made it out in time or not.

THE NIGHT MY NUMBER CAME UP

(1955)

Ealing Films/Continental Distributing • B&W/94 Minutes

CREDITS

Director: Leslie Norman; *Producer*: Michael Balcon; *Screenplay*: R.C. Sherriff, based on a story by Victor Goddard; *Cinematographer*: Lionel Banes; *Editor*: Peter Tanner; *Music*: Malcolm Arnold; *Art Director*: Jim Morahan.

CAST

Air Marshal John Hardie: Michael Redgrave; *Owen Robertson*: Alexander Knox; *Flight Lt. McKenzie*: Denholm Elliott; *Mary Campbell*: Sheila Sim; *Mrs. Robertson*: Ursula Jeans; *Pilot*: Nigel Stock; *Lord Wainright*: Ralph Truman; *Commander Lindsay*: Michael Hordern; *Soldiers*: Bill Kerr and Alfie Bass; *Navigator*: David Yates; *Engineer*: Victor Maddern; *Copilot*: David Orr; *Wing Commander*: Hugh Moxey; *Bennett*: George Rose.

* * *

Civil servant Owen Robertson (Alexander Knox) gets the disquieting news that he is to join Hardie's (Michael Redgrave) Tokyo-bound flight.

Forget about *Airport, The Hight and the Mighty, Fate Is the Hunter,* and all those other big-budget, all-star, disaster-in-the-air spectaculars. If you're a white-knuckle flyer like me, the little-known but absolutely terrifying *The Night My Number Came Up* is the skybound thriller for you—although I wouldn't recommend seeing it if you've got an upcoming flight scheduled. Under those circumstances, I suggest giving the film the widest berth possible.

It begins in Bangkok a decade after World War Two. A Tokyo-bound, twin-engine Dakota with eight passengers and five crew members has run into trouble and presumably crashed somewhere in a remote part of Japan. But where? The plane had lost radio contact, probably wandered off course, and no one knows where to look for it. Commander Lindsay arrives at rescue H.Q. and suggests a possible location, right down to the most detailed landmark, but he won't reveal how he knows this for fear that the Wing Commander will think him crazy and refuse to take his suggestion. The film then flashes back to reveal the source of Lindsay's uncanny information.

At a dinner party in Hong Kong a few days earlier, attended by Air Marshal Hardie, civil servant Owen Robertson, and several others, Lindsay is coaxed into revealing the details of a troublesome dream he'd experienced recently. It was about a twin-engine Dakota whose radio burns out midflight to Tokyo, gets lost in dark storm clouds and snow, runs out of fuel, and finally crashes along the Japanese coastline, a spot vividly landmarked by several small fishing villages, a lighthouse, and rocky terrain. On board are five crew members and eight passengers—notably Hardie himself, an unnamed bigwig in the British foreign office, an attractive blonde woman, and a flashy civilian with a loud voice. Prior to the crash, one of the passengers goes berserk with fear and has to be restrained by the others. Hardie, who is scheduled to fly to Tokyo in a Liberator, not a Dakota, initially dismisses the dream as pure fancy. But then his Liberator flight is cancelled and he's rescheduled on a Dakota. Soon, other parts of Lindsay's dream start coming true as well.

If you're a white-knuckle flyer, The Night My Number Came Up *is the skybound thriller for you—just don't see it if you've*

got an upcoming flight scheduled. With Michael Redgrave, Nigel Stock, Sheila Sim, and Alexander Knox.

Lord Wainright, a senior official in the foreign office bound for an important Tokyo conference, unexpectedly joins the passenger list with his secretary, Mary Campbell, an attractive blonde, and insists that Robertson, a nervous first-time flyer now even more edgy because of the dream, go along as his aide. When two British soldiers who have missed their bus to Okinawa show up at the gate and book passage as well, the dream's passenger list of eight is now complete—though its details are not precisely correct for none is a flashy civilian with a loud voice.

The plane stops over in Okinawa and the two soldiers disembark, reducing the passenger list to six—at which point the loud-mouthed type, a salesman named Bennett who's on a trade mission for the British government and must get to Tokyo fast, turns up on cue and requests seats for himself and his male secretary. Feeling the supernatural net closing in, Hardie initially refuses—much to the relief of Robertson and the others on the plane, including the pilot, who are all aware of Lindsay's dream by now. But Bennett is not the sort of man who easily takes no for an answer, and Hardie is compelled to reconsider. Robertson is furious with Hardie's decision ("You're deliberately gambling with peoples' lives!"), but Lord Wainright casts the deciding vote ("It's the twentieth century; we mustn't be slaves to 'black magic.'"). And Bennett and his secretary join the plane's company for the initially uneventful but ultimately hair-raising last lap of the journey.

As Lindsay's dream predicted, the Dakota's radio goes out, the plane gets lost when it runs into dark storm clouds and snow, one of the passengers goes berserk and must be restrained, the fuel runs out and the pilot must attempt a forced landing on a snow-covered rice paddy near several fishing villages and a lighthouse along the rugged Japanese coast. Though intimating all on board are killed, the finale of

127

"It's the twentieth century; we mustn't be slaves to black magic." From left to right: Denholm Elliott, Sheila Sim, Alfie Bass, Bill Kerr, Ralph Truman, Michael Redgrave, and Alexander Knox in Leslie Norman's absolutely terrifying The Night My Number Came Up.

Robertson (Alexander Knox) and Flight Lt. MacKenzie (Denholm Elliott) are justifiably concerned when the dream's "flashy civilian (George Rose, left) with a loud voice" turns up on cue.

The other passengers (Denholm Elliott, standing, Sheila Sim, and Alexander Knox) feel the supernatural net closing in when Hardie grants Bennett (George Rose) passage on the Tokyo-bound flight.

"You're deliberately gambling with people's lives!" Air Marshal Hardie (Michael Redgrave) and Owen Robertson (Alexander Knox) embark on the initially uneventful but ultimately hair-raising last lap of the journey.

Lindsay's otherwise vivid dream had actually been inconclusive. In reality, everyone is rescued—thanks to Lindsay himself.

Directed in low key but chillingly effective style and played by a first-rate cast, there is nothing foolish or over-the-top about *The Night My Number Came Up*, no stiff-upper-lip heroics, no unbridled hysteria— except for the passenger who goes berserk, of course. But given the terrifying situation and the fact that he's an asthmatic who almost hyperventilated when the pilot climbed to 14,000 feet to escape the storm (the plane doesn't carry an oxygen supply because it normally doesn't fly that high), his actions are wholly believable. In fact, *everything* about this film is credible and convincing—from its white-knuckle recreation of being shut up in a small plane buffeted about in a storm (filmed entirely in a studio) to the close-ups of Robertson's ashen face glued to his window, as if the mere *sight* of land will somehow make him safe.

As Lindsay's precognitive dream starts coming true and the characters are challenged with struggling between reason and unreason—their rational beliefs versus their atavistic fears—*The Night My Number Came Up* gets straight to the heart of the matter. The next time you're 30,000 feet up, enjoying your lunch, and secure in the belief that you stand a better chance of being killed in a car than in a plane, yet find your palms have inexplicably begun to sweat, you'll know what I mean.

THE NIGHT OF THE HUNTER

(1955)

United Artists • B&W/93 Minutes

CREDITS

Director: Charles Laughton; *Producer*: Paul Gregory; *Screenplay*: James Agee and Charles Laughton (uncredited), based on the novel by Davis Grubb; *Cinematographer*: Stanley Cortez; *Editor*: Robert Golden; *Music*: Walter Schumann; *Art Director*: Hilyard Brown.

CAST

Preacher Harry Powell: Robert Mitchum; *Willa Harper*: Shelley Winters; *Rachel*: Lillian Gish; *Mrs. Spoon*: Evelyn Varden; *Mr. Spoon*: Don Beddoe; *Ben Harper*: Peter Graves; *John Harper*: Billy Chapin; *Pearl Harper*: Sally Jane Bruce; *Uncle Birdie*: James Gleason; *Ruby*: Gloria Castillo.

* * *

Kaleidoscopic in its styles—from the traditional to *film noir* and avant-garde—breathtakingly cinematic yet boldly theatrical with a marvelously intricate and evocative soundtrack and an extraordinary music score that's as much a character as the people we see and hear, *The Night of the Hunter*, actor/stage director Charles Laughton's debut as a feature filmmaker, is the *Citizen Kane* of movie thrillers.

Published in 1953, Davis Grubb's Depression-era thriller about a serial killer preacher relentlessly pursuing two orphans in order to get at a cache of stolen loot in their possession shot immediately to the top of the bestseller list, and stayed there for four months. The book was brought to the attention of Laughton by a business associate, producer Paul Gregory, who thought it could be a commercial winner as a film as well and therefore ideal for Laughton's debut as a motion picture director. Although Laughton was still in demand as a stage actor and director (his recently mounted Herman Wouk's *The Caine Mutiny Court-Martial* was a Broadway hit), his film career had hit the skids, and he'd been reduced to roles in minor horror films and Abbott and Costello comedies. To help Laughton regain some of his former film prestige, Gregory felt his colleague should move away from movie acting into directing where he might

Mrs. Spoon (Evelyn Varden, back to camera) acts as matchmaker between Preacher Harry Powell (Robert Mitchum) and widow Willa Harper (Shelley Winters).

reestablish himself as a creative talent. Laughton agreed and felt that *The Night of the Hunter* might do the trick.

Laughton and Gregory quickly purchased the rights and secured a deal with United Artists to bankroll and distribute the film which they intended to shoot mostly on Hollywood soundstages on a comparatively small budget of $497,000. Feeling they needed a "name" screenwriter to adapt the book, they hired James Agee, but when Agee turned in a draft that was "the size of a telephone book" (according to Laughton's wife, Elsa Lanchester), he was dismissed and Laughton adapted the novel himself. Agee received solo screen credit, however.

One of the screen's premier maniacs: Robert Mitchum as Preacher Harry Powell in Charles Laughton's masterful The Night of the Hunter. With Sally Jane Bruce and Billy Chapin as the victimized children.

Powell (Robert Mitchum) gently coaxes Pearl (Sally Jane Bruce) to tell where the money is, then flies into a rage, calling her a "poor, silly disgusting little wretch," when she obeys her brother's instructions to keep silent.

The orphans, John (Billy Chapin) and Pearl (Sally Jane Bruce), whose mother has been murdered by Preacher Harry Powell.

Robert Mitchum was Laughton's only choice to play the con-man preacher, Harry Powell, whose warring inner demons are symbolized by the words "love" and "hate" tattooed on the knuckles of his right and left hands. "Miss" (as she was billed on the screen) Shelley Winters was selected to play the emotionally fragile and sexually frustrated wife, Willa Harper, whose husband, Ben, had briefly shared a prison cell with Powell while waiting to be executed for bank robbery and murder. Prior to being captured, Harper had secreted the stolen $10,000 with his young son, John, who then stashed it in a doll belonging to his sister, Pearl. When Powell is released, he heads for the town where the Harpers live, establishes himself in the community as a man of the cloth and a paragon of virtue, and marries the lonely, vulnerable Willa to get at the cash, which she knows nothing about. When she catches on, Powell cuts her throat, dumps her body in the river, and informs her employers, the Spoons, that she ran off and left him to care for the children. They believe him, but John knows better, and escapes with Pearl down the river, with Powell in pursuit. The desperate pair is finally taken in by a kindly farm woman named Rachel, a sort of Mother Courage figure with a houseful of orphans, who manages to scare Powell off with a shotgun and finally see him brought to justice.

To prepare for the film, which he wanted to exude an atmosphere of early rural Americana, Laughton went to New York's Museum of Modern Art and studied its collection of silent films by the undisputed master of such atmosphere, D.W. Griffith—then, in a further nod to Griffith, cast Griffith's greatest leading lady, Lillian Gish, in an important role. The many striking similarities between *The Night of the Hunter* and Mary Pickford's silent melodrama, *Sparrows* (see separate chapter), suggest that he may have been influenced by that film as well. Laughton may also have studied the work of some of the German masters like F.W. Murnau, for his film is also highly expressionistic, particularly its interior scenes. It is also stamped with dream-like surrealism, Brechtian theatricality, and *film noir.* The result was a pictorially striking but decidedly unusual combination of picaresque adventure, fairy tale, and psychological thriller that eluded most critics—the *New York Herald Tribune* put the film on its annual ten-best list and the *New York Times* gave it a fairly good notice, but the majority of reviewers voted "thumbs-down," as did the Academy of Motion Picture Arts and Sciences, which completely ignored the film come Oscar time. The movie fared even less well with audiences, who chose to stay away from it in droves. Subsequently, Laughton made an attempt to bring Normal Mailer's bestseller, *The Naked and the Dead,* to the screen, but difficulties with the script coupled with his no-hit track record caused the project to fall through (the film was eventually made in 1958 by Raoul Walsh), and Laughton gave up and went back to acting. He died of cancer in 1962.

Over time, however, *The Night of the Hunter* has come to be viewed as a masterpiece, a work so chock full of memorable performances and scenes that it puts many of the more highly touted films of its period to shame. Some examples: the tense wedding night when the psychosexual preacher suppresses his bride's natural ardor by converting her into a Holy Roller; the subdued yet frightening murder scene of

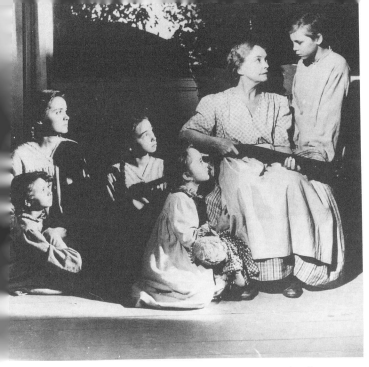

The desperate John and Pearl (Billy Chapin and Sally Jane Bruce) are given sanctuary by a kindly farm woman (Lillian Gish), a sort of Mother Courage figure with a houseful or orphans, who scares Powell off with a shotgun and sees him brought to justice.

The nightmare finally over, John (Billy Chapin) expresses delight at a Christmas present Rachel (Lillian Gish) has given him.

Willa, which Powell ritualistically plays out as if he were giving the woman benediction inside some hellish church; the nightmarish discovery of Willa's corpse tied to an automobile at the bottom of the river by the children's only confidant, the drunken riverboat captain Uncle Birdie; John and Pearl's flight down the river as viewed from the shoreline and above by various wildlife; Rachel and Powell performing a duet of "Lean on Jesus" as she sits in the house with a shotgun on her lap waiting for Powell to make his murderous next move; and many, many more. Very few first-time film directors have displayed such a natural gift for the medium as Laughton does here, which makes it a shame that he never got the opportunity to direct another movie.

The performances Laughton drew from his cast are as remarkable as the visuals he achieved with the help of his brilliant cameraman, Stanley Cortez. But the film's standout performance is Robert Mitchum's, whose frequent deceptively listless manner in other films disguises what a fine actor he can be given the proper guidance. With Laughton, he got it and his performance as Harry Powell is one of the screen's most chilling portraits of perversity and genuine evil. He is astonishingly convincing as he gently coaxes Pearl to tell where the money is, then flies into a rage calling her a "poor, silly, disgusting little wretch" when she obeys John's instructions to keep silent, scaring the wits out of both children—and the audience—in the process. And his frustrated cry of sheer animal rage when the skiff carrying the fleeing children slips inches from his grasp as he wades into the river after them is one of those isolated moments when the viewer can't help but feel a cold breeze from hell run up his spine. As the *New York Times* noted in its review of the film, "The locale is crushingly real, the atmosphere of the 'sticks' is intense, and Robert Mitchum plays the murderous monster with an icy unctuousness that gives you the chills. There is more than malevolence and menace in his character. There is the strong trace of Freudian aberration, fanatacism and iniquity."

So expertly made and definitive is Laughton's memorable screen version of Davis Grubbs's novel that it would seem foolhardy for anyone to attempt to remake and improve upon it. But director David Greene tried to do so in a 1991 version made for television, starring a miscast Richard Chamberlain as Powell. Astonishingly, the telefilm dispensed with the important final third of Grubbs's novel. Only Diana Scarwid's touching performance as the doomed Willa saved the remake from being totally dismissed—unlike Charles Laughton's version, which remains unforgettable in every way.

ABANDON SHIP!
(1957)

[a.k.a. *Seven Waves Away*]
Columbia Pictures • B&W/100 Minutes

CREDITS

Director: Richard Sale; *Producer*: John R. Sloan; *Screenplay*: Richard Sale; *Cinematographer*: Wilkie Cooper; *Editor*: Ray Poulton; *Music*: Sir Arthur Bliss; *Production Designer*: Wilfred Shingleton.

CAST

Alec Holmes: Tyrone Power; *Julie*: Mai Zetterling; *Frank Kelly*: Lloyd Nolan; *Will McKinley*: Stephen Boyd; *Edith Middleton*: Moira Lister; *"Cookie" Morrow*: James Hayter; *Mrs. Knudson*: Marie Lohr; *Sparks Clary*: John Stratton; *Major General Barrington*: Clive Morton; *John Merritt*: Gordon Jackson; *Captain Darrow*: Laurence Naismith; *Michael Faroni*: Eddie Byrne; *Aubrey Clark*: Noel Willman; *Willie Hawkins*: Victor Maddern; *Solly Daniels*: Ferdy Mayne; *Seaman*: Finlay Currie.

* * *

Former matinee idol Tyrone Power gave one of his best, most convincing and distinctly unglamorous performances in this disturbing disaster-at-sea thriller made in England for the actor's own short-lived production company. (Power's independent filmmaking activities came to abrupt end when he died of a heart attack just two years later.)

Writer-director Richard Sale (who wrote the script for the taut presidential assassination thriller, *Suddenly*—see separate chapter), based his gripping screenplay on a real-life tragedy which befell the crew and passengers of an American freighter bound from England to Philadelphia in 1841. The freighter struck an iceberg, broke in half, and went down in the North Atlantic. As the ship was equipped with insufficient lifeboats to hold all the survivors, the captain was faced with the grim responsibility of playing God and deciding who should be cast adrift to perish so the rest might have a better chance at survival.

After the boats were rescued, however, several survivors insisted that murder charges be brought against the captain. But he was subsequently cleared of any wrongdoing since he had the legal right and responsibility under maritime law to act as he did— and had he not faced up to this awesome challenge, very likely *no one* would have survived.

Taking his cue from this unsettling incident, Sale updated his tale and included elements of the Titanic disaster by transforming his ill-fated ship into a 1,076 passenger liner on a world cruise. Striking a derelict World War Two mine, the liner sinks swiftly beneath the waves of the North Atlantic, claiming all but one lifeboat and twenty-seven passengers and crew members.

The dying captain gives the job of commanding the lone lifeboat, which is barely large enough to hold half the number of survivors, to his executive officer, Alec Holmes, who is determined at first to get everyone through the ordeal. But Holmes soon realizes that this is not to be.

The lifeboat is already dangerously overcrowded— and weighted down even more by other survivors in the water who are clinging precariously to its sides, threatening to capsize it. Many are in desperate need of medical attention if they are to make it. There's not enough food or water to sustain everyone. And a ferocious storm is looming that will likely swamp and sink the lifeboat if something isn't done to lighten the load.

Another crew member, Frank Kelly, who is himself seriously wounded, makes the reluctant Holmes confront the inevitable. With no immediate hope of rescue in sight, Holmes must sacrifice the older, the weaker, and the wounded so that the rest will have a better chance at survival. As Holmes and the others watch in horror, the dying Kelly throws himself overboard, calls on Holmes to face up to his grim task, and disappears beneath the waves.

Over the vehement protests of the ship's nurse, Julie (who also is Holmes's fiancée), and another junior officer, Will McKinley, the grim-faced Holmes begins the seemingly heartless process of selecting who is to be given a chance to survive and who is to be cast overboard to face certain death. It's a tough, morally repugnant decision that gets even more so when Holmes is faced with expanding his definition

When the luxury liner Crescent Star strikes a derelict mine, it explodes and sinks, claiming all but twenty-seven passengers and crew and a single lifeboat—which is equipped to hold no more than fourteen.

The dying Kelly (Lloyd Nolan) makes the reluctant Holmes (Tyrone Power) confront the inevitable: that the older, the weaker, and the wounded must be sacrificed so that the others will have a better chance at survival.

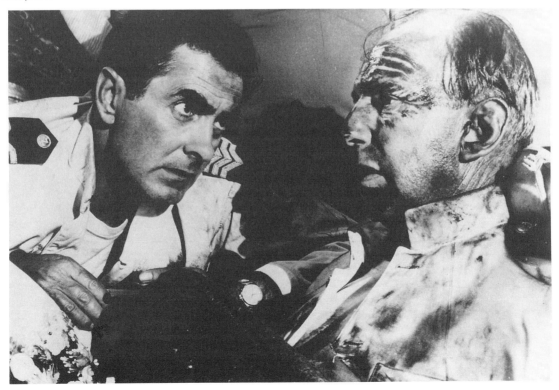

Over the vehement protests of another officer (Stephen Boyd, right), Holmes (Tyrone Power) begins the selection process and starts ordering the "unfit'" from the lifeboat.

Tyrone Power, Marie Lohr, Clive Morton, and Gordon Jackson in Richard Sale's disturbing disaster-at-sea thriller, Abandon Ship!

Some of the passengers go willingly and bravely to their deaths so that others may live. Far more of them refuse, however, and

Holmes (Tyrone Power) must force them into the water or away from the lifeboat at gunpoint.

of "the fittest" to exclude not only those who are sick or wounded, but the idle rich, the elderly but not infirm, and those whose professions are less vital to the current situation—a singer and a playwright, for example, as opposed to a nurse and an experienced seaman like Holmes himself.

Some of the passengers concur with the Holmes decision and go willingly and bravely to their deaths so that others may live. Far more, including McKinley, refuse, however, and Holmes must force them into the water or away from the lifeboat at gunpoint.

Due to Holmes's actions, the lifeboat and its remaining fourteen occupants successfully weather the violent storm when it hits, and several of the survivors finally admit to Holmes, whose haggard face and hollow eyes grimly reflect the awful weight of his decisions, that he was right to do what he did. But

when the lifeboat is rescued, all but the nurse, who stands loyally by Holmes's side even though she doubted him at first, turn against the man who saved them, and they shun and condemn him as a murderer.

Is Holmes a murderer? Or is he a hero? The makers of this tough, unsentimental, convincingly staged, and persuasively acted British thriller,* which generates most of its tension not with fake heroics and stereotypical acts of disaster film derring-do but by posing unsettling—and perhaps unanswerable— questions about leadership and "the survival of the fittest," leave that one up to you.

---

*A made-for-TV version in 1975, called *The Last Survivors*, starred Martin Sheen as the officer in charge of the lifeboat who must make the life or death decisions.

ORDERS TO KILL

(1958)

A Lynx/United Motion Picture Organization Release • B&W/93 Minutes

CREDITS

Director: Anthony Asquith; *Producer*: Anthony Havelock-Allan; *Screenplay*: Paul Dehn and George St. George, based on a novel by Donald Downes; *Cinematographer*: Desmond Dickinson; *Editor*: Gordon Hales; *Music*: Benjamin Frankel; *Art Director*: John Howell.

CAST

Major MacMahon: Eddie Albert; *Gene Summers*: Paul Massie; *Mrs. Summers*: Lillian Gish; *Naval Commander*: James Robertson Justice; *Leonie*: Irene Worth; *Marcel Lefitte*: Leslie French; *Kimball*: John Crawford; *Interrogator*: Lionel Jeffries.

* * *

Underrated by the critics and a box office failure at the time of its release, Anthony Asquith's low-key but compelling WWII espionage tale, *Orders to Kill*, has since gained in reputation, particularly among British film critics and historians, as one of the most outstanding, yet unorthodox, war thrillers ever made. In his massive (1,280 pages) *The Story of Cinema*, for example, critic David Shipman calls it, "The best British war movie of the period." As David Lean's classic *The Bridge on the River Kwai* came out during the same period as *Orders to Kill*, this is scarcely faint praise. But *New York Times* critic Bosley Crowther's contemporary view was a whole lot different. He called *Orders to Kill* "a promising melodrama that loses steam and credibility and ends in a sad heap of sentiment that should make an old cloak-and-dagger boy turn gray." One must keep in mind that Crowther originally found little favor with *Citizen Kane* or *Bonnie and Clyde* either, but to be fair, he was not alone in his dismissal of *Orders to Kill* as just another run-of-the-mill spy yarn.

So, who's right? The Shipmans or the Crowthers? These days, it's a bit difficult to judge because despite the revisionist accolades that have been heaped on *Orders to Kill* over the years, the film has fallen through the distribution cracks and stubbornly refuses to emerge. Released independently of a major

American counterintelligence expert Major MacMahon (Eddie Albert) gives Summers (Paul Massie) some last minute pointers before sending him into German occupied France.

studio and probably in the public domain by now, it seldom turns up on television and hasn't even been released on video—not in America anyway.

I personally side with the Shipmans, though I can also understand why the film's merits may have eluded its detractors at the time, for like Hitchcock's *Secret Agent* (which was likewise critically drubbed and a commercial failure when it debuted), *Orders to Kill* boasts an atypical action movie hero—one who, like Hamlet, is plagued by conscience and indecision, character traits that tend to work against the fast-paced action audiences and critics generally demand from espionage films.

This is not to say that *Orders to Kill* isn't suspense-

Grounded bomber pilot and spy-in-training Gene Summers
(Paul Massie) shares a quiet moment with his mother (Lillian
Gish) in Anthony Asquith's Orders to Kill.

Summers (Paul Massie) links up with Leonie (Irene Worth), his
contact in the French underground, who pinpoints Summers's
quarry for him.

Convinced that Lefitte, the man he's been ordered to kill, is innocent, Summers (Paul Massie) asks Leonie (Irene Worth) to radio his superiors in London and have them reexamine their evidence against Lefitte.

ful, however. It is, and to a very high degree. But its tension and suspense do not stem from a lot of conventionally exciting bits of derring-do. They emerge rather from the moral issues the film imposes on its psychologically pressured hero (and, through him, the audience). Namely, "Will he go through with it?" And, more important, "Should he?" We don't know until the end, at which time director Asquith and writers Paul Dehn and George St. George pull a clever double whammy that clouds things even more.

The reluctant hero of the piece is Gene Summers, an American bomber pilot who is used to killing the enemy at a remote distance (and has likely claimed the lives of innocent civilians with his bombs as well) with little crisis of conscience. When he's grounded, he transfers to an espionage unit near London and undergoes rigorous training to become a spy and a killer by American counterintelligence expert Major MacMahon and his British counterpart. Summers is then dropped into occupied France and links up with a woman named Leonie, his contact in the French underground, who pinpoints Summers's quarry for him—another member of the resistance suspected of being a turncoat. (Ironically, the man is accused of causing the deaths of Resistance radio operators by supplying their names and locations to Nazi collaborators; in short, he kills from a distance just as Summers had.)

But actually meeting his target—a gentle little lawyer and dedicated family man named Lefitte who expresses fervent anti-Nazi sentiments and demonstrates a fondness for cats—Summers begins to wonder if Allied intelligence may be in error. Befriended by the man and his family, Summers grows more and more convinced that the person he's been ordered to kill is innocent and his cold-blooded training suffers severe cracks. Hesitant to go through with the job until his suspicions are either confirmed or denied, he asks Leonie to radio his superiors in London and have them reexamine their evidence against Lefitte. But she tells him in coolly professional terms to suppress his doubts and follow orders. Which, eventually, he

The murder of Lefitte (Leslie French).

does.

Prefiguring the lingering, bloody execution of the enemy agent in Hitchcock's *Torn Curtain*, Lefitte's murder is portrayed as a graceless, ugly, and brutal business, his final death rattle delayed just long enough for him to look into Summers's face and ask an astonished, "Why?" (The people whose names he allegedly turned over to the Nazis probably looked into the faces of their executioners and asked the same question.)

Returning to Leonie's, Summers learns that she contacted London after all and was told too late to stop him that the man he just murdered really was innocent. This shattering news sends Summers on a downward spiral of guilt and self-destruction that threatens to blow the whole operation. But he's pulled back at the last moment when, in the film's final twist, his superiors inform him that Lefitte's disputed treachery has since been confirmed.

This finale raises more questions than it answers, however, for Summers's superiors not only train

people in duplicity but are experts in it themselves and are probably lying to him. Not that it really matters, of course, for the point of the film is not whether Lefitte was guilty and deserved what he got. Rather, as George Perry states in his book, *The Great British Picture Show*, "The Film is concerned with the morality of war and the conscience of the individual when ordered to carry out inhuman orders. By allowing the victim a chance, the young spy begins to ask the questions that war has no time for." In this thriller, it is the drama of doubt not deeds that glues you to your chair.

Anthony Asquith began his directorial career in the closing days of the silents. The son of a former British Prime Minister, he tended to be a bit upper class in his choice of screen material and classical (Crowther called it "soft") in his filmmaking style. His most famous and successful films on both sides of the Atlantic were high gloss adaptations of plays by G.B. Shaw (*Pygmalion*), Oscar Wilde (*The Importance of Being Earnest*), and Terence Rattigan (*The Winslow Boy, The Browning Version*), Asquith's most frequent screen collaborator.

Although he made a number of excellent war films throughout his career, most of them conformed to the conventions of the time in which they were made (World War Two itself) and were more patriotic affairs than the cynically hard-edged and gritty *Orders to Kill*. This one came late in the director's career and was so dismally received that he went back to making glossy, upper crust entertainments such as *The V.I.P.s* (written by Rattigan) and *The Doctor's Dilemma* and *The Millionairess* (both adapted from Shaw). To the end of his days, however, Asquith, who died in 1968, looked upon the anomalous *Orders to Kill* as a personal favorite among his films, and one of his best—which it is.

It is a film whose effectiveness is heightened considerably by a very credible performance from Canadian actor Paul Massie as the conscience-ridden hero (Massie's career never really took off and he later soured on acting and went into teaching) and Paul Dehn's tension-filled script. A former film critic, Dehn had earlier won an Oscar for contributing the story (written with composer James Bernard), though not the script, for another excellent British thriller, *Seven Days to Noon*. He later adapted two John Le Carré espionage novels to the screen, including *The Spy Who Came in From the Cold*, a Cold War thriller whose disillusioned and embittered title character (played by Richard Burton) suggests what *Orders to Kill*'s Gene Summers might have turned into in his later years. Dehn's best known script though was for *Goldfinger*, one of the most enjoyable and, not surprisingly, most suspenseful of the James Bond thrillers.

VERTIGO

(1958)

Paramount Pictures • Color/128 Minutes

CREDITS

Director: Alfred Hitchcock; *Producer*: Alfred Hitchcock; *Screenplay*: Alec Coppel and Samuel Taylor, based on the novel *D'entre les morts* by Pierre Boileau and Thomas Narcejac; *Cinematographer*: Robert Burks; *Editor*: George Tomasini; *Music*: Bernard Herrmann; *Art Directors*: Hal Pereira and Henry Bumstead.

CAST

John "Scottie" Ferguson: James Stewart; *Madeleine Elster/Judy Barton*: Kim Novak; *Midge*: Barbara Bel Geddes; *Gavin Elster*: Tom Helmore; *The Coroner*: Henry Jones; *Pop Liebl*: Konstantin Shayne; *McKittrick Hotel Landlady*: Ellen Corby.

* * *

Everyone has his or her own favorite Hitchcock film. Mine is *Vertigo*, which I believe to be the master of suspense's best movie and the most mesmerizing romantic thriller ever made.

By all accounts a very personal film for Hitchcock, *Vertigo* was not a big hit with audiences or critics when it first came out—one critic, in fact, dismissed it as a "Hitchcock and bull story." Once the rights to the film reverted to Hitchcock, he removed it from distribution together with four other films to which he owned the rights (including *Rear Window*—see separate chapter) and kept it from being shown for almost twenty years. During this period, many of the new breed of auteurist critics began writing about it in glowing terms and the film began popping up on numerous critic polls of the ten best movies ever made. By the time *Vertigo* was finally rereleased after Hitchcock's death, it had received more critical ink than any of his films with the possible exception of *Psycho* and had attained cult status. With the reissue its reputation soared, for like all legitimate classics, *Vertigo* had not only weathered the test of time but also improved with age. Audiences and critics who'd never seen it were bowled over by its technical brilliance and emotional richness and power, and were rightly bewildered that such a remarkable movie could have been so quickly and easily dismissed by contemporaries. And for those of us who knew and loved the film, the experience of seeing it again simply confirmed what we already believed: that *Vertigo* was one of the truly great ones—a genuine cinematic masterpiece and timeless screen love story masquerading as a top-notch thriller.

Hitchcock based *Vertigo* on a bizarre French tale by the authors of *Les Diaboliques*, which Hitchcock had considered bringing to the screen himself at one time. After learning that he had almost bought their novel *Les Diaboliques*, the authors, Boileau and Narcejac, set about writing a follow-up that the director wouldn't be able to pass on this time around. He didn't, and the film Hitchcock made follows the novel in many particulars, although it departs from it in significant ways, too.

Set in France during World War Two, the book is a gritty, Georges Simenon-like detective story that typically reveals its twist ending almost on the last page. In both versions, the hero, a detective suffering from vertigo, is hired by an old friend to tail the latter's beautiful wife, who seems possessed by the spirit of a dead ancestor pushing her to suicide. The detective and the wife fall in love, but the seemingly haunted woman kills herself, leaving the detective bereft with grief as it was his inability to conquer his fear of heights that prevented him from saving her. The death is ruled an accident.

Subsequently, the still-grieving detective meets another woman who bears a striking resemblance to his dead love and he pushes her into making herself over in the deceased woman's image. The twist is that they're actually the same person—the woman who died was the real wife of the detective's friend, who had set the detective up to unwittingly participate in and play witness to an elaborate murder scheme disguised as suicide. In the book, the detective, Roger Flavieres, learns the truth at the very end—at which point he strangles the girl (Renee) in retribution. In the film, however, Hitchcock lets us in on the girl's (Judy Barton) guilty secret well before the detective, Scottie Ferguson, discovers it, shifting the focus of the absorbing last act from surprise to suspense as we wonder what will happen to the desperate girl (who genuinely loves Scottie and whom we come to like)

*James Stewart as Scottie Ferguson, the obsessed lover who is
literally "left hanging" during the tension-filled opening scene
of Alfred Hitchcock's* Vertigo.

*Midge (Barbara Bel Geddes) tries to help Scottie overcome the
vertigo that inadvertently led to the death of a policeman and
sent Scottie into retirement. But only another shock will do the
trick for him.*

Former college chum Gavin Elster (Tom Helmore) hires Scottie (James Stewart) to tail Elster's beautiful wife, Madeleine, who is possessed by the spirit of someone dead pushing her toward suicide.

Scottie and Madeleine (Kim Novak) fall in love, but the haunted woman kills herself, leaving Scottie bereft with grief as it was his inability to conquer his fear of heights that prevented him from saving her.

Scottie (James Stewart) and Judy/Madeleine (Kim Novak) confront one another during Vertigo's *climactic bell tower scene—one of the most suspensefully staged, movingly acted,* and emotionally shattering sequences in Hitchcock's cinema *(indeed,* all *cinema!).*

Dismissed upon release as a "Hitchcock and bull story," Vertigo *is now considered to be one of the cinema's truly great films—a genuine masterpiece and timeless screen love story masquerading as a top-notch thriller.*

once Scottie finds her out.

The moment of truth arrives when she puts on a necklace she'd worn while posing as the dead woman, Madeleine Elster, and Scottie takes her back to the scene of the murder for the film's devastating conclusion. "The necklace...that was your big mistake, Judy. You shouldn't keep souvenirs of a killing. You shouldn't have been so...*sentimental,*" Scottie says, his voice breaking and his eyes filling with tears as he drags her to the top of the bell tower of the Spanish mission from which Madeleine supposedly hurled herself—and conquers his vertigo at last. Clinging to him, Judy replies in anguish, "I was safe when you found me. There was nothing that you could prove. When I saw you again, I couldn't run away, I loved you so. I walked into danger and let you change me because I loved you and I wanted you. Oh, Scottie, you love me...please keep me safe." At which point, a shrouded figure rises from the floor, and Judy, believing it to be the ghost of Madeleine herself, backs away from Scottie gasping "Oh, no!" and falls to her own death from the bell tower. The film concludes with Scottie staring down at the girl's body as the ghostly figure, a nun, tolls the bell for help. I have seen *Vertigo* as part of a large audience on several occasions, and at each of them, one could have heard the proverbial pin drop during the ten minutes or so that it takes this scene—one of the most suspensefully staged, movingly acted, and emotionally shattering climaxes in Hitchcock's cinema (indeed, *all* cinema!)—to unfold. It alone makes *Vertigo* a not-to-be-missed experience.

But the bell tower finale is only one of many spellbinding sequences in this hypnotic film—in which James Stewart gives the performance of his career as the tormented Scottie. The pain in the actor's eyes and voice as his character realizes he's been duped and finally comes to terms with the fact that he's romantically obsessed with the memory of a woman (the fake Madeleine) who never existed is heartbreaking indeed. As is the scene in Judy's hotel room where Scottie coerces the reluctant Judy into making her transformation into Madeleine complete by styling her hair like Madeleine's. While she's in the bathroom doing this, the camera focuses on Scottie waiting anxiously for her to emerge, Bernard Herrmann's lush romantic score building slowly to a crescendo on the soundtrack. The bathroom door opens, the camera moves in on Scottie, his eyes filled with the wonder and emotion of a man whose desperate yearning has finally been fulfilled, and Herrmann's music powerfully crescendos as Hitchcock at last lets us see what Scottie sees—the ghostly figure of his resurrected love assuming solid shape as she (the fully transformed Judy) slowly crosses the floor to him. As Scottie and Madeleine/Judy embrace and kiss, Hitchcock's camera pans vertiginously around them, the background shifting from the hotel room to the scene of Scottie's last tryst with Madeleine then back again, making us experience the same distortion Scottie himself is feeling at this emotional moment.

Though by no means a great actress, Kim Novak gives a great performance (and the performance of *her* career as well) in *Vertigo* under Hitchcock's Svengali-like direction. Originally, the part was to have gone to Vera Miles, but when Miles got pregnant and had to bow out, Hitchcock opted for Novak instead. (Curiously, there is one scene where Novak, her face half hidden by shadow, actually looks like Miles!) Hitchcock was never satisfied with Novak, but fans of the film (including Stewart himself) find it difficult to imagine anyone else in the dual role—even Grace Kelly, who would surely have been a perfect Madeleine, but probably wouldn't have been able to convincingly pull off the earthy, vulnerable Judy.

In his controversial biography of Hitchcock, *The Dark Side of Genius*, Donald Spoto calls *Vertigo* the "...ultimate disclosure of his [Hitchcock's] romantic impulses and of the attraction-repulsion he felt for the object of those impulses: the idealized blonde he thought he desired but really believed to be a fraud." That may be, but I don't think it explains why the film strikes such a familiar and emotional chord with audiences. My own explanation of this reaction is that at one time or another most people in the audience have been in Scottie's position. That is of having a deep attachment abruptly terminated (for whatever reason) and of being unable to work through the loss and finally come to terms with it unless or until the object of that attachment can be confronted one more time—in other words to be "left hanging," as Scottie is in the film's metaphoric opening scene. In *Vertigo*, Scottie gets this universally wished-for opportunity, seizes it, and finally exorcises himself—as does Rick (Humphrey Bogart) in *Casablanca*, the screen's other great romantic drama, a much less Freudian variation on the very same theme.

THE LAST VOYAGE

(1960)

Metro-Goldwyn-Mayer • Color/91 Minutes

CREDITS

Director: Andrew L. Stone; *Producer*: Andrew L. and Virginia Stone; *Screenplay*: Andrew L. Stone; *Cinematographer*: Hal Mohr; *Editor*: Virginia Stone; *Music*: Rudy Schrager.

CAST

Cliff Henderson: Robert Stack; *Laurie Henderson*: Dorothy Malone; *Captain Adams*: George Sanders; *Second Engineer Walsh*: Edmond O'Brien; *Hank Lawson*: Woody Strode; *Jill Henderson*: Tammy Marihugh; *Chief Engineer Pringle*: Jack Kruschen; *Third Officer England*: Joel Marston; *Third Engineer Cole*: Richard Norris; *Osborne*: George Furness; *Quartermaster*: Marshall Kent.

* * *

A genuine Hollywood maverick, writer-producer-director Andrew L. Stone, who worked in tandem with his editor-wife Virginia, basically made three categories of films during his nearly fifty-year Hollywood career: musical comedies, thrillers, and schmaltzy musical biographies like *The Great Victor Herbert* and *Song of Norway*.

While some of his early musical comedies are quite zestful, Stone did his best work in the fifties and early sixties when he concentrated almost exclusively on making moderately budgeted thrillers, several of which—*The Night Holds Terror* and *Cry Terror!*—are exciting and quite suspenseful indeed.

Stone's best thriller though is *The Last Voyage*, a forerunner of the Irwin Allen disaster films that flooded theaters in the seventies and eighties. Stone was able to lavish a larger budget than usual on *The Last Voyage*, and he used the money to good effect. A stickler for detail and realism who began his Hollywood career working with the great silent star Harold Lloyd on some of Lloyd's most amazing thrill comedies, Stone was determined to give audiences their money's worth by shooting every cliff-hanging sequence on board an actual ship, which he would actually sink in the final scene as the cameras grinded away.

Vacationing couple Cliff and Laurie Henderson (Robert Stack and Dorothy Malone) share a quiet moment aboard ship shortly before all hell breaks loose.

Stone found the ship he required in Osaka, where it was being held for scrap by a Japanese salvage company. Stone and MGM paid off the Japanese and got permission to shoot the entire film on board the condemned ship, the Ile de France. Contrary to rumor, however, Stone did not actually sink the legendary liner. This the Japanese owners wouldn't have allowed, no matter how much of a stickler for realism the director was. Instead, Stone flooded the ship and set off myriad explosions on board to make audiences believe the ship was going down.

Stone and MGM got permission to shoot The Last Voyage aboard the doomed ship, Ile de France. Contrary to rumor, however, Stone did not actually sink the liner for his film. It just looked like he did.

Dorothy Malone, Tammy Marihugh, and Robert Stack in Andrew L. Stone's ultra-realistic disaster film, The Last Voyage.

The Captain finally gives the order to abandon ship when it becomes clear there's no hope the sinking luxury liner can be saved.

Trapped beneath a ruptured beam in her stateroom, which is fast filling with water, Laurie (Dorothy Malone) bids farewell to her daughter (Tammy Marihugh).

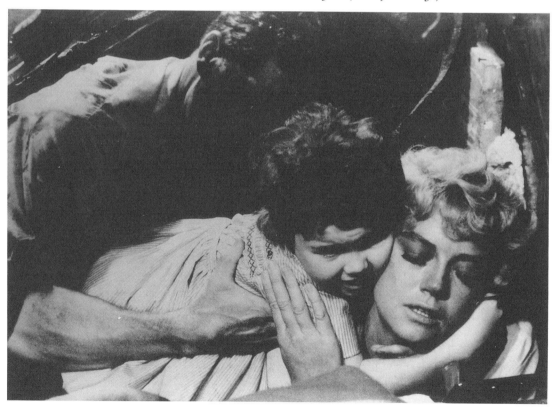

Hank Lawson (Woody Strode), Second Engineer Walsh (Edmond O'Brien), and Cliff (Robert Stack) rescue Laurie (Dorothy Malone) just seconds before the ship finally goes under.

While the plot of *The Last Voyage* is fairly standard disaster movie stuff, the film itself exudes a powerful sense of atmosphere and authenticity. "He [Stone] has got an extraordinary feeling of the actuality of being aboard a ship, the creeping terror of a disaster, and the agony of a great vessel's death," wrote the critic for the *New York Times*. "And in all of his performances, he has got a moving reflection of frenzy, futility and fear."

In many cases, the on-screen frenzy and fear looked so good because they were very real indeed.

In his autobiography, *Straight Shooting*, star Robert Stack writes of the experience:

> The use of the real ship made *The Last Voyage* exceptionally hazardous. When we ran up and down ladders, instead of finding neatly designed stairs built for the action of the film, we found ourselves on ladders with forty-five years of grease and slime on them. Great chunks of glass flew freely through the air on deck as dynamite explosions rocked the boat with regularity. The special effects men decided that the only way to sink the ship visually was to put the cameras inside and photograph the sea rushing in. Using fireboats, which shoot streams of water several hundred feet high, they stretched giant hoists up the sides of the ship through the portholes, and sealed them off. The water came through with such ferocity that we literally were thrown head over heels. Electricity [from the arc lights] combined with salt water to produce a small electrical storm on board. Great waves poured through the ship. For yours truly, *The Last Voyage* very nearly lived up to its title.

Like the *Ile de France*, the film's luxury liner is well past its prime and ready for retirement. Unlike the real one, however, the movie ship puts out to sea for one cruise too many. A boiler room accident rocks the liner with a tremendous explosion that splits through the hull, causing the ship to list and, finally, to sink. As the desperate crew struggles in vain to seal the hole and stop the water from rushing in, the career-concerned captain strives to keep the passengers from panicking but only succeeds in making things worse. Cliff Henderson spends much of the film's ninety-one nail-biting minutes working feverishly to find and rescue his daughter and wife, the latter trapped beneath a ruptured beam in her stateroom, which is fast filling up with water.

Virginia Stone's editing builds maximum excitement and tension by cutting swiftly from one scene of mounting disaster to another as the ocean gradually swamps the entire ship and everyone aboard finds him or herself waist deep, then chest deep, then chin deep in water as the beleaguered liner slips out from under their feet and sinks to the bottom.

Her editing is so seamless—and her husband's direction so convincing—that for years audiences and critics thought the *Ile de France* really went down in the film. Not so. As cameraman Hal Mohr recounted to film historian Leonard Maltin in the book, *Behind the Camera*: "The only shot we made that was not made on that boat was the final shot of them [the passengers] running up the deck with the boat going under the water; finally the boat goes under the water, they jump overboard, and the camera goes under the water with the boat. We did that out at the beach in Santa Monica—because obviously, you couldn't have actors working on a sinking boat. But nobody ever knew it wasn't made on the boat, it was that realistic."

Indeed it was. In fact, despite all the advances in screen special effects over the years, disaster movies still don't come much more realistic and convincing than Andrew L. Stone's one-of-a-kind white-knuckler, *The Last Voyage*.

CASH ON DEMAND

(1962)

A Columbia Pictures Release of a Hammer Films Production
B&W/84 Minutes

CREDITS

Director: Quentin Lawrence; *Producer*: Michael Carreras; *Screenplay*: David T. Chantler and Lewis Greifer, based on the play *The Gold Inside* by Jacques Gillies; *Cinematographer*: Arthur Grant; *Editor*: Eric Boyd-Perkins; *Music*: Wilfred Josephs; *Production Designer*: Bernard Robinson.

CAST

Fordyce: Peter Cushing; *Hepburn*: André Morell; *Pearson*: Richard Vernon; *Harvill*: Barry Lowe; *Sanderson*: Norman Bird; *Miss Pringle*: Edith Sharpe; *Collins*: Charles Morgan; *Detective Inspector Mason*: Kevin Stoney; *Kane*: Alan Haywood; *Sally*: Lois Daine; *Mrs. Fordyce*: Vera Cook.

* * *

Cash on Demand is a minor gem of a thriller made by England's Hammer Films during the studio's heyday when it was turning out what have since come to be called "mini-Hitchcocks" (modern day, black-and-white horror/suspense films in the vein of *Psycho*) in between its colorful Gothic horror movies. Unlike most of Hammer's "mini-Hitchcocks," however, *Cash on Demand* is not a horror film. Nor does it owe very much to the master. On the contrary, its inspiration stems from a very different, though no less famous, British storyteller and tale.

The film opens on a cold Christmas Eve morning at a small bank in Haversham, England, where one of the tellers, Miss Pringle, is trying to brighten the holiday spirits of her fellow staffers by putting up a Christmas card display and handing out Yuletide crackers and party hats. The arrival of Mr. Fordyce, the stiff-necked manager of the bank, puts a stop to that, however. "Banking is one of the few dignified businesses left in the world," he snaps at her. "Do you mind terribly if we keep it that way?" Fordyce then vents his spleen on his loyal chief clerk, Pearson, threatening the man, who is preoccupied over his wife's illness, with dismissal for a minor mistake.

As the clock strikes ten, Pearson unlocks the bank doors to let in customers. An expensive car draws up outside and an obviously wealthy man in a camel hair coat gets out. In a cultured voice, he asks Pearson if he may park there. Pearson replies, "For thirty minutes, sir," and the man hands him his card, asking to see Mr. Fordyce. The man, Hepburn, tells Fordyce that he represents the Home and Mercantile Bankers Insurance Company, and due to a large number of robberies in the area, is on a tour of inspection of the security measures carried out by the banks his company insures. Fordyce says he'll be happy to show Hepburn around, and as the phone rings on his desk, he invites the man to take a chair.

Fordyce picks up the receiver and hears the distorted and terrified voice of his wife on the other end. "For God's sake do as he tells you," she urges him. Hepburn coolly takes the phone from Fordyce's paralyzed hand and hangs it up. "If you want to see your wife and child again, you will do as I say," Hepburn instructs him and then outlines his ingenious plan to rob the bank using Fordyce himself as his main accomplice. The robbery is to be carried out methodically and unhurriedly, Hepburn says. "No noisy guns, no stolen cars, no working through the night. Just a social affair."

Fordyce has to appear normal to his staff as if conducting Hepburn on a routine investigation, yet he is constantly reminded that any slipup on his part will result in the deaths of his wife and child. When Fordyce protests that he cannot bear the thought of what his family is suffering, Hepburn, who seems to know quite a bit about him, reminds the officious bank manager that he has never shown much affection for his family, or anyone else for that matter. Fordyce is psychoanalyzed by his unwelcome visitor and made to squirm. "I've had a chance to study you under ideal laboratory conditions," Hepburn says to him. "The most interesting part of your character is what it lacks—charity. Each man is his own bank, Fordyce, and it's the gold inside that counts."

With Fordyce's help, the robbery takes just forty-five minutes. The businesslike Hepburn stuffs the cash in his briefcase, warns Fordyce that any attempt

The tyrannical Fordyce (Peter Cushing) reads the riot act to one of his employees (Barry Lowe) for not following exact procedure regarding proper initialing of the bank's ledger.

Sanderson (Norman Bird) and Pearson (Richard Vernon) discuss the funds they're collecting for the office Christmas party, which will soon be scotched by all work and no play bank manager Fordyce.

Hepburn (André Morell) orders the offscreen Fordyce to hurry up with the vault and get the money in the suitcase.

Fordyce (Peter Cushing) considers taking a drink to quell his nerves. In the background sits Hepburn (André Morell), the bank robber posing as an insurance inspector, who has Fordyce at his mercy.

For the sake of his wife and son, who are being held hostage by Hepburn's men, Fordyce (Peter Cushing) pleads with Detective Inspector Mason (Kevin Stoney) to release the wily bank robber.

to inform the police will bring disaster to the man's family, then leaves the bank with a friendly goodbye and "Happy Christmas" to the staff.

Pearson enters Fordyce's office moments later and is perplexed to find his agitated boss pouring himself a whiskey—something Fordyce has never done on the job before. He tells Fordyce that after hearing Hepburn's lecture on bank security measures and how people in such a business can never be too cautious, he'd dutifully checked up on Hepburn, discovered the man to be an imposter, and has just phoned for the police. Panicked, Fordyce confesses what's happened, explains that his family's life is at stake, and urges Pearson to conspire with him in putting the police off by acting as if nothing has happened.

Pearson sympathetically agrees, but when the police arrive, he and Fordyce are informed that based on Pearson's excellent description of the man, Hepburn has already been picked up. Horror-struck, Fordyce pleads with the police to release their prisoner for the sake of his wife and child.

The screw tightens further for Fordyce when the suspicious Inspector Mason puts a call through to the bank manager's wife and learns from the bewildered woman that she and her son are okay and that no such hostage-taking ever took place. At this point, it looks even to Pearson that Fordyce and Hepburn must have been in cahoots. But this being Christmas after all, the tormented bank manager is spared the final disgrace of being hauled off to the hoosegow when Hepburn charitably reveals the man's innocence in the nick of time. Having learned a valuable lesson in charity and humility, Fordyce undergoes a transformation of character, joins in the holiday spirit, and begins treating Pearson and everyone else as human beings for the first time.

It doesn't take much critical insight to discern that *Cash on Demand* is Charles Dickens's *A Christmas Carol* replayed as a crime thriller. Fordyce is Scrooge. Pearson is Bob Cratchit. And Hepburn is a combination of Jacob Marley and the other unwelcome ghostly visitors who give Dickens's venerable "Mr. Humbug" an important lesson in life. But the variation works quite well as a thriller. The film is extremely taut due to the remarkable degree of character tension created by Cushing and Morell as they force our sympathies to shift back and forth between them. Cynics may argue that the film might have concluded on a much sharper and more powerful note if the initially very unlikable Fordyce had actually gone to the slammer. I thought so myself when I saw the film the first time, but after repeated viewings, I've since revised that opinion because, like Dickens's *A Christmas Carol*, the story would have had little point otherwise.

THE MANCHURIAN CANDIDATE

(1962)

A United Artists Release • B&W/126 Minutes

CREDITS

Director: John Frankenheimer; *Producers*: George Axelrod and John Frankenheimer; *Screenplay*: George Axelrod, based on the novel by Richard Condon; *Cinematographer*: Lionel Lindon; *Editor*: Ferris Webster; *Music*: David Amram; *Production Designer*: Richard Sylbert.

CAST

Bennett Marco: Frank Sinatra; *Raymond Shaw*: Laurence Harvey; *Raymond's Mother*: Angela Lansbury; *Senator Iselin*: James Gregory; *Rosie*: Janet Leigh; *Yen Lo*: Khigh Deigh; *Senator Jordan*: John McGiver; *Jocie*: Leslie Parrish; *Chunjin*: Henry Silva; *Corporal Melvin*: James Edwards; *Zilkov*: Albert Paulsen; *Army Psychiatrist*: Joe Adams; *Holborn Gaines*: Lloyd Corrigan; *Bobby Lembeck*: Tom Lowell; *Ed Mavole*: Richard LaPore.

* * *

World War Two is rife with true stories about daring and ingenious escapes made by Allied POWs. America's next conflict in Korea revealed a lack of similar derring-do, however, for the startling reason that not a single U.S. prisoner of war attempted to escape from his Communist Chinese captors during the entire conflict. The explanation for this amazing turnabout was not a sudden lack of courage on the part of America's imprisoned fighting men, but a lack of will, for the enemy, in cooperation with their Soviet allies and advisors, had engineered their captives' docility and compliance by subjecting them to sophisticated experiments in mind control—later dubbed "brainwashing" by the C.I.A.

Novelist Richard Condon, a onetime advertising man not unfamiliar with very different but no less effective forms of mind control, picked up on the "brainwashing" story and speculated "What if?" in his landmark political satire-cum-espionage thriller *The Manchurian Candidate*, which became an immediate bestseller when published in 1959. The book was snapped up for the movies by screenwriter-producer George Axelrod and John Frankenheimer, the *wunderkind* Hollywood director of his day, but they encountered little enthusiasm from the major studios until Frank Sinatra, a big fan of the book, signed on as executive producer (uncredited) and star. On the strength of Sinatra's name and participation, United Artists agreed to bankroll the film, which was released in October 1962.

As is the case with so many daring and innovative films, *The Manchurian Candidate* found little favor with most contemporary critics, who notably absented it from all major newspaper and magazine "ten best" lists that year, or the Academy of Motion Picture Arts and Sciences, which gave the film only one Oscar nomination—Angela Lansbury for Best Supporting Actress.

Those who disliked the film dismissed it as "confusing" and "improbable." And many were incensed by its scathing portrait of American extremist politics as exemplified by the character of Senator Iselin, an empty-headed and opportunistic Commie witch-hunter with eyes on the presidency. They apparently had short memories, for Iselin was but a thinly-veiled portrait of Senator Joe McCarthy and the film's admittedly satiric view of his antics did not stray all that far from the truth. Critics on the other hand who were dazzled by the film's wit, sophistication, and power also tended to slough it off, however, as a bright but "far-out fantasy thriller."

The truth of the matter is that *The Manchurian Candidate* was never a difficult and "confusing" film to follow. I had no trouble following it and I was no experienced and presumably savvy film critic at the time, just a college freshman. Frankenheimer did use some techniques that were challenging and ahead of their time to propel the film's plot along, but they were by no means obfuscating. Essentially, it unfolds in a linear and straightforward manner. Critics were "confused" by the film because they tended to view it not as the subtle and devilish black comedy that it is but as a "reality-based" thriller (which it also is), and they found its premise—that Communist Chinese mind control experts could actually brainwash and condition someone to be a remote-controlled killer—

Captain Marco (Frank Sinatra) is plagued by recurring nightmares in which he sees his Communist Chinese captors order Raymond Shaw to coldbloodedly murder two fellow prisoners.

The bravura sequence where Frankenheimer puts us into the brainwashed soldiers' heads and shows us the elaborate mind game the Communist Chinese are playing on them by panning his camera 360 degrees around a room that changes from an imagined ladies' garden party in New Jersey to an austere lecture hall in Manchuria.

Frank Sinatra as Captain Marco and Laurence Harvey as
Sergeant Raymond Shaw in John Frankenheimer's The
Manchurian Candidate, *one of the most powerful, cleverly
written, and technically ingenious thrillers America has ever
produced.*

*Rosie (Janet Leigh) bails out Marco (Frank Sinatra) at the
police station for having beaten up Raymond Shaw's Korean
houseboy.*

Romance blossoms between Rosie (Janet Leigh) and Marco (Frank Sinatra).

more than a bit hard to swallow. As it turns out, however, they were simply being naïve for the Soviets and the Communist Chinese were engaged in precisely such activities at the time, and so was our C.I.A. And as events a little over a year later would demonstrate, many details of *The Manchurian Candidate*'s premise were neither far-out nor improbable, but horrifyingly prescient indeed. For however one views the 1963 assassination of John F. Kennedy—either as the work of a lone gunman or the product of an elaborate conspiracy—*The Manchurian Candidate* hits the mark.

Similar to JFK's alleged single assassin, Lee Harvey Oswald, *Candidate*'s Raymond Shaw is a mother-dominated loner with a fondness for guns and a reputation as a skilled marksman whose insecure and unstable personality draws him to authority figures and makes him a likely prospect for manipulation. On the other hand, if you favor the theory that JFK's murder was planned and carried out by a group of conspirators, some of them in high places inside our own government, *The Manchurian Candidate* eerily foreshadows that possibility as well.

In the early seventies, the rights to the film reverted

159

Marco (Frank Sinatra) pieces the puzzle together and succeeds in applying the conspirators' posthypnotic suggestion technique to finally deprogram Raymond—or so Marco thinks.

Disguised as a priest, the brainwashed Raymond (Laurence Harvey) enters the Madison Square Garden convention center to carry out his bloody assignment.

to Frank Sinatra. Due to a financial dispute with United Artists, he pulled the movie from distribution and let it sit on the shelf for almost two decades. In 1987, Sinatra finally permitted it to be re-released theatrically and on home video, and it at last received the critical accolades it had long deserved. Though now thirty years old, *The Manchurian Candidate* has aged very little. It remains one of the most powerful, cleverly written, and technically ingenious thrillers America has ever produced, its message as relevant and disturbing today as it was back in 1962.

As the film begins, Sergeant Raymond Shaw returns home from Korea a Congressional Medal of Honor winner for having saved the lives of all but two of his platoon members during a nighttime skirmish. His fellow survivors, led by Captain Bennett Marco, are convinced that Raymond's a hero and sincerely refer to him as "the kindest, bravest, warmest, most wonderful human being I have ever known"—even though a pre-credits sequence has revealed to us that Raymond is a cold and unlikable person who holds these men in contempt, and vice versa. The truth is that the platoon was taken captive and the men were brainwashed into believing that Raymond saved their lives. Raymond unknowingly has been programmed to return home as an assassin. (Mavole and Lembeck, the two men who didn't survive the fabricated skirmish, were actually killed by Raymond himself as a test of the programming technique's effectiveness.) Raymond's ultimate assignment is to assassinate the moderate presidential candidate during the nominating convention at Madison Square Garden so that the vice-presidential candidate (Raymond's extremist stepfather, Senator Iselin) can step in and take the dead man's place. The mastermind behind the insidious plot is Raymond's unscrupulous and power hungry mother.

Plagued by recurring nightmares in which he sees his Communist Chinese captors order Raymond to kill Mavole and Lembeck, Marco manages to piece the puzzle together and succeeds in applying the conspirators' inventive posthypnotic suggestion technique on Raymond to finally deprogram him—or so Marco thinks. But Raymond gets away and heads for the convention where, at the appointed moment, he unexpectedly shoots his mother and stepfather instead. Marco breaks in on him and the luckless young man spins around, saying, "You couldn't have stopped them...the Army couldn't...so I had to...Oh, God, Ben..." And then he turns the rifle on himself.

"Poor Raymond...poor friendless, friendless Raymond," Marco mourns at the film's conclusion. "He was wearing his medal when he died."

The Manchurian Candidate is an emotional roller coaster—bitingly funny one minute, violent the next (Lembeck's shooting is particularly grisly), tense all the way through (the Madison Square Garden sequence alone ranks with the best of Hitchcock and clearly recalls the Albert Hall sequence in his two versions of *The Man Who Knew Too Much*), and ultimately quite moving and powerful. The scene where Frankenheimer puts us into the brainwashed soldiers' heads and shows us the elaborate mind game the Communist Chinese are playing on them by panning his camera 360° around the room that changes from an imagined ladies' garden party in New Jersey to an austere lecture hall in Manchuria without a single cut is just one of many bravura sequences in the film.

But the key to the film's emotional wallop is character. Like Marco, we never come to actually *like* Raymond, but we do come to *feel* for him. He is ultimately a very tragic character whose fate is inescapable and has been since birth. Early in the film when we see Raymond cover his ears like a child in a futile attempt to shut out the diatribes of his domineering mother, we get a good idea of what his unhappy childhood must have been like and why he is like he is. And when Raymond shoots the liberal Senator Jordan and milk streams from the hole the bullet made in the carton the victim is holding before him, we're offered a symbolic reminder of what this particular mother's deadly "nurturing" has produced.

It's worth noting that Raymond's mother is the only character who is not given a name. That's because, unlike everyone else in the film (including Raymond and the buffoonish Iselin), she is not so much a person as a symbol of what happens when the lust for power consumes all other human emotions. And lust is the operative word, especially if you accept Henry Kissinger's view that power is "the ultimate aphrodisiac," for Raymond's mother is clearly hooked. As she sits watching and listening to Iselin parrot her scripted, extremist accusations into the TV cameras, her back and forth movements suggest sexual excitement—in fact, she seems to be "riding" her chair. When she reveals the assassination scheme to the hypnotized Raymond for the first time and rhapsodizes over being "swept into the White House with powers that will make martial law seem like anarchy," her excitement is almost orgasmic. And after she gives Raymond his final instructions, she kisses him in a manner not at all motherly before sending him on his way. Raymond's mother is truly a monster, and Angela Lansbury plays her to the hilt in the performance of her career.

CAPE FEAR

(1962)

Universal-International • B&W/105 Minutes

CREDITS

Director: J. Lee Thompson; *Producer*: Sy Bartlett; *Screenplay*: James R. Webb, based on the novel *The Executioners* by John D. MacDonald; *Cinematographer*: Samuel Leavitt; *Editor*: George Tomasini; *Music*: Bernard Herrmann; *Art Directors*: Alexander Golitzen and Robert Boyle.

CAST

Sam Bowden: Gregory Peck; *Max Cady*: Robert Mitchum; *Peggy Bowden*: Polly Bergen; *Nancy Bowden*: Lori Martin; *Mark Dutton*: Martin Balsam; *Dave Grafton*: Jack Kruschen; *Charlie Sievers*: Telly Savalas; *Diane Taylor*: Barrie Chase.

* * *

Though not like *Psycho* an outright horror film, *Cape Fear*, one of a string of psychological thrillers turned out by Hollywood in the wake of the Hitchcock film's stunning impact and success, put audiences of 1962 through the emotional wringer almost as effectively as its classic forebear. And it still has the power to chill due to the fact that it has not suffered the influential *Psycho*'s fate of being constantly ripped off or imitated to death.

Cape Fear's memorably brutal sexual psychopath, Max Cady, has little in common with *Psycho*'s Norman Bates, but, as directed by J. Lee Thompson, the film itself does. A major suspense sequence in which the heroine, Peggy Bowden, suffers a nightmare about the victimizing Cady, wakes up to find her husband gone, and goes downstairs to investigate is staged and assembled (by Hitchcock's longtime cutter, George Tomasini) in a style that mimics Hitchcock's to a T. One or two of the interior sets—the entryway and stairway of a drab boarding house, a cluttered bedroom—look like redressed sets from *Psycho* itself, which is more than possible since both films were shot on sound stages at Universal and made use of the same set and prop departments. There is the appearance of Martin Balsam (*Psycho*'s doomed private detective, Arbogast) in the supporting role of yet another lawman. And then there is the nerve-shattering music score by longtime Hitchcock composer,

After spending eight years in prison for assault and battery due to the damning eye witness testimony of Sam Bowden (Gregory Peck), the sadistic Max Cady (Robert Mitchum) returns to get even in Cape Fear.

Bernard Herrmann—although it admittedly sounds less like the one he composed for *Psycho* and more like the one he would later do for Brian De Palma's Hitchcock pastiche, *Sisters*.

Cape Fear, in addition to Hitchcock and *Psycho*, offers a few nods to Charles Laughton's *The Night of the Hunter* (see separate chapter). The most superficial nod is Robert Mitchum's being featured in the role of the loathsome Cady, a character roughly similar to and almost as frightening as the deranged preacher, Harry Powell, he played in the Laughton film. But Thompson and Mitchum subtly deepen the connection by having Mitchum strike some very Powell-like poses during the course of the film. One notable example of this is a bedroom scene where the sexually twisted Cady hovers over the semi-dressed form of an attractive girl he's picked up and we see in his body language and the expression in his eyes that he's pervertedly arousing himself to commit murder (or close to it), not make love. Mitchum's looks and gestures—even the content of the scene itself—intentionally recall the hellish scene in which he murders

Cady's vengeful campaign of terror against Bowden (Gregory Peck), his wife (Polly Bergen) and daughter (Lori Martin) includes poisoning the family dog, although Bowden can't actually prove Cady did it.

The diabolical Cady (Robert Mitchum) threateningly follows Nancy (Lori Martin) to school, but the police's hands are tied unless Cady commits an overt criminal act.

Nancy (Lori Martin) flees from the school yard and is almost hit by a car.

Bowden hires some local toughs to put Cady (Robert Mitchum) in the hospital, but the plan misfires when Cady makes mincemeat of them.

Cady (Robert Mitchum) tracks Bowden's wife (Polly Bergen) and daughter to their secret hideaway on a remote part of the Cape Fear river.

Shelley Winters in the Laughton film. These nods and connections tend to strike one as acknowledgments of past film history rather than in-jokes or plagiarism. As a potent thriller, *Cape Fear* stands very sturdily on its own.

After spending eight years in prison for assault and battery due to the damning eye witness testimony of Sam Bowden, a prominent small-town attorney, the sadistic Cady returns to take up residence in Bowden's town and launch a vengeful campaign of terror against his accuser and his wife and daughter. He stalks the family and even poisons their dog, although Bowden can't actually prove Cady did it. Bowden turns to the police chief, Mark Dutton, for help, and Cady is rousted on several trumped up charges but released for lack of evidence. The wily criminal turns the tables on Bowden by hiring an ambulance chasing lawyer, Dave Grafton, and threatening to sue Bowden and the police for harassment. Dutton regretfully informs Bowden that the law's hands are now tied unless Cady commits an overt criminal act and suggests that Bowden hire a local private detective, Charlie Sievers, to follow Cady and get the goods on him.

While Sievers is following him, Cady picks up a girl, Diane Taylor, in a local bar, returns to his boarding house room and takes out his twisted sexual urges on her by beating her within an inch of her life. Sievers calls in the cops, but the terrified girl refuses to press charges and blows town. Sievers tells Bowden that the only way to scare off an animal like Cady is to act just like him and suggests hiring some local toughs to put Cady in the hospital. But the upright lawyer balks at this and tries buying Cady off instead. The malevolent Cady, however, turns him down flat and guardedly hints at his horrific intentions—to humiliate the lawyer and ruin his serene home life by raping Bowden's underage daughter. Knowing that the girl can't be watched twenty-four hours a day for who knows how long and that Cady will make good on his threat the first chance he gets, Bowden hires the toughs Sievers recommended, but the plan backfires when Cady makes mincemeat of them and they confess who hired them. Through his attorney, Cady initiates disbarment proceedings against the professionally tarnished Bowden, who must fly to Atlanta to appear before a judicial panel, leaving his family alone and defenseless for several days. This frightening prospect gives Bowden an idea for drawing Cady into the open and finally nailing him. To pull it off, however, he must use his own family as bait.

Bowden ships his wife and daughter off to a secret hideaway on a remote part of the Cape Fear river and makes arrangements for Sievers to deliver food and provisions knowing that Cady will likely follow the private detective. As Cady is no fool and will keep a close eye on him, Bowden actually does fly to Atlanta and schedules a return flight for several days later. Upon arriving in Atlanta, however, he rents a car and rejoins his family on the Cape Fear to await Cady and kill him if necessary. As the film winds to a tense close, Bowden's carefully premeditated scheme—which is as diabolically clever and, ultimately, as morally repugnant as Cady's—runs into several snags, resulting in a climax with enough unpredictable twists to raise the blood pressure of any audience.

Though arguably not as frightening as *The Night of the Hunter*'s preacher Harry Powell, Mitchum's Max Cady is still a fearsome fiend indeed, and it is chiefly due to his skin-crawling performance that *Cape Fear* reaches the tension-filled heights it does and deserves its status as a classic screen thriller. But Gregory Peck's equally convincing performance as the stoic, morally upright Bowden, who gradually deteriorates into a violent, wild-eyed avenger due to the pressure Cady puts on him, should not be overlooked either.

Predictably, this memorable thriller, like so many others in this book, has also undergone remake treatment. Martin Scorsese's 1991 update starred Nick Nolte in the role of Sam Bowden, Jessica Lange as his wife, and Robert DeNiro as the villainous Max Cady. In an acknowledgment to the original, Gregory Peck, Robert Mitchum, and Martin Balsam appeared in cameos. Bernard Herrmann's classic score was re-orchestrated by Elmer Bernstein and used for the remake as well.

HIGH AND LOW

(1963)

Continental/Toho • B&W/143 Minutes

CREDITS

Director: Akira Kurosawa; *Producers*: Tomoyuki Tanaka and Ryuzo Kikushima; *Screenplay*: Ryuzo Kikushima, Ei jiro Hisaita, Hideo Oguni, and Akira Kurosawa, based on the novel *King's Ransom* by Ed McBain; *Cinematographers*: Asakazu Nakai and Takao Saito; *Music*: Masaru Sato; *Art Director*: Yoshiro Muraki.

CAST

Kingo Gondo: Toshiro Mifune; *Reiko (Gondo's wife)*: Kyoko Kagawa; *Kawanishi*: Tatsuya Mihashi; *Aoki (the chauffeur)*: Yutaka Sada; *Inspector Tokura*: Tatsuya Nakadai; *Director*: Takashi Shimura; *Commissioner*: Susumu Fujita; *Detective Taguchi*: Kenjiro Ishiyama; *Detective Arai*: Ko Kimura; *Ginji Takeuchi (the kidnapper)*: Tsutomu Yamazaki.

* * *

Akira Kurosawa has often been called the most Western of all Japanese filmmakers due to the strong influence Western writers and directors have had on his work—and the widespread acceptance and popularity his work has achieved in the West as a result of that influence.

In *Throne of Blood, The Bad Sleep Well*, and *Ran*, for example, Kurosawa breathed new life into Shakespeare's classic tragedies *Macbeth, Hamlet*, and *King Lear*, respectively, when he powerfully transposed their stories and themes to medieval and modern Japan. In his masterpiece, *Seven Samurai*, Kurosawa did for the traditional Japanese samurai film (or costume drama) what John Ford's intimate yet epic scale studies of America's West did for the traditional horse opera. In fact, many of Kurosawa's period films seem so much like Westerns that several Western directors have reversed the cultural shift and transposed them to *American* settings—thus *Seven Samurai* was remade as *The Magnificent Seven, Rashomon* became *The Outrage*, and *Yojimbo* (whose story Kurosawa had actually derived from Dashiell Hammett's detective novel *Red Harvest*) was turned into the archetypal "spaghetti Western," *A Fistful of Dollars*.

High and Low was Kurosawa's first stab at making

Gondo (Toshiro Mifune) listens to his fellow executives outline their plans to turn the shoe company's fortunes around by manufacturing a more profitable but inferior product once Gondo helps them take control of the firm. What they don't know is that he is secretly buying up stock to take control of the company himself.

an outright suspense thriller in the vein of Alfred Hitchcock and Fritz Lang (whose *M* clearly had an influence on the way Kurosawa handles the details of police procedure in the film). And though Kurosawa never dabbled in the genre again, he proved the equal of Hitchcock and Lang with this single film—one of the most spellbinding of all thrillers.

That this powerfully performed, technically dazzling, and thematically rich work failed to achieve the critical acceptance of some of Kurosawa's other films—*Seven Samurai*, for example—simply confirms the critical disregard to which the thriller genre and its masters (like Hitchcock and Lang) have been unfairly subjected for far too many years. Quite simply, *High and Low* (whose Japanese title, *Tengoku to Jigoku*, translates literally as "Heaven and Hell") ranks with *Seven Samurai* among the top achievements the cinema has given us.

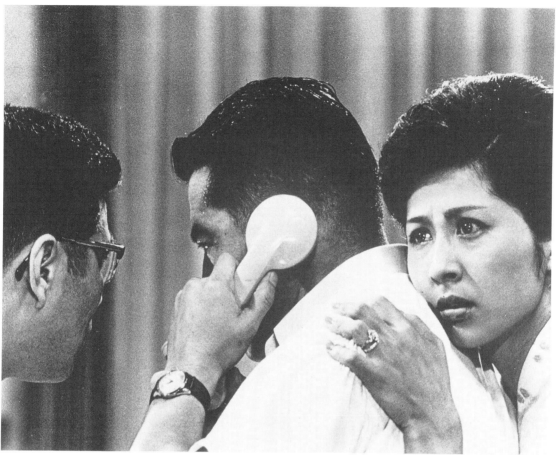

Gondo's assistant, Kawanishi (Tatsuya Mihashi), and Gondo's wife, Reiko (Kyoko Kagawa), listen in as Gondo (Toshiro Mifune) takes the phone call from the kidnapper demanding a king's ransom for his son's life. Actually, the son of Gondo's chauffeur has been snatched by mistake.

The child leads the detectives to the abandoned lair where he was held prisoner.

Detectives Taguchi (Kenjiro Ishiyama, left) and Arai (Ko Kimura, center) radio details of the kidnapper's movements to colleagues as they stalk their elusive prey through the teeming streets of Yokohama.

Loosely based on an American crime novel, *King's Ransom* by Ed McBain, which, I believe, also was adapted for American television during the late fifties or early sixties, *High and Low* is about a high stakes Japanese industrialist, Kingo Gondo (the magnetic Toshiro Mifune in yet another bravura performance), who is brought to financial ruin yet simultaneously reborn, personally and professionally, by a brutal act of kidnapping.

A self-made man, Gondo is secretly maneuvering to win control of the major shoe company into which he's put thirty years of his life away from his greedy fellow executives, who seek to cut costs by turning out an inferior but more profitable product. Having mortgaged himself to the hilt to buy the additional shares of stock he needs to put him in the driver's seat, Gondo's on the verge of closing the deal when his young son is kidnapped and the ransom demand is virtually the same amount of capital involved in the stock transaction. The distraught Gondo feels he has no choice but to agree to the kidnapper's demands and is about to pay up when his son reappears, and Gondo realizes the kidnapper has snatched the wrong child—he's taken the boy's playmate, the chauffeur's son, instead. Believing himself to be off the hook because the kidnapper will undoubtedly return the boy once he realizes his mistake, Gondo turns the case over to the police. But he finds himself once more in the hot seat when the kidnapper rings back and insists that the ransom be paid anyway, or the chauffeur's boy will be killed. Though quick to give in to the kidnapper's demands when the life of his own son was at stake—even though doing so would have caused him to miss the stock transaction deadline and led to his professional ruin—Gondo now faces a moral dilemma. Is the life of another man's son worth the same sacrifice? Initially, Gondo says no. But his wife's pleas and his own conscience soon persuade him otherwise and he finally agrees to fork over the ransom money and help the police nab the kidnapper. Though at first disapproving of the seemingly selfish rich man, the police (as well as the press and the public) develop a deep respect for Gondo as they begin to comprehend the reality of his sacrifice. As the shoe company's corporate sharks and Gondo's creditors move in to relieve him of his position and

Unaware that the police are closing in on him, the kidnapper (Tsutomu Yamazaki) picks up a prostitute on whom to test the effectiveness of the lethal heroin he intends to use to murder his accomplices.

even his house, the police turn the matter of bringing the kidnapper to justice into a personal crusade.

Gondo is ordered by the kidnapper to pack the cash into two small cases and rendezvous with him on the high speed Bullet Train to turn the money over. Teams of detectives board the train as well and prepare to grab the kidnapper as soon as he makes his move. But the wily abductor places a phone call to the train instead and instructs Gondo to toss the money off at a specified location. As Gondo and the frustrated detectives watch from the moving train, the kidnapper's disguised male and female accomplices grab the money and leave the boy behind to be picked up.

During the equally absorbing and suspense-filled second half of the film, Gondo fairly disappears from the action, but his presence is felt throughout as the teams of detectives diligently work round the clock to run the kidnappers to ground and return the money to the all but impoverished Gondo. Their search takes them from the barren coastline overlooking scenic Mount Fuji to the teaming bars and hellish "drug alleys" of Yokohama harbor. The abductor murders his two accomplices with an overdose of pure heroin, but the press assists the police by publishing a false story that they are still alive, and the kidnapper is

lured out into the open and caught. The bulk of the ransom money is returned to Gondo, who proceeds to rebuild his life and career by opening a small, quality-conscious shoe company where *he* is now the boss.

The title of this dense, multilayered thriller refers not only to the contrasting domains of the hero and villain—Gondo lives high on a hill overlooking the Yokohama slums where the kidnapper resides—but also to the gulf in status that seemingly separates yet ultimately binds the two men together. Both men are "at war with society"—Gondo with the society of corporate wolves who threaten to undermine his pride in his life's work by taking control of the company and turning out an inferior product; the kidnapper with an affluent society that looks down on him—as Gondo's luxurious house does—but refuses to take notice of him unless he rebels and takes action against that society. Despite the gulf that separates them, both men are, in a sense, very much alike. Each "loves to play violent games" and feels the need to "attack or be attacked." And in the film's visually stunning final scene, they are, in fact, united—their faces merging in the glass of the cell separating them as they confront one another for the first and last time.

THE GREAT ESCAPE

(1963)

United Artists • Color/173 Minutes

CREDITS

Director: John Sturges; *Producer*: John Sturges; *Screenplay*: James Clavell and W. R. Burnett, from the book by Paul Brickhill; *Cinematographer*: Daniel L. Fapp; *Editor*: Ferris Webster; *Music*: Elmer Bernstein; *Art Director*: Fernando Carrere.

CAST

Hilts: Steve McQueen; *Hendley*: James Garner; *Bartlett*: Richard Attenborough; *Ramsey*: James Donald; *Danny*: Charles Bronson; *Blythe*: Donald Pleasence; *Sedgwick*: James Coburn; *Ashley-Pitt*: David McCallum; *MacDonald*: Gordon Jackson; *Willie*: John Leyton; *Ives*: Angus Lennie; *Cavendish*: Nigel Stock; *Kommandant Von Luger*: Hans Messemer; *Werner*: Robert Graf.

* * *

There have been a number of excellent, edge-of-your-seat suspense films about prisoner-of-war escape attempts which might have served equally well for inclusion in this book about great movie thrillers. Jean Renoir's *Grand Illusion* (admittedly more of a moving antiwar statement than an outright thriller), Jack Lee's *The Wooden Horse*, and Guy Hamilton's *The Colditz Story* are some examples that spring to mind. But I selected John Sturges's *The Great Escape* instead because it's not only a terrific piece of entertainment but also the epic last word on its subject.

The Great Escape, like *The Wooden Horse* and *The Colditz Story*, is based on an actual World War Two incident and strives to be an authentic record of that incident. It was filmed on location in Germany and employed some of the people who took part in the incident as technical advisers and bit-players. But it eschews the almost documentary approach of *Horse* and *Colditz* in favor of *Grand Illusion*'s emphasis on style, pictorialism, and character. So, it is largely fictional, too.

Many of the real-life characters in the grim, hard-hitting, non-fiction account by Paul Brickhill (an actual participant in the breakout) are deleted, combined, or embroidered upon, or have their names

Three of the Allied prisoners introduce the Spirit of '76 to the escape-proof Stalag Luft Norden.

changed, and events are telescoped so as not to make the film last any longer than it already does—nearly three hours. But the film basically follows the details of Brickhill's story even including its ironic and bittersweet ending.

The Great Escape tells of an early experiment in behavior control conducted by the Nazis. The object was to prevent widespread escape attempts by removing the most incorrigible Allied P.O.W. escape artists from camps all over Germany and putting them all together under a single, escape-proof roof such as Colditz Castle, or, in *The Great Escape*, Stalag Luft

While the Allied prisoners celebrate the Fourth of July, the Germans locate one of the three tunnels, prompting the stir-crazy Ives (Angus Lennie, center) to attempt a daytime breakout which results in his death.

Steve McQueen as Hilts, the "Cooler King," in John Sturges's epic take on the World War II POW breakout movie, The Great Escape.

Hendley (James Garner), Hilts (Steve McQueen), and Willie (John Leyton) manufacture a still to bring their fellow POWs some wartime refreshment.

Norden in a remote part of Bavaria. But the experiment backfired. Rather than being confounded or inhibited by their confinement, these incorrigibles, who were threatened with being shot if they got up to their old tricks, pooled their talents and energies and mounted even more elaborate escape attempts. In the case of Colditz, the escape was successful. Not so with *The Great Escape*, the more intricate mass breakout of the two. Most of the seventy-six men who broke out were recaptured. Realizing that imprisoning them again would likely result in another escape attempt requiring another costly and time-consuming manhunt, the Nazis made good on their threat and shot many of those recaptured as spies.

For dramatic clarity and audience identification, the film synthesizes Brickhill's huge cast of incorrigibles into a dozen major characters—Hilts, Hendley, Bartlett, Blythe, Ashley-Pitt, Sedgwick, Danny, Willie, Ives, etc.—whose escape attempts begin as soon as they arrive at the newly constructed stalag and the opening credits fade. Several try mixing in with a

Russian work detail passing through the prison's gates, while another, Hilts, probes a blind spot between two guard towers. All are caught and Hilts lands in solitary confinement, a place dubbed "the cooler."

Kommandant Von Luger suggests to the prisoners' acting C.O., Group Captain Ramsey, that although it is a prisoner of war's duty to attempt to escape and confound the enemy, a wiser course of action (given the camp's tight security and the threat of execution if an attempt to escape is made) would be to cooperate and sit out the rest of the war comfortably. Ramsey acknowledges the Kommandant's warning, but as soon as Squadron Leader Bartlett, a top organizer known as "Big X," arrives in the camp, plans are immediately mounted for a massive breakout of two hundred and fifty men, each of whom will be provided with civilian disguises, forged identity papers, passports, bogus train tickets, and so on. The plan is to dig three separate tunnels—dubbed Tom, Dick, and Harry—so that in the event the "goons"

The breathless final hour of the film chronicles the escapees' efforts to reach Allied lines while the Gestapo mercilessly hunts them down. Here, Hilts (Steve McQueen) vaults some barbed wire with the help of a stolen German motorcycle.

Only three of the seventy-six escapees actually reach Allied territory. Hilts (Steve McQueen) isn't one of them.

discover and shut down one or even two of them the escape can still be carried out.

Like "Big X," each of the main characters is given a nickname which not only defines his particular area of expertise in the escape plan, but, after so many years of imprisonment, interestingly redefines his wartime role—in criminal terms. Hendley is no longer an upright American fighter pilot, he's "the scrounger," a skillful procurer, pickpocket, and thief; Blythe, a former reconnaissance man, is now "the forger"; Allied airmen Danny and Willie are "tunnel kings"; and so on. In other words, as a result of their wartime experiences, they individually have taken on a trade that would brand each a criminal if he carried it over into civilian life, a common occurrence following the war and the subject of many a good *film noir*.

Needing a layout of the surrounding countryside, "Big X" persuades the hotheaded loner Hilts (known as "the cooler king"), who intends to go through with an escape plan of his own, to get the information required, then allow himself to be recaptured. (A plot twist that would be lifted whole cloth for John Huston's 1981 P.O.W. escape film, *Victory*.) Hilts goes through with this in return for being the first man out of the tunnel. On the night of the breakout, the escapees discover the tunnel's opening falls just short of the trees and is in full view of the stalag's guards. Hilts climbs out and arranges a signal with a rope that proves effective in enabling seventy-six men to escape before the breakout is at last discovered.

The breathless final hour of the film chronicles efforts of the P.O.W.'s to reach Allied lines while the Gestapo mercilessly hunts them down. Only three of the seventy-six actually do reach Allied territory. Fifty are recaptured by the Gestapo, rounded up, and machine-gunned as spies. (The film is dedicated to these fifty.) The remainder are returned to the prison camp, whose Kommandant, a professional soldier with a sense of chivalry who is just as repelled by the news of the mass execution as the surviving Allied prisoners, is replaced by a member of the Gestapo.*

Though admittedly it does indulge in a cliche or two, *The Great Escape* is a grand summation of every P.O.W. escape film ever made and (pardon the pun) great escapist fare. It is funny yet grimly realistic with a sting in its tail, exciting and suspenseful throughout, and vividly acted by its ensemble cast. That its huge critical and popular success is probably what spawned TV's *Hogan's Heroes* should not be held against it.

---

*In 1988, a two-part TV-movie, *The Great Escape II: The Untold Story*, recapitulated the original film in a vest-pocket version in the first part and then went into a what-happened-afterward addendum in the second part, leading the survivors on a postwar hunt for their Nazi captors.

FAIL-SAFE

(1964)

Columbia Pictures • B&W/111 Minutes

CREDITS

Director: Sidney Lumet; *Producer*: Max E. Youngstein; *Screenplay*: Walter Bernstein, based on the novel by Eugene Burdick and Harvey Wheeler; *Cinematographer*: Gerald Hirschfeld; *Editor*: Ralph Rosenblum; *Art Director*: Albert Brenner.

CAST

The President: Henry Fonda; *General Black*: Dan O'Herlihy; *Groeteschele*: Walter Matthau; *General Bogan*: Frank Overton; *Colonel Cascio*: Fritz Weaver; *Buck*: Larry Hagman; *Secretary Swenson*: William Hansen; *General Stark*: Russell Hardie; *Congressman Raskob*: Sorrell Booke; *Ilsa Wolfe*: Nancy Berg; *Foster*: Dana Elcar; *Sergeant Collins*: Dom DeLuise.

* * *

It's well known among film buffs that Stanley Kubrick's black comedy *Dr. Strangelove* started out as a serious and straightforward thriller about nuclear jitters, but the deeper he and his collaborators dug into the material, the more ironic and absurd that material became, so they shifted gears entirely and transformed it into a nightmarish end of the world cartoon. It's not often that moviegoers get the opportunity to see the film that might have been, but with *Dr. Strangelove*, we did, for Sidney Lumet's *Fail-Safe* is very probably what the early drafts of *Strangelove* were like. Except that one film is a comedy and the other a sober thriller, the sum and substance of both are virtually identical. There are even striking similarities between characters, situations, and the look of both films, which were shot almost simultaneously (one in England, the other in the U.S.) and released practically on top of one another by the same studio, Columbia.

As Kubrick's film was derived from a novel (*Red Alert* by Peter George) published several years before the bestseller upon which *Fail-Safe* was based, he threatened a law suit for plagiarism to prevent the Lumet movie from being released and competing with his own. The studio apparently mollified Kubrick by agreeing to really get behind *Strangelove*

Russian specialist (Larry Hagman) tries to interpret the Soviet premier's emotions as well as his words for the President (Henry Fonda).

promotionally and release it first, then slip *Fail-Safe* into the theaters with considerably less fanfare two months later—at which point the two films distinctly went their separate ways. *Strangelove* became a big critical and commercial success whereas *Fail-Safe*, though not unfavorably reviewed, died a quick box office death. Frankly, I think *Strangelove* would have achieved the same notoriety and success even if *Fail-Safe* had reached theaters first with equal fanfare, for the former is definitely the more daring and original work of the pair. But *Fail-Safe* is not without its merits, too. It's a first-class thriller which might have achieved even greater commercial success had it been directed by someone other than the dreary Sidney Lumet, whose heavyhandedness tends to wring the

Political scientist and megadeath numbers man Groeteschele
(Walter Matthau) recommends to the chiefs of staff that the
U.S. take advantage of the accident to finish the Commies off
once and for all.

The President (Henry Fonda) and his interpreter (Larry
Hagman) wait to hear back from the Russians.

Compared to the hawkish civilian Groeteschele (Walter Matthau), most of the military men in Fail-Safe *seem like doves and "peaceniks."*

Realizing there is no chance of stopping the lone bomber from reaching Moscow, the distraught President (Henry Fonda) has no choice but to offer up a comparable U.S. city for sacrifice— even though his own wife will be killed in the blast.

Having been trained to resist all efforts at being recalled, Colonel Grady (Edward Binns) heads his B-52 toward Moscow to deliver the deadly nuclear payload.

life (if not the hysteria) out of most everything he touches. (Ironically, Stanley Kubrick is often criticized for having a similar touch.) *Fail-Safe* suffers from a certain dryness as well, particularly its opening scenes where too many messages (however well meant) about the perils of technology and dehumanization in the nuclear world are rammed down the viewer's throat with an annoying lack of subtlety. But once the central nightmare of the story gets underway and the scene shifts to the war room and the President's bunker beneath the White House as Armageddon approaches, *Fail-Safe* moves into high gear and Lumet manages to keep it there.

In the Lumet film, the superpowers' day of reckoning with their nuclear arsenals is triggered by a technical malfunction in Washington's automated command and control system that transmits an erroneous order to a squadron of SAC bombers to fly beyond their fail-safe points and nuke Moscow. This technological disaster is compounded by the efficiency of the Russians' sophisticated jamming devices which prevent American military officials from communicating with the planes until too late, for once the planes have passed fail-safe, the pilots and crew are instructed to cease all radio communication until they've reached their target. At this point, even a direct order from the President won't be able to stop them, for his voice could easily be imitated by the Russians. (Burdick and Wheeler's book was written during the administration of John F. Kennedy, whose distinctive Boston accent was always being mimicked by comic impressionists, who no doubt existed in Russia, too.)

Faced with the terrifying prospect that the Russians will launch a counterstrike if Moscow is destroyed and that the U.S. will have to respond, triggering World War Three, the President contacts the Russian Premier, convinces him that it's all a mistake, and orders SAC personnel in Omaha to assist their Russian counterparts in shooting down the planes. As each side trades heretofore top secret information in an effort to avert catastrophe, bitter conflicts arise between the hawks and the doves in both camps that delay action and allow one plane to get through. Interestingly, the most extreme hawk in *Fail-Safe* is not a military man, but a civilian—a coldly pragmatic political scientist and megadeath numbers man named Groeteschele, who recommends that the U.S. take advantage of the accident to finish off the dangerous Commies once and for all. Most of the military men in the film seem like doves by comparison.

Realizing there is little chance of stopping the lone plane and that Moscow will likely be destroyed, the President has no choice but to offer up a comparable American city for sacrifice as a grim gesture of "good faith." A nuclear-armed B-52, piloted by the President's close friend, General Black, is sent aloft. As the fireball hits Moscow and the U.S. ambassador's telephone line melts with a high-pitched shriek, the President gives Black the horrifying order to nuke New York City, aware that Black's family and the First Lady, a Jackie Kennedy lookalike on a visit to the city, will be among the millions who will perish.

As the distraught President and Russian premier ring off vowing to make sure nothing like this ever happens again, the screen fills not with Strangelovian fireballs but with a series of freeze-frames showing life in the Big Apple coming to a stop—and symbolic end.

The final credits to this tense and disturbing thriller conclude with a Pentagon-inspired disclaimer insisting that the events portrayed in *Fail-Safe* couldn't possibly happen.

GOLDFINGER

(1964)

Eon Productions—A United Artists Release • Color/108 Minutes

CREDITS

Director: Guy Hamilton; *Producers*: Harry Saltzman and Albert R. Broccoli; *Screenplay*: Richard Maibaum and Paul Dehn, based on the novel by Ian Fleming; *Cinematographer*: Ted Moore; *Editor*: Peter Hunt; *Music*: John Barry; *Production Designer*: Ken Adam.

CAST

James Bond: Sean Connery; *Pussy Galore*: Honor Blackman; *Auric Goldfinger*: Gert Frobe; *Jill Masterson*: Shirley Eaton; *Tilly Masterson*: Tania Mallet; *Oddjob*: Harold Sakata; *M*: Bernard Lee; *Felix Leiter*: Cec Linder; *Mr. Solo*: Martin Benson; *Miss Moneypenny*: Lois Maxwell; *Q*: Desmond Llewelyn.

* * *

Goldfinger holds the distinction of being the last James Bond film to adhere to its Ian Fleming source novel with any degree of fidelity while also serving as the prototype for the louder, more expensive and spectacular Bonds that have come our way since.

As the series progressed, Ian Fleming's already fanciful superspy would evolve into a figure of total fantasy and the plots would depart so outlandishly from the books from which they were adapted that by the time *The Spy Who Loved Me* reached the screen in 1977, there would be little or no trace left of Fleming's Bond. In fact, with that film, the makers of the immensely successful series retained nothing from the book on which it was based but the title. (Fleming who had died by this time, had insisted that this particular book, his least favorite, not be adapted to the screen. A low key but quite suspenseful tale of survival in New York's rugged Adirondack mountains, *The Spy Who Loved Me* was a very atypical Bond novel in that it was more of a John D. McDonald or William McGivern reality-based thriller. The filmmakers got around this problem by concocting a wholly different storyline more in keeping with the series' emphasis on spectacular action and stunts, but retaining Fleming's title. For people who see the film then read the book, or vice versa, the differences between the two versions come as quite a shock.)

In one of the film's more unusual suspense set pieces—a close and critical golf match between Bond (Sean Connery) and the duplicitous Auric Goldfinger (Gert Frobe)—007 outwits the greedy bullion magnate by catching him cheating.

By the time Roger Moore took over the role of Bond, the character had become a cartoonish superhero whose life-supporting gadgetry made him so impervious to the dangers threatening him that the films contained very little tension or suspense. They

*Bereft of gadgets up his sleeve courtesy of Q Branch, Bond
(Sean Connery) must again resort to his wits to outsmart
Goldfinger (Gert Frobe), or risk being emasculated by a laser
machine.*

Bond (Sean Connery) gets the nuclear device open but can't figure out what to do next. A U.S. government official steps in and disarms it with only 007 seconds to spare. Note the appropriately worried look on the face of Felix Leiter (Cec Linder), Bond's C.I.A. counterpart.

noting which ingredients went over with audiences better than others and developing future Bond scripts on the basis of what they found out. They discovered that audiences particularly liked the high-tech Astin Martin with its machine guns and passenger ejector seat, developed by Q Branch for Bond's use in the field. And so ever more elaborate gadgetry, which had taken somewhat of a backseat in the first three Bond outings, became the series' main hallmark. While this didn't diminish the action or entertainment value of subsequent Bonds, it did lessen their ability to generate much tension or suspense. No matter what tight situation Bond got himself into, he was able to escape with ease. He no longer had to rely on his wits to get himself out of impossible scrapes the scriptwriters put him in. Like Batman, he always had some kind of gizmo on hand specifically designed for just such a situation.

In *Goldfinger*, 007 has to rely mostly on his wits. Even his wondrous Astin Martin doesn't stand him in very good stead for long. It gets cracked up early on when Bond drives it into the wall of one of Goldfinger's warehouses to avoid a head-on collision (actually the reflection of his own car's headlights in a specially rigged mirror). He is captured, spread-eagled on a table, and threatened with emasculation by a laser beam, and it genuinely looks like curtains for our intrepid hero until he verbally plants an important suspicion in Goldfinger's mind that persuades the diabolical genius to spare his life, at least for a time. Breathing a sigh of relief over his resourcefulness, Bond then finds himself staring down the barrel of a gun, which is fired at point blank range into his chest. It turns out to be a tranquilizer gun.

There are many surprises like this scattered throughout the script of *Goldfinger*, which, perhaps due to the contribution of cowriter Paul Dehn (a specialist in taut espionage thrillers), is structured more like a suspense film than an action movie. We're constantly kept guessing. Even the details of Goldfinger's centerpiece scheme (rendering the gold in Fort Knox radioactive so that his personal wealth will increase in value) is held back from Bond, and the viewer, until the film's final half hour.

Bond's celebrated brawn also takes a backseat to his wits in the film. He wins a critical golf match with the devious Goldfinger not by skill (Goldfinger is clearly his equal on the links) but by taking advantage of his adversary's predilection for cheating. And in the film's major fight scene with Oddjob, Goldfinger's Oriental bodyguard with the lethal bowler, Bond takes a real pounding until he resorts to his wits rather than his obviously inferior muscle power to take out his adversary. Even his wits fail him, however, when it comes to disarming the nuclear device set to go off inside Fort Knox. A government official switches it off for him—with only 007 seconds to spare!

Fans of the Bond series have their individual favorites, but most agree that the Sean Connery Bonds were, on the whole, superior to most later entries in the series. And of the Sean Connery Bonds, the first three are considered by fans to be the best because the series was still evolving and fresh. Suspense, not just mindless, gadgety action, was the main emphasis. This is certainly true of *Goldfinger*, my personal favorite (with *From Russia With Love* coming in a very close second). It still has the power to grip an audience.

OPERATION CROSSBOW

(1965)

[a.k.a. *The Great Spy Mission*]
Metro-Goldwyn-Mayer • Color/116 Minutes

CREDITS

Director: Michael Anderson; *Producer*: Carlo Ponti; *Screenplay*: Richard Imrie, Derry Quinn, and Ray Rigby; *Cinematographer*: Erwin Hillier; *Editor*: Ernest Walter; *Music*: Ron Goodwin; *Art Director*: Elliot Scott.

CAST

Curtis: George Peppard; *Frau Van Omstagen*: Sophia Loren; *Professor Linderman*: Trevor Howard; *Captain Bradley*: Jeremy Kemp; *Bob Henshaw*: Tom Courtenay; *Ziemann*: Paul Henreid; *Duncan Sands*: Richard Johnson; *Gestapo Officer*: Anthony Quayle; *Group Leader Linz*: Helmut Dantine; *Hotel Concierge*: Lilli Palmer; *Winston Churchill*: Patrick Wymark; *Air Marshall*: Maurice Denham.

* * *

Inspired by the blockbuster success of *The Guns of Navarone*, film studios began turning out one big budget, big name, World War Two impossible mission/

espionage thriller after another in the sixties. Many of these spectaculars—*The Train, Von Ryan's Express, The Dirty Dozen, Where Eagles Dare*—were big hits too and, like *Navarone*, are just as popular today. All still rack up impressive ratings on television and have been big hits in the home video rental and sales market as well.

Operation Crossbow, another spectacular, extremely popular wartime thriller made during this period, has not fared so well. It is less frequently shown on television than the others, and only recently has been released on video. In some respects, the reason why is easy to fathom. Despite its comparable star power and budget, *Crossbow* is not as anarchic or funny as *The Dirty Dozen*, not as exciting as *The Train* or *Von Ryan's Express*, and lacks the visual sweep and exotic locales that contributed so much to *Navarone* and *Where Eagles Dare*. It also has some major structural problems. There's an overreliance on coincidence, and the characters who take part in the film's impossible mission are so thinly drawn that we never come to

Sophia Loren stars as the widow of a German engineer whose identity has been assumed by Allied saboteur George Peppard.

The Germans set up shop at an impenetrable underground installation near Hamburg and recruit engineers from all over *Nazi-occupied Europe to work on their V-1 and V-2 rocket project.*

identify with them even though we *are* caught up in their plight. (Ron Goodwin's bombastic, military march music score is an even more severe liability.) As an indication that all was not right in the script department, cowriter Emeric Pressburger, the prestigious collaborator with director Michael Powell on some of the best British films of the forties and fifties, insisted that his name be removed from the credits and instead took a pseudonym, Richard Imrie.

At this point, you're probably wondering why, with all these problems, I've chosen *Operation Crossbow* for this book, which is supposed to be about the best, not

Curtis (George Peppard) tries to convince Frau Van Omstagen (Sophia Loren) that he means her no harm.

Even up to the fiery conclusion, we expect that somehow Curtis (George Peppard) and Bradley (Jeremy Kemp) will manage to get away. But they don't.

Curtis (George Peppard) completes his mission, but at a most unhappy cost in Operation Crossbow.

the worst thrillers. The reason is that despite its deficiencies, *Operation Crossbow* works amazingly well. It is tense, exciting, surprising, well acted (paper-thin characterizations notwithstanding), and spectacularly staged. More important, however, it's an extremely unusual example of this type of big budget, mass audience film in that it refuses to indulge in the one major cliche of its ilk, which is to let the audience off the hook by allowing at least some of the impossible missioners (usually the most likable) to get away after the job. In *Operation Crossbow, nobody* survives. That the film was such a box office success anyway is a tribute to its skillfulness in overcoming the problems I've mentioned, problems which would have sunk lesser films.

The title refers to the British-led mission to destroy Germany's long-range missile manufacturing capabilities during the closing days of the war. As the film opens, Winston Churchill gives top aide Duncan Sands the job of finding out how far along the Germans have gotten in their experiments to develop a secret weapon called a "flying bomb" (later dubbed the V-1 and V-2 rocket) capable of being fired directly into the heart of London and causing mass destruction. British scientists led by the irascible Professor Linderman stubbornly refuse to believe that the Germans have made any significant progress at all since their own experiments in the field have so far come to nothing. Nevertheless, intelligence reports and RAF sightings indicate that the enemy is conducting actual tests of the rocket at a remote spot in the Balkans. Sands orders the site to be destroyed by RAF bombers. The Germans then set up shop at a less penetrable underground installation near Hamburg and recruit engineers from all over occupied Europe to hastily resume work on the project.

The British counterattack by putting together a team of German-speaking operatives, all accomplished engineers in civilian life, to parachute behind enemy lines, obtain work at the factory, and sabotage it from within. To effectively pull off the charade, each operative is supplied with the forged papers of a bona fide German, French, and Dutch engineer (each now deceased) and is thoroughly schooled in the dead men's backgrounds and habits.

Curtis and Henshaw are the first to be flown in. But things immediately go wrong for both of them. Henshaw is arrested by the Gestapo because the man whose identity he is assuming is wanted on a murder charge. (British Intelligence stumbles upon this information too late to prevent Henshaw from being dropped into harm's way and sends in another operative, Captain Bradley, to make sure Curtis is alerted to the potential danger of associating with Henshaw.) In

one of the film's many intriguing twists, Henshaw realizes he must play along by assuming this less savory aspect of his identity's past as well. He can't admit that the alleged murderer is dead and that he's an imposter or he'll risk exposing the mission. And so, when he's threatened with standing before a lineup of eyewitnesses to the crime, he has no alternative but to confess to the murder charge. In yet another surprising turnabout, the Gestapo, anticipating Allied sabotage of the rocket factory, agrees to forget about the murder charge if Henshaw will take a job there and keep an eye out for Allied infiltrators. Seeing that this arrangement will put him in the ideal position of carrying out his mission while supplying false information to the Nazis at the same time, Henshaw quickly seizes the opportunity. But just as he's about to be sent on his way, a Gestapo officer who had tried but failed to infiltrate the Operation Crossbow team in London recognizes the hapless Henshaw, who soon finds himself back to square one, standing before a firing squad.

Curtis's cover is almost blown too when Frau Van Omstagen, the ex-wife of the man whose identity he has assumed, tracks him to his hotel to sign papers giving her custody of their children. When she discovers he's an imposter and that her husband is dead, she almost gives him away to the authorities, but Curtis and a resistance leader (the hotel's female concierge) prevent her from doing so just in time and hold her captive in the room as they try to figure out what to do with her. Sympathetic to the woman's plight, Curtis comes up with a solution that will save both their skins. Able to forge the dead man's signature perfectly, he agrees to sign the woman's custody papers. As she will only get herself in trouble (and probably lose her children in the bargain) if she admits the signature is false and that her husband is dead, her silence is thus assured. Curtis goes on his way, and the thankful Frau Van Omstagen, whom we have come to like, prepares herself to be set free. But then the concierge, who is obviously much less trusting than Curtis, unexpectedly puts a bullet through the woman's head. This came as quite a shock to audiences of the day—and still packs a punch—because the victim is the film's top-billed female star, Sophia Loren, and big budget movies like this don't usually bump off their female lead—especially if she also happens to be the producer's wife.

But *Operation Crossbow* runs counter to many such expectations, and that's why it works as well as it does. Even up to the fiery conclusion, we expect that somehow, some *way*, Curtis and Bradley too will get away, but they don't. They do accomplish their mission, but at a most unhappy cost.

THE FLIGHT OF THE PHOENIX (1966)

Twentieth Century-Fox • Color/147 Minutes

CREDITS

Director: Robert Aldrich; *Producer*: Robert Aldrich; *Screenplay*: Lukas Heller, based on the novel by Elleston Trevor; *Cinematographer*: Joseph Biroc; *Editor*: Michael Luciano; *Music*: DeVol; *Art Director*: William Glasgow.

CAST

Frank Towns: James Stewart; *Lew Moran*: Richard Attenborough; *Captain Harris*: Peter Finch; *Heinrich Dorfmann*: Hardy Kruger; *Cobb*: Ernest Borgnine; *Crow*: Ian Bannen; *Sergeant Watson*: Ronald Fraser; *Dr. Renaud*: Christian Marquand; *Standish*: Dan Duryea; *Bellamy*: George Kennedy; *Carlos*: Alex Montoya.

* * *

In addition to being a riveting thriller and a richly detailed study of characters in conflict, Robert Aldrich's *The Flight of the Phoenix* offers a unique twist on the familiar cinematic theme of group survival in a hostile setting.

A twin-engine cargo plane piloted by Frank Towns experiences radio trouble and encounters a ferocious sandstorm on a hop to Bengazi. Rather than turning to an alternate destination for safety, Towns, an old-time seat-of-the pants air jockey, decides to weather the storm, but the plane crashes and breaks up in the Sahara, killing several passengers. After trying to justify his actions, which have now placed the lives of everyone on board in jeopardy, the independent-minded Towns, who dislikes being wrong even more than he dislikes being told what to do, in the ship's log crosses out what he's written and inserts the words "pilot error" with humiliation.

With no chance of repairing the aircraft, Towns, his alcoholic navigator, Lew Moran, and the surviving passengers, a group that includes several oil company workers, two British soldiers, a French doctor, and a German engineer named Dorfmann, set about making themselves as comfortable as possible until help arrives. After several days of living on rationed water and pressed dates, however, it becomes clear that as the plane drifted hundreds of miles off course due to

Pilot Frank Towns (James Stewart) and navigator Lew Moran (Richard Attenborough) encounter radio trouble and a ferocious sandstorm on a perilous hop to Bengazi.

Moran (Richard Attenborough) explains to the group why Captain Harris' (Peter Finch, center, with military cap) plan to go for help is courageous but foolhardy.

The survivors of Robert Aldrich's The Flight of the Phoenix. Left to right: Christian Marquand, Ian Bannen, James Stewart, Dan Duryea (behind Stewart), Richard Attenborough, Ronald Fraser, George Kennedy (crouching), and Peter Finch.

The arrogant Dorfmann (Hardy Kruger) and the irascible Towns (James Stewart) angrily engage in one of their frequent contests with each other over who's in charge.

the storm it is unlikely they will be found until it's too late.

One of the soldiers, Captain Harris, decides to go for help and orders his sergeant, Watson, to accompany him on the perilous journey. But the cowardly Watson fakes a sprained ankle and one of the oil company workers goes with Harris instead.

As there is just enough water to sustain those left behind for ten or eleven days, Dorfmann comes up with an alternative plan in case Harris's mission fails. Dorfmann has examined the crippled aircraft and checked the equipment and supplies on board, and believes they have everything they need to build a workable single-engine plane from the wreckage. But Towns dismisses the plan as being impossible due to the men's weakened condition—and too dangerous even if it does work, as the jerry-rigged plane would likely break apart as soon as the engine was fired up, killing everyone on board. Believing the irascible Towns to be a man who "behaves as if stupidity were a virtue," the reproached Dorfmann goes off in a snit and the idea is dropped.

When Cobb, an American oil worker bound for home due to nervous exhaustion, wanders off to join Harris and disappears, Sergeant Watson runs to inform the others and Towns discovers Watson's pro-

nounced limp has miraculously vanished. Disgusted with the man but in no position to cast stones due to his own foibled behavior, Towns keeps the man's secret even from Captain Harris, who survives his ordeal and later returns to camp alone (the other man perished in the broiling sun).

Having enough deaths on his conscience, Towns stubbornly sets out to rescue Cobb. After Towns is gone, Moran learns that Dorfmann is not just an engineer but an airplane designer. The arrogant German is convinced his plan is sound, but as a pilot will be needed to fly the plane once it's built and Towns has "stupidly" wandered off into the desert to rescue a "useless madman" probably never to return, the disdainful Dorfmann and Moran, angered by Dorfmann's cold pragmatism, agree the discussion is moot.

But Towns does return (sans Cobb), and despite his protestations, everyone agrees that Dorfmann's plan, longshot though it may be, is their best chance. And as Captain Harris had argued earlier, it will at least occupy them and keep them distracted from brooding upon their probable fate.

Working practically around the clock, the exhausted men struggle to convert the wreckage into the insufferable Dorfmann's new plane, which one of them, a meek accountant named Standish, dubs the "Phoenix" after the mythical bird that crashed and burned from flying too close to the sun but rose again from its ashes. As the "Phoenix" begins to take shape, Captain Harris spots a small caravan of Arabs. Believing the "Phoenix" will never get off the ground, he suggests going to them for help even though they might be dangerous. In the event they are hostile, Harris and Dr. Renaud circle the Arab camp and enter it from another direction so as not to give away the location of their comrades. By morning, the Arabs have gone, and when Towns and Moran enter the camp, they find the bodies of Harris and Renaud outstretched in the sand, their throats cut from ear to ear.

The "Phoenix" their only hope now, the men hasten to complete it before their water runs out. As excitement and anticipation mount on the morning of the flight, the plot takes a stunning twist, however, as Towns and Moran discover that Dorfmann is a specialist in designing remote controlled *model* aircraft, not the "big stuff." Dorfmann points out that successful model aircraft flight predated the Wright Brothers by fifty years. Nevertheless, as the shock registers and hope of survival drains from their faces, Towns and Moran persuade the confident Dorfmann to keep this revelation secret from the other men.

Having suffered Dorfmann's authoritarianism for days, Towns now assumes control of the project and

*Although suffering from dehydration, the hallucinating
Sergeant Watson (Ronald Fraser) appears to have something on
his mind other than a drink of water. The mirage is dancer
Barrie Chase.*

Captain Harris (Peter Finch) and Towns (James Stewart) spot a small caravan of Arabs and speculate on the possible dangers of approaching them for help.

climbs into the pilot's seat as the film rushes to its thrilling conclusion. Towns must use shotgun cartridges to fire the plane's engine and start the propeller, but there are only seven rounds left. Suspense mounts as Towns fires one cartridge after another to no avail. The hysterical Dorfmann accuses Towns of wasting them, but the wily oldtimer knows what he's doing and the prop catches on the sixth try. As the men cling to its wings, the rickety "Phoenix" bounces and skips along the sand. Then, under Towns's skillful control, it finally lifts off, soars into the air, and the beleaguered men fly away from the scene of their ordeal to safety.

In a terrible irony, however, whereas the "flight of the Phoenix" is successful on film, in reality is wasn't. The single-engine plane crashed on landing and its pilot, veteran stunt flyer Paul Mantz, was killed. Director Aldrich dedicated the film to him.

WAIT UNTIL DARK

(1967)

Warner Bros. • Color/108 Minutes

CREDITS

Director: Terence Young; *Producer*: Mel Ferrer; *Screenplay*: Robert and Jane-Howard Carrington, based on the play by Frederick Knott; *Cinematographer*: Charles Lang; *Editor*: Gene Milford; *Music*: Henry Mancini; *Art Director*: George Jenkins.

CAST

Susy Hendrix: Audrey Hepburn; *Harry Roat, Jr.*: Alan Arkin; *Mike Talman*: Richard Crenna; *Carlino*: Jack Weston; *Sam Hendrix*: Efrem Zimbalist, Jr.; *Lisa*: Samantha Jones; *Gloria*: Julie Herrod.

* * *

Frederick Knott may not have been one of Britain's most prolific and acclaimed playwrights, but he was certainly one of the most influential and financially successful—and one of the luckiest as well in terms of having his work faithfully transposed from stage to screen. Knott was a specialist in thrillers who began his writing career with BBC radio, but his reputation rests with just two plays: *Dial M for Murder* and *Wait Until Dark*, each an established classic of the genre. Both were huge hits on the London and Broadway stage and have become staples of regional and community theaters, as well as high school drama groups.

To bring *Dial M* to the screen, Knott secured a deal with no less than Alfred Hitchcock himself. Though not classic Hitchcock by any means, the film version of *Dial M*, which launched his short but fruitful association with Grace Kelly, his definitive ice-cool blonde, was one of his biggest successes of the fifties and has been imitated countless times since. The 1981 made-for-television remake directed by Boris Sagal starring Angie Dickinson in the Kelly role even duplicates shots from Hitchcock's film.

Wait Until Dark, Knott's second stage thriller (and last as far as I know) had just as great an impact. The more tension-filled of the two works, it put Big Apple theatergoers through the emotional wringer—and, in one notable scene, lifted them straight out of their seats—when it debuted on Broadway in the mid-sixties, directed by Arthur Penn and starring Lee Remick. An unqualified critical and commercial suc-

Mike Talman (Richard Crenna) gains entrance to the Hendrix apartment where the heroin-stuffed doll is supposedly hidden by posing as a former service buddy of Susy's (Audrey Hepburn) husband.

cess, *Wait Until Dark* offered a wonderfully theatrical combination of intricate, topsy-turvy plotting, deadly charades, and visceral thrills (Knott's signature), and spawned a number of plays in the same vein. Most of them failed to match the original in thrills or cleverness. Only Anthony Shaffer's *Sleuth* and Ira Levin's *Deathtrap*, both clearly influenced by the work of Frederick Knott and Knott's *Wait Until Dark* especially, managed to hit the mark and stand effectively on their own as inventive and exciting theatrical experiences.

Although Arthur Penn and Lee Remick were by no means obscure names to moviegoers, Warner Bros. passed over them for the film version in favor of

The terrified but resourceful Susy (Audrey Hepburn) flees the wounded Harry Roat (Alan Arkin) during the film's exciting climax in which director Terence Young at times allowed the screen to go completely black so that the viewer would become as blind as Susy.

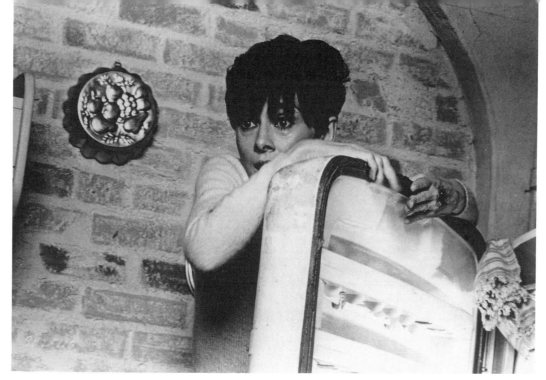

The valiant Susy (Audrey Hepburn) emerges from her hiding spot behind the open refrigerator door in the final scene of Frederick Knott's classic stage and screen thriller.

volved in a murder case, his only connection to which is a missing doll that accidentally fell into his hands. To get Sam off the hook, Talman agrees to help the blind woman ransack the apartment for the doll and get rid of it for her. The ruse works except that the doll is nowhere to be found. As the con men step up their game, Susy begins to believe that Roat and Carlino are in cahoots and may be pulling some kind of scam. With the help of a little girl named Gloria living upstairs who turns out to have taken the doll (when she gives it back, Susy immediately hides it), Susy confirms her suspicions, but is horrified to discover that Talman is part of the plot as well. As Gloria goes for help, Susy prepares to defend herself the best way she knows. She smashes all the lights in the hall and in the apartment so that her adversaries will be as blind as she.

When Talman returns and finds that she's on to him yet refuses to turn over the doll, he is impressed by her courage and backs off, assuring her that the dangerous Roat will be taken care of by Carlino and that she will not be harmed. But the wily Roat gets Carlino first, then kills Talman, setting the stage for the film's justly acclaimed climax where the crazy, knife-wielding Roat and the terrified but resourceful Susy confront one another in the darkness. To increase audience involvement, director Young allows the screen to go completely black at times so that all we hear are the sounds of their struggle. (During the

film's original run, some theaters even dowsed the house lights at this point to make the climax even more chillingly effective.)

Sam and the police arrive with Gloria to find Roat dead from a knife wound. But when the valiant Susy emerges from cowering in terror behind the open refrigerator door, her husband (who's always insisting that she be "the world champion blind lady") stubbornly stays put and offensively encourages her to come to him, which she does, locking her arms around him in an emotional embrace. Considering what the poor woman has just been through, however, I think a good swift kick in the groin would have been more appropriate.

As I said, for the film to work on you, it's best not to look at the plot too closely. For example, as the maniacal Roat obviously has no compunction about killing Susy to get at the doll—and ultimately tries to do so—it seems likely that in a real-life situation he would have chosen precisely that course of action initially rather than bothering with an elaborate hoax involving two untrustworthy henchmen that had so much built-in potential for failure. And why did Roat find it necessary for his equally elaborate "old man" disguise, which would be lost on a blind victim in the first place?

But *Wait Until Dark* is not intended to be a mirror of real life. It's intended to be thrilling theater. And that it undeniably is.

DELIVERANCE

(1972)

Warner Bros. • Color/105 Minutes

CREDITS

Director: John Boorman; *Producer*: John Boorman; *Screenplay*: James Dickey, based on his novel; *Cinematographer*: Vilmos Zsigmond; *Editor*: Tom Priestly; *Music*: Eric Weissberg and Steve Mandel; *Art Director*: Fred Harpman.

CAST

Ed Gentry: Jon Voight; *Lewis Medlock*: Burt Reynolds; *Bobby Trippe*: Ned Beatty; *Drew Ballinger*: Ronny Cox; *Mountain Man*: Bill McKinney; *Toothless Man*: Herbert "Cowboy" Coward; *Sheriff Bullard*: James Dickey.

* * *

Survival in an alien and hostile environment was certainly not a new movie subject when John Boorman tackled it in *Deliverance*, but his adaptation of James Dickey's bestselling novel was such a critical and commercial success and proved so influential that it launched an entire movie subgenre: the "city slickers versus the backwoods" thriller. Subsequent examples include *Shoot, Open Season, Southern Comfort, Hunter's Blood*—even *The Texas Chainsaw Massacre* to some degree—and many others.

But *Deliverance* towers above most of the films in this subgenre because in addition to being the first of them, it remains the best: an intense and disturbing tale not just of survival but of man's struggle to overcome the powerful forces of nature and his search for deliverance from the primitive "evil" that lurks in his own heart.

Though it now seems obvious that Boorman was the ideal choice to direct the film, he was not the studio's first selection to bring poet-turned-novelist Dickey's adventure tale to the screen. Directors such as Sam Peckinpah and Robert Aldrich were strongly in the running before him, but Boorman campaigned so vigorously for the job that the studio finally gave in to him. Though an adaptation of another man's work, the film proved to be a perfect match between the director and his material, for Boorman's other films (*Hell in the Pacific, Exorcist II: The Heretic, Excalibur, The Emerald Forest*) have much in common with Dickey's novel, especially the sharing of its central theme. As a

After humilating Bobby, the brutish mountain men (Herbert "Cowboy" Coward, left, and Bill McKinney) turn on Ed but are stopped in their tracks when Lewis gets off a deadly shot with an arrow.

result, *Deliverance* turned out to be an uncommonly faithful translation of a literary work to the screen.

Shot along a forty-mile stretch of Georgia's treacherous and boulder-strewn Chattooga River, *Deliverance* was an extremely difficult film to make. When studio location scouts returned form their forays into Chattooga county, they advised Boorman that it would be virtually impossible to film there, that there would be no way to get to the shooting sites except for the river itself because large populations of cottonmouths, rattlers, and copperheads guarded the overgrown river banks along the way. But Boorman was determined to use this location because it was the authentic site of the city slickers' ordeal in Dickey's novel (though Dickey had renamed it in his book). He also wanted his stars to perform much of their own stuntwork.

The other mountain man flees, having lost his gun to Ed (Jon Voight), as Drew (Ronny Cox) pursues him, brandishing an oar.

The four "city slickers" argue over what to do with the body.

Heavy-duty U.S. Navy Underwater Demolition Team rafts operated by experienced crews were used to get to and from the location site. These rafts were also outfitted with cameras so that much of the film could be shot on the river itself, placing the audience squarely in the center of the action. As in the novel and film, the river proved a tough foe. Actor Jon Voight's canoe was dashed to splinters twice and he was dumped into the churning river a dozen times. ("I lost fifteen pounds paddling that canoe," he has said. "I spent so much time underwater, I thought we were doing a Jacques Cousteau documentary!") Jagged rocks tore the bottoms out of several other rafts carrying soundmen and equipment and many times these crewmen and their equipment were stranded along the riverbank waiting for the "evening pickup," an auxiliary raft which made an evening sweep of the river for stragglers. However arduous it may have been for his crew and his actors, Boorman's insistence on authenticity paid off, for the film's numerous point of view shots on the river and scenes of his stars actually shooting the treacherous rapids and flailing about in the rolling foam give *Deliverance* a powerful sense of credibility that similar films tend to lack.

Another element that makes the film work more credibly than most of its subgenre—and why it produces such tension—is that there is nothing foolish or preposterous about the nightmarish situation the four city slickers find themselves in. These men are not stock types but very believable people with whom we can all identify, and what happens to them could, given the right set of circumstances, happen to any one of us.

The four set out on a weekend canoe trip in the unfamiliar and threatening wilds—an activity pursued across this country every weekend by urbanites with a yen for the outdoors. As they proceed deeper and deeper into the wilderness, they encounter a pair of dangerous backwoods rednecks who confront two of the party, Ed and Bobby, with a shotgun. Ed and Bobby try to bluff their way out of this situation, but this only makes things worse. At gunpoint, Bobby is ordered to undress and is sodomized by one of the animalistic mountain men. As the two turn on Ed, one of them is centershot with an arrow fired by Lewis and the other escapes into the woods.

The four trekkers must now decide what to do. Take the body of the mountain man, whose death was clearly a matter of self-defense, to the police and risk being tried by a jury of the dead man's vengeful backwoods peers, possibly even his relatives? Or bury the body in the woods, which is scheduled to be flooded with water? Only Drew opts for the legal alternative, regardless of the consequences, but he's outvoted and they bury the body deep in the forest. As they escape down the river, a strong current draws

As they flee down the river, Drew is shot from above by the other mountain man and falls overboard. The canoes overturn, one of them shattering against a rock, and Lewis (Burt Reynolds), Bobby (Ned Beatty), and Ed (Jon Voight) are sucked down a high falls into a pool at the base of a gorge.

*After killing the other mountain man, Ed (Jon Voight) descends
the precarious cliff face to rejoin Bobby and Lewis.*

The baldly wounded Lewis lying between them on the floor of the canoe, Bobby (Ned Beatty) and Ed (Jon Voight) shoot the rapids to safety at the river's end.

them into a stretch of violent rapids leading to a gorge overlooked by a high cliff. Drew is struck by a bullet fired from above and topples into the water. The canoes overturn and are sucked down the falls into the gorge where Lewis breaks his leg. The three survivors are trapped. Ahead lie more rapids while above the other mountain man stands poised to draw on them again if they budge.

That night, bow in hand, Ed scales the cliff. At dawn, the mountain man appears. As the man bears down on him, Ed lets loose an arrow. At first it looks as though he's missed, but then the mountain man crumbles and we see the arrow lodged in his throat. Ed lowers the body down the cliff face and he and Bobby weight it with rocks and sink it into the river. As the incapacitated Lewis drifts in and out of consciousness, Ed and Bobby shoot the rapids and come upon Drew's lifeless body lodged between a fallen tree and a rock. Since they cannot afford to tell the authorities how Drew came to be shot, Ed and Bobby are compelled to sink Drew's body into the river as well.

After shooting more dangerous rapids, the men finally reach the end of the river at the town of Aintry, where an ambulance speeds Lewis to the hospital. Ed and Bobby are given medical treatment and are put up in a hotel for questioning by the police, who are suspicious of Ed's explanation that Lewis broke his leg and that Drew was drowned due to a bad spill at the river's end because several facts contradict the man's story—notably that one of their shattered canoes was found upstream. In addition, a man who was hunting in the woods has been declared missing. It happens that he is related to the deputy sheriff who believes that Ed and Bobby might have met up with him. Ed and Bobby make up a new story and rush to the hospital to tell Lewis so that he will confirm it when the police question him.

The sheriff strongly hints that he suspects something as well but as he has no proof he lets Ed and Bobby go with the ominous line, "We'll wait and see what comes out of the river."

Ed and Bobby agree not to see one another for a while and Ed returns to his family. At this point, we breathe our first sigh of relief in over a hundred minutes. But then Boorman cuts back to the river and we see the bone white hand of one of the dead men rise to the surface.

Ed snaps up in bed, his body drenched in sweat, and we realize we have been witness to his recurring nightmare—a nightmare from which he has yet to experience deliverance, and probably never will for as long as he lives.

CHARLEY VARRICK
(1973)

Universal Pictures • Color/101 Minutes

CREDITS

Director: Don Siegel; *Producer*: Don Siegel; *Screenplay*: Dean Riesner and Howard Rodman, based on the novel *The Looters* by John Reese; *Cinematographer*: Michael Butler; *Editor*: Frank Morriss; *Music*: Lalo Schifrin; *Art Director*: Fernando Carrere.

CAST

Charley Varrick: Walter Matthau; *Harman Sullivan*: Andy Robinson; *Molly*: Joe Don Baker; *Maynard Boyle*: John Vernon; *Sybil Forte*: Felicia Farr; *Jewell Everett*: Sheree North; *Nadine Varrick*: Jacqueline Scott; *Damon Garfinkle*: Norman Fell; *Howard Young*: Woodrow Parfrey; *Sheriff Horton*: William Schallert; *Gun Store Owner*: Tom Tully.

* * *

After soaring in the late sixties and seventies when the critics finally "discovered" him, veteran director Don Siegel's cinematic fortunes declined precipitously in the early eighties. The successive box office disasters of *Rough Cut* (1980) and the appropriately titled *Jinxed* (1982), two troubled productions meddled with by the studios and the films' respective stars, Burt Reynolds and Bette Midler, caused a disheartened Siegel subsequently to disown both films and decide to retire from moviemaking. It's unfortunate that Siegel's career had to end on such a sour note. These two misfires notwithstanding, Siegel's overall body of work—much of it in the thriller genre—remains impressive, and his reputation as one of Hollywood's front-rank action directors and most skillful craftsmen is fixed and untarnished.

Fittingly subtitled "The Last of the Independents" (the independent-minded Siegel's personal view of himself at the time), *Charley Varrick* came fairly late in the director's nearly four decade career—one that produced such grade A "B" movies as the classic *Invasion of the Body Snatchers, Riot in Cell Block 11, Baby Face Nelson*, and *The Line-Up*, as well as Elvis Presley's *Flaming Star* and the original *Dirty Harry* (the only really good entry in the otherwise tepid Clint Eastwood

Charley Varrick (Walter Matthau), "the last of the independents," discusses strategy with his impetuous partner, Harman Sullivan (Andy Robinson).

wood, *The Beguiled* and *Escape From Alcatraz*, and many other notable thrillers, Westerns, and war films. Perhaps because Siegel identified so closely with the plight of the film's antihero title character, *Charley Varrick* revealed the director at the top of his form not only as an action specialist but also as a master of tough-tender characterization.

Ironically, Siegel almost didn't get to make the film (one of his best). The novel by John Reese upon which it is based had been passed about Hollywood for several years. At one point, Howard Hawks was set to direct it (with Hawks acolyte Peter Bogdanovich serving as producer), but then Hawks went on to make *Rio Lobo*, and *Charley Varrick* fortuitously crossed the desk of Don Siegel, who by this time had achieved

Varrick (Walter Matthau) and Sullivan (Andy Robinson) discover that the bank they just robbed was a "drop" for laundered Mafia money—and the Mafia wants its money back.

enough clout in the industry to green light his own projects. He immediately jumped at doing the film which, befitting its personal overtones, became the first to bear his own handwritten signature ("A Siegel Film") above the title during the opening credits. He then begins with a bang—a viscerally charged bank robbery sequence that is pure Don Siegel.

Following a series of bucolic shots of the serene, early morning Nevadan landscape, a Lincoln Continental bearing an elderly man and a young woman (she's driving) pulls up to the entrance of a small town bank and parks in a "no parking" zone. Two policemen passing by in a patrol car spot the illegally parked Continental (Siegel puts the innocent looking occupants—and us—immediately on guard by observing the patrol car from the interior of the Continental itself.) One of the policemen asks the woman to move. She smilingly agrees to do so, but the old

man, who is wearing a plaster cast on his foot, requests that they be allowed to park there briefly because he doesn't want her cashing his disability check and he can only walk so far on his game leg. Empathizing with the woman (presumably the crotchety old man's long-suffering daughter), the officer says okay and the patrol car drives off as the old man hobbles into the bank to cash his check.

Once inside, however, he informs the teller that he's sticking the place up. His two henchmen, posing as customers and now wearing masks, pull guns, backing up his claim. Meanwhile, one of the patrolmen, with a penchant for memorizing license plate numbers, recalls seeing the Continental's on a hot sheet. He follows up with the dispatcher and finds out the Continental is indeed stolen. The patrol car returns to the bank, pulling up cautiously behind the still-parked Continental. As the robbery continues

*Varrick (Walter Matthau) engages photographer Jewell Everett
(Sheree North) to make him some phony passport photos so
that he and his partner can get out of the country and escape
the Mafia hit man on their tail.*

*Varrick (Walter Matthau) works a deal to get a false passport—
part of his cunning scheme to cover his tracks, turn his crooked
pursuers against one another, and get away with all the loot.*

Varrick (Walter Matthau) sets up bank director Maynard Boyle (John Vernon) to take the heat.

inside the bank, one of the officers unholsters his gun and approaches the woman behind the wheel, asking to see her license and registration. She places her purse on her lap in full view, reaches inside, and a bullet explodes through the cloth into the policeman's forehead. As he falls back, his gun discharges, the bullet penetrating the car door and hitting the woman. A bank employee surreptitiously triggers the alarm system and in the melee that follows, one of the security guards and one of the robbers are killed. The old man rips off his fake plaster cast as he exits the bank with the stolen loot. As he and his remaining henchman scramble inside the waiting Continental and it peels out, police cars swarm into the area. The fleeing Continental broadsides one of them and its hood flies open, obscuring the wounded woman's vision as another patrol car crosses her path, the two cars just missing one another. (Though the visceral effect of this stunning sequence, which Siegel shoots entirely from the viewpoint of the Continental's mo-

Former stunt pilot Varrick (Walter Matthau) pulls his last deadly trick on his pursuers and makes off with the stolen cash.

mentarily blinded occupants, tends to be lost in the "panned and scanned" versions of the film circulating on television and videocassette, its impact on the wide screen is heart-stopping indeed.)

Due to the woman's skillful driving, the robbers get away. In a trademark example of Siegel's tough-tender approach to movie romance, the mortally wounded woman expires in the arms of the old man, who is actually her husband, Charley Varrick, in disguise, and Varrick gives her several goodbye pecks on the lips before getting on with the urgent business at hand—rigging the car to explode so that her body cannot be identified. Then he and his youthful accomplice, Harman Sullivan, disguising themselves as crop dusters, drive off with the stolen loot in a waiting van emblazoned with the logo, "Charley Varrick—Last of the Independents." The two immediately run into trouble, however, when they discover that the bank was a "drop" for laundered Mafia money and that they've made off with a lot more cash than the bank reported stolen—and the Mafia wants it back. In addition to being hunted by police, they are soon stalked by a Mafia hit man—a leisurely, pipesmoking

but cold-blooded and brutal professional thug with the bizarre name of Molly whom Siegel subtly develops into a weirdly fascinating character.

When Harman refuses to go along with Charley's suggestion that they lay low for several years and not spend any of the stolen cash until things blow over, Charley sets him up to take the heat ("You called it, Harman") and the younger man is tracked down and killed by Molly. The remainder of the film deals with Charley's convoluted and cunning scheme to cover his tracks, turn his crooked pursuers against one another, and get away with all the loot.

Only once does this intricately woven thriller suffer a lapse in credibility—when Charley beds down the secretary of the bank's national manager, Maynard Boyle, and, for motives that are both unclear and unconvincing, she agrees to help Charley set her boss up for a double-cross. Otherwise, the film is a prime example of director Don Siegel's taut, tough (though never repellently violent) approach to thriller-making, with a wonderfully wry performance by Matthau as the duplicitous but engaging Charley and an ending that leaves the viewer both surprised and satisfied.

JUGGERNAUT

(1974)

United Artists • Color/109 Minutes

CREDITS

Director: Richard Lester; *Producer*: Richard De Koker; *Screenplay*: Richard De Koker; *Cinematographer*: Gerry Fisher; *Editor*: Antony Gibbs; *Music*: Ken Thorne; *Production Designer*: Terence Marsh.

CAST

Anthony Fallon: Richard Harris; *Charlie Braddock*: David Hemmings; *Ship's Captain*: Omar Sharif; *Inspector McCloud*: Anthony Hopkins; *Mrs. Bannister*: Shirley Knight; *Nicholas Porter*: Ian Holm; *Cruise Director*: Roy Kinnear; *Sidney Buckland (Juggernaut)*: Freddie Jones.

* * *

American born British director Richard Lester burst upon the world cinema scene with *A Hard Day's Night* (1964) and *Help!* (1965), his Beatles comedies whose nonstop visual gags and anarchic spirit launched Lester's reputation as the British cinema's reigning farceur and set the "mod" tone for most other British movies of the late sixties and early seventies, comedy and drama.

Though the "Lester style" no longer pervades the British cinema as it once did, Lester himself has never abandoned it. Even though his output over the years includes Westerns (*Butch and Sundance: The Early Years*), adventure films (*The Three Musketeers, The Four Musketeers*), dramas (*Petulia, Cuba*), and special effects extravaganzas (*Superman II, Superman III*), his unique sense of outrageousness and absurdity—his comic signature, if you will—has remained as distinct as ever. This is true even of *Juggernaut*, his only outright thriller, which contains as many visual sight gags aimed at tension-relieving laughter as it does moments of palm-sweating suspense and high drama. In fact, Lester's skillful balancing act between humor and suspense is probably why the film works as well as it does, for it succeeds in disguising some significant loopholes in writer Richard De Koker's credibility-stretching plot.

The film's title refers to the pseudonym of a terrorist who has placed seven steel barrels aboard the Britannic, a twelve-hundred passenger and crew luxury liner bound for America from Southhampton.

A navy demolition team headed by explosives expert Anthony Fallon (Richard Harris) is parachuted to the ship to disarm the bombs in Richard Lester's Juggernaut.

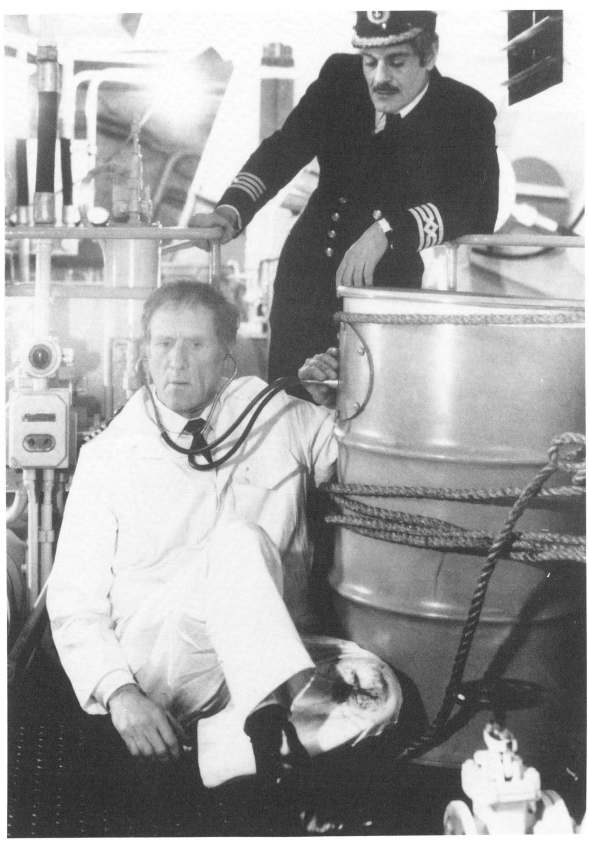

The ship's captain (Omar Sharif) and his crew chief (Jack Watson) cautiously examine one of the oil drums containing one thousand pounds of explosives and sophisticated boobytraps left on board by "Juggernaut."

Each drum contains one thousand pounds of explosives and sophisticated triggering devices set to detonate at dawn, when the liner is in the mid-Atlantic, unless Juggernaut's £500,000 ransom demand is met. Once he gets the money, he agrees to instruct the ship's captain and crew how to disarm the bombs, each of which is rigged with a series of booby traps designed to trigger the explosives prematurely if anyone attempts to tamper with the bombs on their own. Any attempt to remove the barrels from the ship will also trigger the bombs, he says, for the booby traps are set to go off at the slightest jostling or swaying. As a demonstration that he's not bluffing, he has timed one of the bombs to explode early in a less critical section of the ship, which it does, injuring one of the crew.

Due to stormy seas, the captain can't lower everyone away on lifeboats and he urges that the ship line's managing director, Nicholas Porter, comply with Juggernaut's demands. Porter is initially inclined to do this, but is dissuaded by a government official who insists that giving in to the demands of the likes of Juggernaut will only lead to more acts of terrorism. He also hints that the line will lose its government subsidies if Porter gives in. As Porter awaits the next phone call from Juggernaut, Scotland Yard goes to work. Led by Inspector McCloud, whose wife and children are on the ship, the police launch a manhunt for Juggernaut by leaning on every IRA sympathizer (Juggernaut has an Irish accent, which turns out to be bogus) and explosives expert in London for information. But they turn up nothing.

At the same time, a navy demolition team headed by bomb expert Anthony Fallon and second-in-command Charlie Braddock is parachuted aboard the ship with equipment to disarm the bombs. Fallon assigns a man to each bomb and has the compartments they're in sealed off. A communications link is established among the ship's captain, Fallon's team, and the officials in London so that they can all hear and talk to one another. It is Fallon's intention to disarm the first bomb himself, reporting each step of the guesswork procedure to his teammates so that they can repeat the steps. In this way if Fallon makes a misstep and is blown up, the others will know not to repeat the same mistake themselves.

Fallon successfully unscrews the face plate of the barrel and gets his first good look at the bomb itself, a maze of multicolored wires and a half dozen trigger devices which must be snipped through in order to reach the main timer. As he is about to cut through a contact wire, the ship lurches and he is knocked backward. Braddock proceeds with the step prematurely and is blown up. Distraught over his friend's death, Fallon tells Porter that the job is too complex and to pay up. But by this time, the petulant Juggernaut is on to the fact that he's being hunted, breaks off negotiations, and intends to let the bombs go off as scheduled.

Having no alternative, Fallon and his men resume their hair-raising work. Eventually, Fallon identifies the signature of the bomb's designer, a deceased Nazi

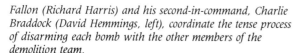

Fallon (Richard Harris) and his second-in-command, Charlie Braddock (David Hemmings, left), coordinate the tense process of disarming each bomb with the other members of the demolition team.

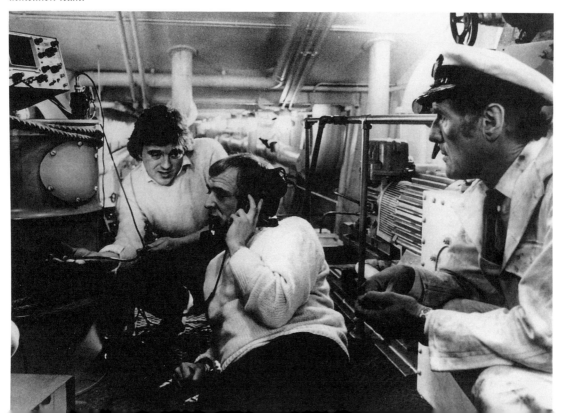

Fallon (Richard Harris) successfully unscrews the face plate of the first barrel and gets a good look at the bomb itself, a maze of colorful wires and a half-dozen trigger devices that must be cut through in order to reach the main timer.

Distraught over Braddock's death, Fallon (Richard Harris) feels the job's too complex and says the captain's (Omar Sharif) employers should agree to Juggernaut's demands and pay up.

When Juggernaut breaks off negotiations, Fallon (Richard Harris) has no choice but to resume his hair-raising work. As *dawn breaks and the explosive deadline nears, Fallon finds himself down to the last wire literally and figuratively.*

explosives expert whose unique devices Fallon and his now-retired mentor, a man named Sidney Buckland, had been challenged with dismantling during the war. The police locate Buckland, an embittered civil servant living on a modest pension, whom they had previously interviewed but dismissed as a suspect. Buckland turns out to be Juggernaut.

With dawn breaking, Fallon, who is down to the last wire both literally and figuratively, trades on his old friend and mentor's conscience and former feelings for him and asks Buckland for guidance. Two remaining wires lead to the main timer—a red one and a blue one. One will disconnect the timer, the other will engage a trembler switch booby trap and detonate the bomb—but which is which? Buckland refuses to answer. Fallon says he's going to cut the blue wire and begs Buckland to tell him if he's right. Buckland finally blurts out yes, but Fallon mistrusts the man's response and at the last second opts to sever the red wire instead. This proves to be the correct decision, Fallon's teammates follow suit, and the ship is saved in the nick of time.

Although Lester's primary aim is to keep the audience on the edge of its collective seat, a feat the

former clown prince of British comedy accomplishes with considerable skill, he also involves the efforts of the ship's dedicated cruise director (the late Roy Kinnear—a Lester regular—in an amusing and ultimately quite endearing performance) to keep the imperiled passengers' minds off their worries by engaging them in a variety of foolish activities, including shuffleboard (no easy task in a storm-tossed sea) and a costume ball. As the ship bobs and weaves in the worsening weather, passengers bang into walls, waiters bump into each other and spill dishes; even more amusingly, some just barely miss colliding with one another thanks to some very clever Chaplinesque footwork.

None of these bits of clowning dissipates the film's relentless tension in any way, however. In fact, as I wrote at the outset, the visceral effect of both tend to keep one's mind off the plot's several implausibilities. The biggest of which is this: How could the elderly Juggernaut, who is working alone, possibly have installed the seven one-thousand-pound barrels aboard the ship by himself? Especially with no one noticing? An engineer's explanation—poor security measures—doesn't quite cut it.

ALL THE PRESIDENT'S MEN
(1976)

Warner Bros. • Color/138 Minutes

CREDITS

Director: Alan J. Pakula; *Producer*: Walter Coblenz; *Screenplay*: William Goldman, based on the book by Carl Bernstein and Bob Woodward; *Cinematographer*: Gordon Willis; *Editor*: Robert L. Wolfe; *Music*: David Shire; *Production Designer*: George Jenkins.

CAST

Carl Bernstein: Dustin Hoffman; *Bob Woodward*: Robert Redford; *Harry Rosenfeld*: Jack Warden; *Howard Simons*: Martin Balsam; *Ben Bradlee*: Jason Robards; *Deep Throat*: Hal Holbrook; *Bookkeeper*: Jane Alexander; *Sally Aiken*: Penny Fuller; *Dardis*: Ned Beatty; *Hugh Sloan*: Stephen Collins; *Frank Wills*: Frank Wills; *Donald Segretti*: Robert Walden; *Kay Eddy*: Lindsay Crouse; *Miss Milland*: Valerie Curtin; *Foreign Desk Editor*: John McMartin.

* * *

When Robert Redford announced in 1975 that he intended to executive produce and star in a movie based on *Washington Post* reporters Carl Bernstein and Bob Woodward's account of the Watergate scandal that led to Richard Nixon's downfall, *All the President's Men*, I couldn't help wondering who would go and see it.

At the time of the Watergate hearings in 1973, I was working at a television station and can still recall the volume of phone calls and letters from irate viewers objecting not only to the "unfair treatment" their President was receiving from the media but to the even worse sin of having their favorite daytime programs canceled so that the hearings could be televised gavel to gavel.

Busloads of protestors arrived at the station practically on a daily basis demanding that we stop all this Nixon bashing and put their favorite quiz shows, talk shows, and soap operas back on the air. Our station was not alone; the same thing happened across the nation during that tumultuous summer and fall. By 1974 when Nixon finally resigned in disgrace, the country had been saturated by Watergate, and was clearly fed up with it. And now Robert Redford was

Dustin Hoffman and Robert Redford as Carl Bernstein and Bob Woodward, the Washington Post *reporters whose exposé of the 1972–74 Watergate scandal led to President Richard Nixon's political downfall.*

Woodward (Robert Redford) and Bernstein (Dustin Hoffman) pool their talents and sources to get at the truth behind the Watergate burglary.

going to sink millions of dollars into making a movie about it? Was he crazy, I asked myself? The theaters would be empty!

Well, I was wrong on both counts. *All the President's Men* captured the attention of audiences and critics and clicked at the box office like no political doc-udrama/newspaper movie before or since. Some say the release of this potent recounting of the Watergate cover-up and scandal during the 1976 election year even led to Gerald Ford's loss of the presidency to Jimmy Carter for having pardoned Nixon. This may or may not be true—Ford was clearly capable of losing the election on his own; nevertheless, the film's timeliness and topicality surely didn't help him.

The marvel of the movie is that it makes the familiar tale seem fresh and exciting even though we already know how it will turn out.

The way it does this is by focusing on that part of the story that is less well known—namely how reporters Bernstein and Woodward latched onto the story of the break-in and cover-up and persevered to uncover and reveal the truth despite seemingly insur-mountable odds. As a result, the movie is as much about the dogged workings of the press—and the importance of having a free press, regardless of its imperfections, in a democracy—as it is about the scandal itself. This intention—and theme—is stated quite clearly (and quite brilliantly) in the film's metaphoric "pen is mightier than the sword" opening scene where a typewriter key slams against a blank piece of paper and we jump out of our seats as if deafened by a gunshot.

Jason Robards plays Washington Post *editor-in-chief Ben Bradlee in Robert Redford and Alan J. Pakula's riveting political thriller/slam-bang newspaper saga,* All The President's Men.

Bernstein (Dustin Hoffman) tells Woodward that he's traced one of the checks found in the possession of the Watergate burglars to Nixon's reelection committee—appropriately acronymed C.R.E.E.P.

Bernstein (Dustin Hoffman), Woodward (Robert Redford), Bradlee (Jason Robards), Rosenfeld (Jack Warden), and Simons (Martin Balsam) watch a Nixon administration spokesperson give yet another "non-denial denial" during a televised news conference.

By personalizing the story—concentrating on how the two reporters uncovered it in the face of overwhelming governmental deceit and chicanery, political stonewalling, condemnation, and even death threats—the film skillfully achieves the kind of tension and suspense that is usually found only in the best fictional thrillers.

As it follows the reporter/sleuths' dogged efforts to expose who done it and why, William Goldman's deservedly Oscar-winning screenplay does a remarkable job of cutting through the tangled web of Watergate and making the ramifications of the scandal clear in a way that the televised hearings themselves failed to do for many people. The film makes eminently clear the often obscured fact that the conspiracy involving the President and all his men was undertaken to cover up not simply a third-rate burglary but also a score of "dirty tricks" dating back several years which had successfully undermined the country's political process. That's a scarifying thought—or should be to every American who truly believes in and cherishes what this country is supposed to stand for. In illuminating this fact, *All the President's Men* often becomes quite scary itself. It not only suc-

cessfully communicates the real and imagined paranoia that consumed everyone involved in this shocking affair and exposé, but skillfully passes that paranoia onto the audience as well in the taut manner of an expert espionage thriller.

Though not a documentary, the film seems like one because the locations are authentic (except for the offices of the *Washington Post*, which were recreated on a Hollywood soundstage) and the performances are amazingly *real* down to the smallest bit player. Except for Dustin Hoffman, who tends to get mannered and "actorish" as the quirky, chain-smoking Bernstein, we forget that the people we're seeing on the screen are acting (only Frank Wills, the Watergate security guard who discovered the break-in, plays himself in the film) and that every scene is staged. Jason Robards won the Oscar as Best Supporting Actor for his portrayal of *Post* editor Ben Bradlee, and William Goldman won for his screenplay.

To his and director Alan J. Pakula's credit, even movie star Redford completely disappears into his role as Woodward in this consummately produced political thriller—and most authentic looking and sounding insider saga of the newspaper business ever made.

TWILIGHT'S LAST GLEAMING
(1977)

Allied Artists/Lorimar-Bavaria • Color/146 Minutes

CREDITS

Director: Robert Aldrich; *Producer*: Merv Adelson; *Screenplay*: Ronald M. Cohen and Edward Huebsch, based on the novel *Viper Three* by Walter Wager; *Cinematographer*: Robert Hauser; *Editors*: Michael Luciano, Maurey Weintrobe and William Martin; *Music*: Jerry Goldsmith; *Production Designer*: Rolf Zehetbauer.

CAST

General Lawrence Dell: Burt Lancaster; *General Martin MacKenzie*: Richard Widmark; *President David Stevens*: Charles Durning; *Secretary of Defense Guthrie*: Melvyn Douglas; *Willis Powell*: Paul Winfield; *Augie*: Burt Young; *Secretary of State Arthur Renfew*: Joseph Cotten; *Professor James Forrest*: Roscoe Lee Browne; *Brigadier General O'Rourke*: Gerald S. O'Loughlin; *Captain Towne*: Richard Jaeckel; *Attorney General Klinger*: William Marshall; *Colonel Bernstein*: Charles Aidman; *C.I.A. Director Whittaker*: Leif Erickson; *General Crane*: Charles McGraw; *Hoxey*: William Smith.

* * *

Railroaded Air Force General Lawrence Dell (Burt Lancaster) takes over Silo 13 in Robert Aldrich's controversial political thriller, Twilight's Last Gleaming.

Like Frankenheimer's *The Manchurian Candidate*, Robert Aldrich's *Twilight's Last Gleaming* is a powerful Cold War thriller that laces its grimly realistic yet bitingly satiric scenario with some very disturbing things to say about the American military and political scene. Of the two, *Twilight* is the much angrier film, however—and the more indignant as well. In it, all lines of moral, ethical, not to mention sane, behavior in our government have become so blurred that it finally takes a madman to point them out. That U.S. military and government officials denied their cooperation in making the film and that Aldrich was forced to shoot it overseas, in Germany, is not surprising. In view of the film's potently critical message about domestic and foreign U.S. policy and policy makers, it would have been much more surprising if they'd granted it.

The madman at the center of things is Lawrence Dell, a railroaded Air Force general who has escaped from a military prison and taken over one of the ICBM missile silos in Malmstrom, Montana. His expressed purpose is to trigger a nuclear exchange with the Soviet Union if President David Stevens refuses to make public the minutes of a secret national security meeting held by a former administration during the early years of the Vietnam War. The minutes, which even outrage Stevens when he reads them, outline the commitment of the United States government to a strategy of limited warfare

Dell (Burt Lancaster) and Powell (Paul Winfield) carefully remove one the many boobytraps aimed at preventing a hostile takeover of the installation's nuclear missiles.

Dell's longtime adversary, General Martin MacKenzie (Richard Widmark), informs the President of the United States of what's happened at Silo 13.

The Pentagon monitors the events at Silo 13.

throughout the world in order to convince the Russians to stay within their own sphere of influence. What this bombshell boils down to, the shocked President announces to his advisers, is that the Vietnam War was nothing more than a "public relations gimmick" aimed at showing the Russians that the U.S. means business. To make matters worse, Stevens's own Secretary of State, who had attended the long-ago meeting, informs him that the reason the strategy was adopted was that the Russians have a similar one, and that such a policy is necessary in a nuclear-armed world in order to avoid any possibility of a face-to-face confrontation that could result in a nuclear holocaust. This strategy, by the way, is not a figment of the filmmaker's imagination; director Aldrich and screenwriters Ronald M. Cohen and Edward Huebsch derived it from a 1957 book called *Nuclear Weapons and Foreign Policy*, in which future Secretary of State Henry Kissinger outlined and endorsed the adoption of just such a policy—a policy which, in view of the Cold War's end and subsequent events, could easily be redirected toward Third World and terrorist nations, and possibly has.

Stevens takes a survey of his advisers, most of whom feel the minutes are too much of a political hot-potato to risk revealing to the American public at this time—especially at the point of a gun. And so, they opt for a military solution to the dilemma posed

by the messianic Dell; ironically, they try to nuke him with a mini-atomic bomb. When this fails, Stevens agrees to Dell's demands. He instructs his Secretary of Defense to reveal the document to the public if anything happens to him and reluctantly agrees to join Dell and his surviving accomplice, Willis Powell, as hostage in their flight to freedom. At the film's devastating conclusion, all three of them are shot down and it is clearly implied that the document will never be made known.

One of the many elements that makes this movie so fascinating is the character of Dell himself. Because the policy he wants to expose is so morally repugnant, he seems like a hero, and we can't help siding with him. And yet the subtle fact is that Dell is really a mirror of that same insane policy. He denounces the government for committing murder in order to prove a point to the Russians—and anyone else; but he is willing to murder millions with nine Titan missiles in order to prove *his* point. He also denounces the government for at first choosing a military solution to the dilemma he poses. Yet his solution to the dilemma the government poses is to threaten military might if it doesn't reveal the truth. Like the superpower he is challenging, he believes that the only way to deal with such strength is to become a superpower himself.

Aldrich believed he failed to make Dell's lunacy

Powell (Paul Winfield) refuses to turn the second key required to launch the missiles. "Nobody honors nothin'," he tells Dell (Burt Lancaster) wearily. "Still, that's no reason to blow up the whole world."

obvious. "My hope was that you gradually came to understand that [Burt] Lancaster is crazy," he said at the time of the film's release. "But I don't think we did it." I disagree. I think the point is eminently clear, and all the more powerful because it is stated so subtly. On the surface, Dell seems quite rational. But so does the strategy of limited war as a way of averting all-out war. Only if you look beneath the surface do you see that each is quite deranged. In Dell's case, this becomes manifestly obvious when, believing the President's acquiescence to all of his demands spells victory, Dell decides to launch the Titan missiles in a fit of pique after the more savvy Powell convinces him that the demands will *never* be honored, no matter what the President says. The only thing that stops Dell from triggering Armageddon is Powell's refusal to turn the second key required to launch the missiles. "Nobody honors nothin'," Powell announces wearily. "Still, that's no reason to blow up the whole world."

But Dell's lunacy is revealed in more cryptic ways, too. Nowhere is this more evident than in the scene in which Powell jokingly suggests that the Air Force might be hiding midget snipers in the tanks outside the installation to shoot them when they come out with the President. With deep indignation, Dell responds, "There are *no* midgets in the United States Air Force!" This statement not only reveals the confused nature of Dell's alliances, but also symbolizes why both he and his morally upright commander-in-chief must die in the end. For when the outcome of a game of real power is at stake, the rules of admission are rigid indeed—and any player exhibiting "weakness" is expendable.

The filmmakers' deeply unsettling suggestion that high ranking government and military officials might acquiesce to and even participate in the assassination of their own president if he got in the way of maintaining the status quo will certainly strike a familiar chord with Kennedy assassination conspiracy theorists, many of whom believe that JFK was "removed" precisely because his desire for detente with the Russians following the Cuban Missile Crisis and hints of a Vietnam pullout following his 1964 reelection jeopardized the exact type of national security policy outlined here. The film doesn't make any overt comparisons between the murder of its fictional president, David Stevens, and JFK, but as Stevens is mowed down in a triangular field of fire by three hidden snipers, one can't help but think of some of the alternative assassination scenarios Kennedy conspiracy theorists have been posing for years. And come to the disquieting conclusion that the muddled truth surrounding that traumatic day in November 1963 was the first indication that twilight's last gleaming was fast approaching.

THE CHINA SYNDROME

(1979)

Columbia Pictures • Color/123 Minutes

CREDITS

Director: James Bridges; *Producer*: Michael Douglas; *Screenplay*: Mike Gray, T.S. Cook, and James Bridges; *Cinematographer*: James Crabe; *Editor*: David Rawlins; *Music*: Stephen Bishop; *Production Designer*: George Jenkins.

CAST

Kimberly Wells: Jane Fonda; *Jack Godell*: Jack Lemmon; *Richard Adams*: Michael Douglas; *Ted Spindler*: Wilford Brimley; *Herman DeYoung*: Scott Brady; *Bill Gibson*: James Hampton; *Don Jacovich*: Peter Donat; *Evan McCormack*: Richard Herd; *Hector Salas*: Daniel Valdez; *Peter Martin*: Stan Bohrman; *Mac Churchill*: James Karen; *Dr. Lowell*: Donald Hotton.

* * *

I have a special fondness for *The China Syndrome* because I saw it on my honeymoon. Nostalgia aside, the film merits its spot in this book because it is an extremely taut tale of nuclear jitters—and one of the few thrillers of its type to focus on the perils of nuclear energy rather than nuclear arms.

As a matter of act, the film isn't really against nuclear energy at all. Its target is corporate greed and the pursuit of the almighty buck at the expense of the truth and the safety of the earth and all living creatures. The film's hero, Jack Godell, makes this point to television reporter Kimberly Wells when he tells her that it isn't his beloved nuclear power plant and its battery of sophisticated safety systems that pose a hazard ("Those systems *work!*" he passionately argues), it's the willingness of the bigwigs who own the plant to undermine the efficiency of those systems if it means cutting costs and growing fatter profits. As if to mirror Godell's argument, the TV station where Wells works at first tries to bury the story of the near-accident at the power plant because exposing it might result in a law suit that would severely affect the station's reputation and bottom line. That the station's viewing audience—indeed, everyone at the station itself, even the corporate honcho, Don Jacovich, who scotches the story—might perish if the truth isn't revealed and the plant suffers a fatal accident next

Plant public relations man Bill Gibson (James Hampton) takes news reporter Kimberly Wells (Jane Fonda) and photographer Richard Adams (Michael Douglas) on a tour of the Ventana nuclear power installation.

time around matters very little. It's money that talks—even though there would be no one around to spend it if the worst finally happened.

While doing a series of shallow television news reports on Southern California energy options, anchorwoman Kimberly Wells witnesses an accident at the Ventana nuclear power plant that could have resulted in a catastrophe—the meltdown of the exposed core all the way to China (the so-called "China syndrome") and the raining of deadly radioactive pollution all over the state. Her cameraman, Richard Adams, secretly captures the incident on film, but the station's management refuses to allow it on the air not only because it fears a law suit but also because it doesn't want Kimberly doing "hard news"—the ratings are markedly up due to the attractive young woman's engaging way with "fluff" and management has no intention of tampering with success.

While doing a shallow news story at a nuclear power plant, TV news photographer Richard Adams (Michael Douglas), reporter Kimberly Wells (Jane Fonda), and sound man Hector Salas (Daniel Valdez) witness a supposedly routine "turbine trip" that could have triggered The China Syndrome.

A crisis of conscience versus job security sparks an angry exchange between TV reporter Kimberly Wells (Jane Fonda) and news cameraman Richard Adams (Michael Douglas).

After taking over the control room at gunpoint, whistleblower Jack Godell (Jack Lemmon) submits to a live TV interview with reporter Wells (Jane Fonda) and cameraman Adams (Michael Douglas).

Furious with the station's irresponsibility and stonewalling of the story, Adams swipes the film from the studio vault and shows it to some nuclear energy experts who confirm his suspicions of the near-fatal accident. As the owners of the unsafe Ventana plant are currently pushing for construction of another potentially unsafe facility at nearby Point Conception, Adams solicits Kimberly's help in getting Ventana control room supervisor Jack Godell, who detected an odd vibration during the incident and has since uncovered evidence of cost-cutting safety infractions that could lead to a fatal accident next time around, to testify before the NRC at the Point Conception hearings.

Godell balks at going on the record himself, but agrees to supply Kimberly and Adams with the damning evidence they need—X-rays of the welding in the Ventana plant's containment area which were deliberately faked in a cost-cutting move to prove to the NRC that all the welds were in equally fine shape. Godell secretly passes the X-rays to Adams's soundman, Hector Salas, to take to the hearings. But Salas is run off the road by plant CEO Evan McCormack's hired goons on the way and almost killed, and the X-rays are stolen. When Kimberly tells Godell what happened, he realizes he has no choice now but to testify at the hearings in person. But McCormack has him tailed, too, and to avoid being killed, he takes

refuge inside the walls of the Ventana plant itself, which, he discovers to his horror, is about to be put back on-line.

Knowing what could happen if the unsafe plant goes back to full power, Godell takes over the control room at gunpoint, orders everyone out, and demands to be interviewed by Kimberly live on television. As the plant is surrounded by newspeople and Kimberly starts to interview Godell inside the control room, McCormack orders his underlings to "scram the plant" so that Godell's attention will be diverted from the interview long enough for a S.W.A.T. team to move in and stop him. The plan works and Godell is shot down in cold blood before he can fully reveal his story. The irresponsible "scramming" maneuver triggers the precise chain of events Godell had feared, however, and the plant almost blows up—but the safety systems Godell had so much faith in do their job once more and this second near-catastrophe is narrowly averted.

The plant's PR man, Bill Gibson, again tries to hide the truth—by painting Godell as a drunken lunatic with a grudge against his employers. But Godell's close friend and coworker, Ted Spindler, objects to this slur on his dead colleague and blurts the truth into Kimberly's microphone as the news cameras grind away. In the film's pointed closing scene, Kimberly's boss, Jacovich, beams at how terrific Kimberly looked

Jane Fonda and Michael Douglas in James Bridges's prophetic The China Syndrome.

doing the story and how much the ratings will probably soar because of it—the seriousness of the story itself obviously of less importance to him than the profit potential of his rising new "hard news" star.

When *The China Syndrome* was released, most critics agreed that it was a tense, well made thriller, but they also felt it to be just a bit farfetched. Several weeks later, however, Pennsylvania's Three Mile Island nuclear power plant experienced a near-fatal accident identical to the one described in the film and these same critics found themselves eating crow. (In an eerily prophetic scene, one of the nuclear energy experts Kimberly and Adams confer with describes what would have happened if the film's fictional plant had suffered a meltdown by saying the radioactive fallout would have contaminated everyone in a state "the size of Pennsylvania.") This chilling instance of life imitating art did wonders for the film's box office but very little for the peace of mind of the people of Pennsylvania.

THE LONG GOOD FRIDAY

(1980)

Embassy Pictures/Handmade Films • Color/105 Minutes

CREDITS

Director: John Mackenzie; *Producer*: Barry Hanson; *Screenplay*: Barrie Keeffe; *Cinematographer*: Phil Meheux; *Editor*: Mike Taylor; *Music*: Francis Monkman; *Art Director*: Vic Symonds.

CAST

Harold Shand: Bob Hoskins; *Victoria*: Helen Mirren; *Charlie*: Eddie Constantine; *Parky*: Dave King; *Harris*: Bryan Marshall; *Tony*: Stephen Davies; *Jeff*: Derek Thompson; *Colin*: Paul Freeman; *First Irishman*: Pierce Brosnan.

* * *

In addition to being one of the most absorbing thrillers of the eighties, John Mackenzie's *The Long Good Friday* is one of the toughest, most fascinating gangster movies ever made. It also has one of the most byzantine plots since Roman Polanski's *Chinatown*.

The story begins with—and hinges upon—a seemingly incomprehensible scene in which Colin, the homosexual hireling of London crime boss Harold Shand, delivers a suitcase full of cash to some shady characters in Belfast. The deal goes bad for some reason, some arrests are made, and Colin's driver and another man are killed and dumped in a ditch—although Colin himself gets away. Not until the last twenty minutes of the film do the full meaning and importance of this baffling opening sequence—which employs music and sound effects but virtually no dialogue—finally become clear.

Shand, a nattily dressed, fiercely patriotic bulldog of a man who has solidified his power and control over all of East London's gangs and rules them with an iron but equitable hand, is cooking up a deal with the American Mafia to cofinance a massive renovation of the harbor area that will transform the city into the moneymaking jewel of Europe and the Common Market. But as soon as the Mafia chief, Charlie, and his lawyer, Tony, arrive to look over Shand's grandiose plans and make their decision, Shand's turf erupts in violence which threatens his power and control and the fate of the entire project.

Shand's private limousine is blown up outside the church where his mother is attending Good Friday services, and the driver is killed. A bomb that failed to detonate is found in one of Shand's nightclubs. And his hireling, Colin, is knifed to death in a public bath.

With the help of Victoria (his mistress, business partner, and loyal confidante), Jeff, his top aide, and Harris, the city councilman in his pocket, Shand manages to keep this catastrophic turn of events secret from his Mafia guests. But when the restaurant where he plans to entertain his overseas visitors is blown up just as they arrive, Shand has no choice but to come clean with them about the "problems" he's having. After reassuring them that he'll make short work of all this nasty business, the usually peace-loving Shand doles out weapons to the normally unarmed members of his inner circle and dispatches them to round up the other gang bosses in the city and find out which one of them is behind the badly-timed insurrection, and why. He also orders Parky, the policeman on his payroll, to do some digging and come up with a name too.

The rounded-up gangsters are rolled into a slaughterhouse and intimidated into talking by being strung upside down next to the bloody animal carcasses—a not-so-subtle warning of their own fate shoud they refuse to cooperate. But they all admit to being genuinely satisfied with the status quo under Shand's rule because there's been no gang warfare for years and everybody's making piles of money. None of them knows anything.

Parky shows up with a significant clue, however. He reveals that the unexploded bomb in Shand's nightclub was the work of experienced IRA terrorists, who obviously have it in for Shand for some reason. As the violence is becoming too public and the involvement of the IRA puts the case under the aegis of Special Branch, Parky bows out of the affair, leaving the furious Shand to sort the mess out on his own.

Shand finally discovers that his top aide and close friend, Jeff, is the source fo the trouble. While Shand was in America paving the way for the Mafia visit,

Victoria (Helen Mirren) assures Mafia rep Charlie (Eddie Constantine) that everything is under control, but the worried look on boss Harold Shand's (Bob Hoskins) face shows that he's not so sure.

One of Shand's henchmen rousts a "grass" (snitch) at gunpoint to find out who's behind the violence threatening Shand's power and control.

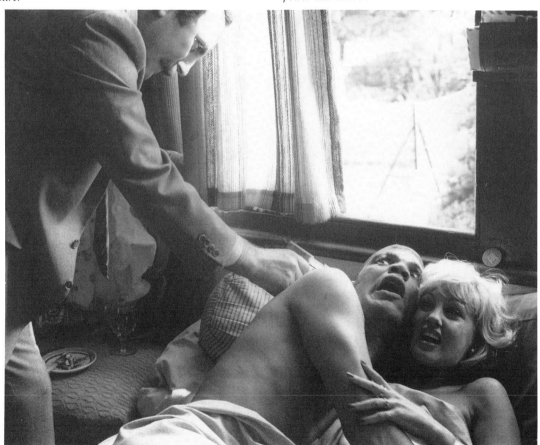

The rounded-up gangsters are rolled into a slaughterhouse and intimidated into talking by being strung upside down next to the bloody animal carcasses—a not-so-subtle warning of their own fate should they refuse to cooperate with mob boss Shand (Bob Hoskins, center).

Councilman Harris had approached Jeff about making a scheduled payment to the IRA in Belfast. Though Shand was unaware of them, Harris had been making similar payoffs to the IRA for years to keep it from stirring up trouble among the predominantly Irish workforce at Shand's various construction sites in and around London—which is why his lucrative building projects had never experienced any strikes. Jeff had assigned the seemingly routine task to Colin, who lifted some of the cash for himself. Coincidentally, three of the IRA terrorists were arrested shortly after receiving the insufficient payoff. Believing Shand

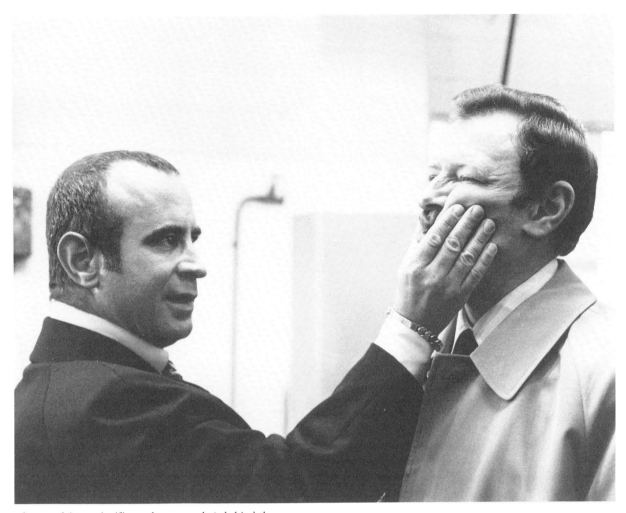

After supplying a significant clue as to who's behind the violence, policeman Parky (Dave King) refuses to do any more digging and Shand (Bob Hoskins) has to show him who's boss.

himself to be behind a double cross, the vengeful terrorists are now bent on destroying Shand's empire and bringing him to his knees.

Stunned by the news that he's been unknowingly financing the hated, anti-British IRA for years just to keep his business interests operating smoothly—and the implication that his power and control are illusory compared to the far-reaching muscle of the IRA— Shand goes berserk, and, in the film's bloodiest and most horrific scene, stabs Jeff to death with a broken bottle.

Overcome with remorse for killing the boy who had been like a son to him, Shand coerces Harris into setting up a meeting with the IRA ringleaders so that he (Shand) can pay them off and put an end to this bloody business. Harris tries to convince Shand to back off and leave bad enough alone because the latter doesn't fully comprehend the powerful force he's dealing with ("They're fanatics!") and that an attempted payoff will do no good now. But the belligerent Shand insists that it is the "murderous Paddys" who don't understand whom *they're* dealing with, and the meeting is arranged. As the IRA ringleaders are counting out the money, Shand's men burst into the room and machine gun them all, including Harris.

Believing the situation to be solved, Shand rejoins his Mafia visitors and is stunned to find them packing for home. They've decided to turn Shand's business deal down as an unsafe risk because the Irish situation has turned England into little more than a "banana republic" and the Mafia does not "do business with

As the IRA ringleaders count out the money, Shand's men burst into the room and machine gun them all. But Shand's troubles are far from over.

gangsters'' (nice touch of irony there). The furious Shand tells them he'll get his financing from the Germans instead and storms out of the hotel to rejoin his mistress, Victoria. But when he climbs into his limousine, he finds she's not there. As the limo lurches away from the curb, Shand catches a glimpse of the terrified Victoria being held down by a bunch of thugs in the back seat of another limo and realizes she's been kidnapped. Turning to his driver and bodyguard for help, Shand discovers two IRA gunmen have taken their place—one of whom has a pistol pointed at Shand's chest—and the beleaguered gangster, who truly didn't understand what he was up against, realizes he's a dead man.

Bob Hoskins gives a superb performance as Shand throughout, but this last scene—a lengthy close-up of the character as his face registers rage, frustration, despair, and, finally, grim acceptance of his fate—is a truly bravura piece of screen acting (Hoskins won the British equivalent of the Oscar as best actor for this performance) that powerfully caps this complex but riveting combination of character study, crime movie, gangster film, and political thriller, which almost didn't get released in its native England due to its controversial IRA subject matter.

BLOOD SIMPLE

(1984)

Circle Films • Color/96 Minutes

CREDITS

Director: Joel Coen; *Producer*: Ethan Coen; *Screenplay*: Joel Coen and Ethan Coen; *Cinematographer*: Barry Sonnenfeld; *Editors*: Roderick Jaynes and Don Weigmann; *Music*: Carter Burwell; *Production Designer*: Jane Musky.

CAST

Ray: John Getz; *Abby*: Frances McDormand; *Julian Marty*: Dan Hedaya; *Visser*: M. Emmet Walsh; *Meurice*: Samm-Art Williams; *Debra*: Deborah Neumann.

* * *

If the benighted characters of *Blood Simple* spent as much time expressing what's on their minds as trying to guess what's on each other's, their fates might not have been so grim. But that's just the point of this commanding stylistic blowout by debuting writer-directors Joel and Ethan Coen. The serpentine plot of this technically brilliant nod to forties *films noir* in general and Edgar G. Ulmer's super-sleazy *Detour* in particular depends on the characters' inarticulateness to work. And work it does—as an absorbing thriller, if not as a superior character study, for the people in this movie are so dim, one-dimensional, and varyingly dishonest that it's hard to arouse much interest in them. It's plot and stylistics that count in *Blood Simple*—and both are riveting indeed.

The title is taken from *Red Harvest*, Dashiell Hammett's 1929 detective story which also served as the inspiration for Akira Kurosawa's classic *Yojimbo* and Sergio Leone's unofficial remake, *For a Fistful of Dollars*. The phrase refers to the state of mind people find themselves in when they allow themselves to become thoroughly swept away by lust, deceit, and murder. In effect, they go "blood simple." And the people in this movie certainly do that.

Low-life nightclub owner Julian Marty hires a sleazy private detective named Visser to tail his wife, Abby, who Marty believes is carrying on an illicit affair—perhaps more than one. His suspicions are confirmed when Visser shows up with photos of Abby romping in bed with one of Marty's own employees, a none-too-bright guy named Ray. Knowing they were tailed and that Marty is aware of their affair, Ray confronts his boss at the club. Marty puts doubts in Ray's mind about Abby's faithfulness and warns him that she'll be two-timing him next. Then he fires Ray and orders him off the premises, still owing him two weeks back pay.

Marty's anger and jealousy build when Abby moves into Ray's apartment until she finds her own place. Marty breaks in to rough her up, but she gets her licks in first and humiliates him by breaking one of his fingers and kicking him in the groin. Driven to rage, Marty hires Visser to kill the pair for $10,000, which Marty steals from his own nightclub safe, throwing suspicion for the theft on Ray.

Visser returns to the club after hours and shows Marty photos of the dead couple in bed, their bodies stained with blood. While Visser isn't looking, Marty stashes one of the incriminating photos in the safe just in case the detective tries to double-cross him. But when Marty hands over the money, Visser shoots him and leaves him for dead. In reality, the unscrupulous detective faked the photos to convince Marty he'd gone through with the double murder. Abby and Ray actually are still alive, and as they will be the prime suspects in Marty's murder, Visser will be able to make off with the ten grand scot-free.

Ray turns up at the club to get his back pay and finds Marty's body. Thinking Abby herself committed the murder, he cleans up the bloodstains, loads Marty's body in his car, and drives to an open field to dispose of it. But Marty isn't dead yet. Ray must now finish the job—for Abby's sake, he thinks—and he buries the mortally wounded man alive.

Horrified by what he's done, Ray rejoins Abby and nervously reassures her that everything's going to be okay. Not having any idea what he's talking about, however, the baffled (and equally none-too-bright) Abby responds in a way that makes Ray think she's pulling a fast one and setting him up to take the rap for Marty's murder.

While burning the incriminating photos, Visser discovers that one of them is missing and realizes

Julian Marty (Dan Hedaya, left) offers Visser (M. Emmet Walsh) ten grand to murder Ray and Abby.

Ray (John Getz) finds the mortally wounded Marty (Dan Hedaya) trying to crawl away from the car and is faced with the unpleasant task of finishing him off.

Abby (Frances McDormand, far left) tells Meurice (Samm-Art Williams) that there may have been trouble between Marty and Ray.

Marty stashed it. He goes back to the nightclub and ransacks the place to find it, but to no avail. Thinking the photo may be locked in Marty's safe, he tries to break it open but is interrupted by Abby's unexpected arrival and beats a hasty retreat. Seeing the mess, Abby puts two and two together and comes to the conclusion that Ray has murdered her husband. She voices her suspicions to Meurice, a coworker of Ray's, but he says she must be mistaken since Marty left a message on Meurice's answering machine about Ray's theft of the ten grand. As neither of them knows that Marty purposely left the message to set Ray up and was subsequently murdered, Abby believes Marty is still alive and playing some kind of deadly game with her and Ray.

Meanwhile, Ray discovers the photograph and realizes there is an insidious third party involved. Believing Ray and Abby are in possession of the incriminating photo and intent on blackmailing him, Visser stalks the pair to Abby's apartment, and as the bewildered Ray tries to stammer his suspicions, Visser shoots him from the building next door. This leads to the film's sensational climax where Visser pursues the terrified Abby from room to room of her apartment in a tense game of cat and mouse that turns quite grisly in the end.

Cornered in her bathroom, Abby escapes through the window into an adjacent room. As Visser reaches around for her, she impales his hand on the sill with a knife. Unable to free himself, the agonized detective fires bullets through the wall, then smashes through the plaster so that he can reach through and pull out the knife.

Abby finds her own gun and, as the shadow of the murderous intruder she believes to be her husband appears at the bottom of the bathroom door, she fires through the door, yelling, "I'm not afraid of you no more Marty!" The dying Visser hits the floor, laughing at the irony of it all, and chortles back, "Well, ma'am, if I see him, I'll sure give him the message."

Though the film's characters are types rather than flesh and blood people, *Blood Simple* still works, for the Coens' primary aim is to play a dazzling cinematic game of cat and mouse with the viewer, and they succeed brilliantly in that aim. Judging from some of their subsequent films, however, it would appear that *Blood Simple*'s lack of interesting and well-rounded characters may be a Coen trademark. Though just as cinematically inventive as *Blood Simple*, the Coens' *Raising Arizona*, a woefully unfunny tale about a gang of comic rube kidnappers, and *Miller's Crossing*, a tedious period gangster piece (and virtual reworking of Dashiell Hammett's novel *The Glass Key*), are full of one-dimensional, dumb, and uncomprehending characters too.

233

Visser (M. Emmet Walsh) struggles to pull his impaled hand free.

Abby (Frances McDormand) takes aim at the shadow of the murderous intruder whom she believes to be her husband.

DIE HARD

(1988)

Twentieth Century Fox • Color/127 Minutes

CREDITS

Director: John McTiernan; *Producers*: Lawrence Gordon and Joel Silver; *Screenplay*: Jeb Stuart and Steven E. de Souza, based on the novel *High Rise* by Roderick Thorp; *Cinematographer*: Jan De Bont; *Editors*: Frank J. Urioste and John F. Link; *Music*: Michael Kamen; *Production Designer*: Jackson DeGovia.

CAST

John McClane: Bruce Willis; *Holly Gennaro McClane*: Bonnie Bedelia; *Hans Gruber*: Alan Rickman; *Sergeant Powell*: Reginald Veljohnson; *Karl*: Alexander Godunov; *Dwayne T. Robinson*: Paul Gleason; *Argyle*: De'Voreaux White; *Thornburg*: William Atherton; *Ellis*: Hart Bochner; *Joe Takagi*: James Shigeta.

* * *

Over the past decade, action thrillers have become bigger, noisier, bloodier, increasingly more plot-thin exercises in the stuntman's art, peopled by wooden actors playing characters with about as much personality and substance as stick figures. *Die Hard*, whose ads hyped that audiences would be blown through the back wall of the theater, looked on the surface like it was going to be yet another nerve-numbing, mindless action fest in this same ignoble tradition. But it turned out to be a nice surprise. In keeping with its *Rambo*-esque forebears, it was big, noisy, bloody, and full of stunts alright. But it also had an intricate and well-developed plot, a great sense of humor about itself, a marvelously Hitchcockian villain played to perfection by Alan Rickman, and some genuinely nail-biting scenes of tension and suspense. It even had a title with a clever double meaning, for *Die Hard* not only characterizes how the various villains meet their end in the film, but the hero's degree of perseverance as well. Except for its torrent of bloodletting and obviously staggering budget, *Die Hard* reminded me in many ways of the type of visceral action thriller turned out by the late, great Don Siegel in his prime.

Though a megabudget extravaganza like *Die Hard* is clearly the work of many hands (particularly those of the special effects and stunt crew), a large part of the film's effectiveness is certainly due to the direction of the talented John McTiernan, who could outstrip all other action directors of his generation and become the Don Siegel of the nineties. Like Siegel, McTiernan doesn't just let his camera *observe* the action sequences he stages, he makes it (and therefore the audience) an integral part of that action by choreographing the movement of his camera and actors as if they were performing a violent duet. As a result, McTiernan's action scenes deliver a visceral punch absent from the work of many of his action thriller colleagues. (To see what I mean, compare McTiernan's work in *Die Hard* with Renny Harlin's work in *Die Hard 2*.)

Like Siegel, McTiernan is as comfortable with actors as he is with the camera. For example, unlike Harlin's *Die Hard 2*, which maintained the stick figure tradition of most contemporary action thrillers, McTiernan imbued even the smallest roles in *Die Hard* with finely tuned shadings of character—something he's done in all his films so far. Unfortunately, until *The Hunt for Red October*, McTiernan was not quite as successful in getting decent performances from his leads. But that shouldn't be held against him, for, after all, look at the non-actors he's been saddled with: Pierce Brosnan in *Nomads* and Arnold Schwarzenegger in *Predator*. And to play the ingratiating, put-upon hero of *Die Hard*, he was given Bruce Willis, one of the most grating and obnoxious actors of our time. Here, however, McTiernan did manage to achieve a not-so-minor triumph—he made Bruce Willis palatable!

New York City cop John McClane (Willis) arrives in Los Angeles to spend the Christmas holidays with his estranged wife, Holly, and their two children. He's picked up at the airport and transported by limousine to the downtown high-tech high-rise offices of the Nakatomi Corporation, a Japanese conglomerate where Holly has an executive position that not only pays a lot more than McClane earns as a cop but also requires her to live three thousand miles away from him—thus the reasons for their marital discord.

After he is introduced to several of Holly's colleagues at the office Christmas party, the estranged couple adjourns to the executive washroom so that he can freshen up after his trip and the two can spend a

John McClane (Bruce Willis), the put-upon but resourceful hero of Die Hard.

Hans Gruber, the marvelously Hitchcockian villain played to cool perfection by Alan Rickman.

few minutes talking in private. But as soon as they're alone, he reopens old wounds and they begin arguing. Holly goes back to the party, leaving McClane alone to brood and kick himself for his emotional immaturity.

While McClane is rebuking himself, a terrorist group led by the smooth-talking Hans Gruber descends on the gathering, takes everyone hostage, and seals off the skyscraper with an arsenal of sopisticated weaponry. Although Gruber's aims at first seem political, it soon becomes clear that he's carrying out an

The blood flows and the bodies pile up courtesy of the diehard McClane (Bruce Willis).

elaborately-staged heist of the company's treasury—a cache of $640 million in bearer bonds locked inside the building's computerized, ultra-secure safe. When the company's CEO, Joe Takagi, refuses to hand over the safe's combination, Gruber cold-bloodedly shoots the man in the head and calmly switches to phase two of his plan, which is actually quite ingenious. Gruber intends to get the police and FBI to shut off power to the building so that the safe's electronic security devices will be automatically released—then time a mini-nuclear device to blow the skyscraper's top floors after he and his men have gotten away so that the cops will think the terrorists took their own lives as well as those of their hostages when they realized they had been surrounded. The one thing Gruber hasn't figured on, however, is the presence of Mc-Clane, who secretly witnesses the arrival of the terrorists and the murder of Takagi, and launches a desperate, one-man crusade to save Holly and the other hostages and bring Gruber and his thugs to their knees.

As the blood flows and the bodies of his henchmen

With the help of a swiftly unraveling fire hose, McClane (Bruce Willis) escapes from his pursuers down the side of the skyscraper.

Gruber (Alan Rickman) uses Holly (Bonnie Bedlia) to draw McClane out into the open.

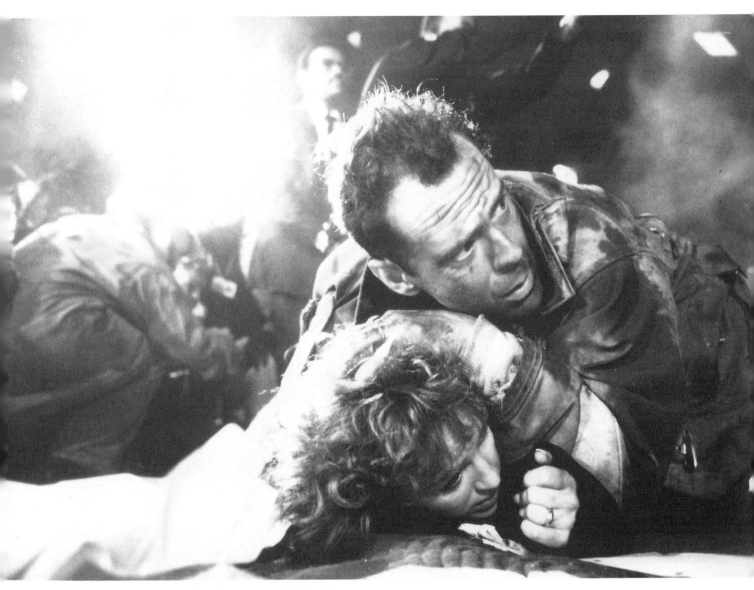

Holly (Bonnie Bedlia) and McClane (Bruce Willis) duck for cover as Sergeant Powell (Reginald Veljohnson, in background) blows away the last villain.

pile up courtesy of the diehard McClane, Gruber finds his carefully laid plans fast going down the drain. But he regains the upper hand when an irresponsible television reporter named Thornburg reveals in a special bulletin that one of the hostages is McClane's wife—a secret McClane and Holly had managed to keep from Gruber up until then. Gruber immediately uses Holly to draw McClane out into the open, but the fast-thinking cop has one more trick up his sleeve, and the villainous Gruber plunges to his death from the skyscraper in the film's tense final showdown, a sequence that mischievously recalls and reworks the heart-stopping Statue of Liberty climax in Hitchcock's *Saboteur*.

There's no doubt that, at heart, *Die Hard* is an adolescent chauvinist fantasy. McClane's self-reproachment for his jealousy over his wife's job status and superior earning power notwithstanding, when he saves her from falling from the skyscraper with Gruber by releasing the catch of her Rolex watch (the affluent symbol of the trouble between them) which Gruber is holding onto, and she falls into McClane's arms instead, the movie's not-so-subtle macho message becomes eminently clear.

Message aside, however, *Die Hard* is a real grabber—a spectacular, action-filled and at times very suspenseful thriller that succeeds in doing precisely what its ad claimed: blowing you through the back wall of the theater.

241

MANHUNTER
(1986)

DeLaurentiis Entertainment Group • Color/120 Minutes

CREDITS

Director: Michael Mann; *Producer*: Richard Roth; *Screenplay*: Michael Mann, based on the novel *Red Dragon* by Thomas Harris; *Cinematographer*: Dante Spinotti; *Editor*: Dov Hoenig; *Music*: The Reds and Michel Rubini; *Production Designer*: Mel Bourne.

CAST

Will Graham: William L. Petersen; *Molly Graham*: Kim Griest; *Reba*: Joan Allen; *Dr. Hannibal Lektor*: Brian Cox; *Jack Crawford*: Dennis Farina; *Freddy Lounds*: Stephen Lang; *Francis Dollarhyde*: Tom Noonan; *Dr. Chilton*: Benjamin Hendrickson.

Brian Cox as Dr. Hannibal "The Cannibal" Lektor in Manhunter.

FBI agent Will Graham (William L. Petersen) goes it bravely alone to meet a twisted serial killer in Manhunter, *based on Thomas Harris's novel,* Red Dragon.

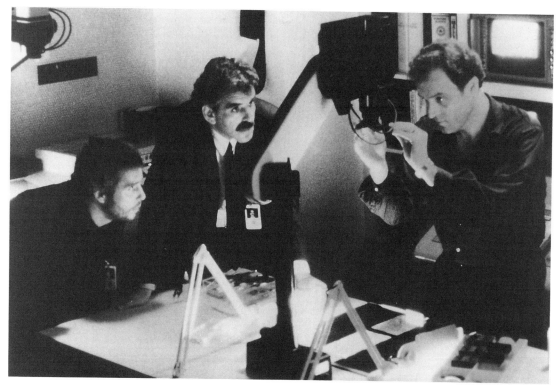

One of the FBI's forensic wizards pieces together fragments of writing found on toilet paper in Lektor's cell, leading Graham (William L. Petersen) and Behavioral Sciences chief Jack Crawford (Dennis Farina) to the horrifying discovery that Lektor has been in communication with Red Dragon.

Red Dragon (Tom Noonan) reveals his ghoulish secrets to the terrified Lounds (Stephen Lang) before killing him.

Dollarhyde a.k.a. "The Tooth Fairy" and "Red Dragon" (Tom Noonan) kidnaps scheming reporter Freddy Lounds (Stephen Lang) for trying to lure him out into the open.

THE SILENCE OF THE LAMBS
(1991)

Orion Pictures • Color/118 Minutes

CREDITS

Director: Jonathan Demme; *Producers*: Kenneth Utt, Edward Saxon, and Ron Bozman; *Screenplay*: Ted Tally, based on the novel by Thomas Harris; *Cinematographer*: Tak Fujimoto; *Editor*: Craig McKay; *Music*: Howard Shore; *Production Designer*: Kristi Zea.

CAST

Clarice Starling: Jodie Foster; *Dr. Hannibal Lecter*: Anthony Hopkins; *Jack Crawford*: Scott Glenn; *Jame Gumb*: Ted Levin; *Dr. Chilton*: Anthony Heald; *Catherine Martin*: Brooke Smith; *Senator Ruth Martin*: Diane Baker; *FBI Director Hayden Burke*: Roger Corman.

* * *

Currently, the serial killer has overtaken the drug dealer, the gangster, the international terrorist, and the supenatural movie monsters of yore as the screen's reigning villain. This is largely due to the epidemic growth of the real-life phenomenon of serial killing itself over the past several decades, a crime the movies—particularly horror movies—have touched upon from time to time throughout their history, but today portray to the point of overkill.

On the thriller side of the ledger (although both of them could arguably be called horror movies as well), Michael Mann's *Manhunter* and Jonathan Demme's *The Silence of the Lambs* are two of the best and most unnerving examples of the recent spate of films dealing with this ugly crime. Not coincidentally, both are adaptations of novels by Thomas Harris, one of the most skillful and successful writers of this type of crime fiction working today. Harris has made a cottage industry of the subject by dealing with it in two of his (to date) three published books (his first novel, *Black Sunday*, was about international terrorists), all of them bestsellers. In fact, *Red Dragon* (renamed *Manhunter* for the movies) and *The Silence of the Lambs* form two-thirds of a potential trilogy whose main recurring character, the brilliant Dr. Hannibal ("The Cannibal") Lecter, is a deranged serial killer himself. The plots of *Red Dragon* and *The Silence of the Lambs*

are extremely suspenseful, creepy, and ingeniously worked out, but they follow a formula, one which becomes more apparent when you compare the two films faithfully adapted from them. Both were made by different companies and different creative talents and featured different actors in identical roles, but are otherwise remarkably similar—even in terms of style, although *Manhunter* is, perhaps, the flashier of the two, and *The Silence of the Lambs* the more low key and grim. Each is extremely well acted and relentlessly suspenseful, though *Lambs* is the more intense of the pair—and the more gruesome—which may be why it was a bigger box office success.

Both films are about psychologically vulnerable FBI agents—connected with the bureau's special Behavioral Sciences section dealing with serial killers—who use the imprisoned Dr. Lecter as a dangerous resource for information and as a conduit in tracking down a sadistic psychopath whose madness is grounded in the twisted belief that he is being reborn by his brutal murders (of both men and women) into a powerful alter ego society will fear and respect. In each tale, as much time is devoted to the psychologically dangerous cat-and-mouse game between the respective FBI agents and the manipulative Dr. Lecter (whose twisted mind and emotions they must connect with in order to ferret out information that will lead them to the killers) as to the pursuit and capture of the killers themselves. In *Manhunter*, the killer is Francis Dollarhyde, who identifies himself by the colorful name "Red Dragon." In *Lambs*, he is Jame Gumb, whom the newspapers have dubbed "Buffalo Bill." (Curiously, *Manhunter* changes Lecter's name to *Lektor*. Nevertheless, in *Manhunter* and *Lambs*, the character is portrayed exactly as Harris wrote him and acted with bone-chilling flair by Brian Cox and Anthony Hopkins, respectively. Cox and Hopkins sound and are even made up to look somewhat alike—although Hopkins's Lecter gets more screen time since his character figures more largely in *Lambs*'s plot.)

In *Manhunter*, FBI chief Jack Crawford coaxes agent Will Graham back into service to solve a series

Lecter (Anthony Hopkins) and FBI agent-in-training Clarice Starling (Jodie Foster) confront each other for the first time in The Silence of the Lambs.

of grisly murders in Birmingham and Atlanta. Graham has a special talent for probing the minds of the murderers he's hunting and developing clues to their motives and methods that escape the attention of everyone else. It was Graham who caught the maniacal Dr. Lektor, a case that wounded him both physically and emotionally and landed him in the hospital with a nervous breakdown. Over his wife's protestations, he agrees to take on the case of this new serial killer whom the FBI calls the "Tooth Fairy" on

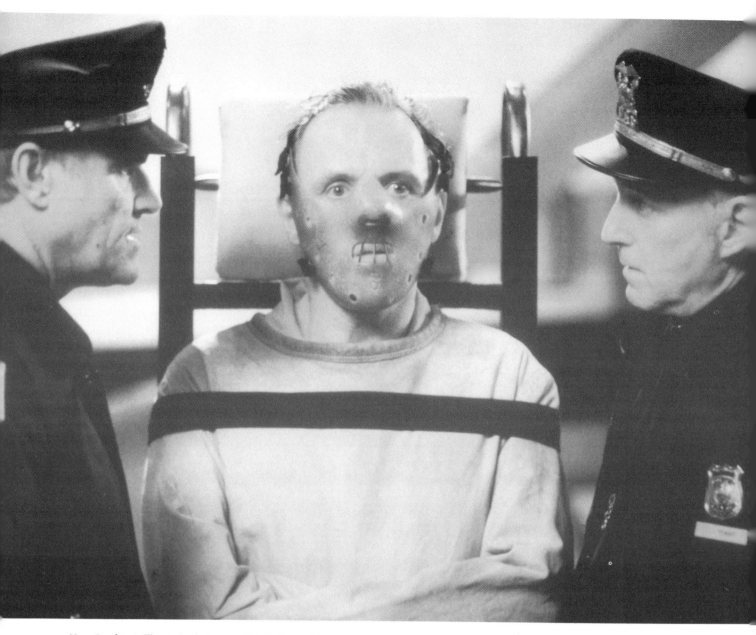

Have Psycho, Will Travel—but not until he's thoroughly subdued. Anthony Hopkins as Dr. Hannibal "The Cannibal" Lecter in The Silence of the Lambs.

account of the unique bite marks the killer leaves on the corpses of his mutilated and molested victims—families with attractive mothers whose dead eyes he covers with pieces of smashed mirror. Graham's investigation of the murder scenes and mind probe of the grisly M.O. lead him to conjecture that the killer puts the pieces of broken mirror over the eyes of his female victims to reflect his image as he rapes and slashes them post mortem—in other words, the killer needs to fantasize that the women can "see" the

powerful creature he is "becoming" through his acts.

To probe the killer's psyche further, Graham pays a visit to the incarcerated Dr. Lektor, who is kept isolated within a brightly lit, white cell encased in glass and bars. At first, Lektor plays diabolical mind games with the still vulnerable Graham, but then agrees to help. He asks for the case file on the "Tooth Fairy" and confirms Graham's theory about the killer's motives and the reason why he will not stop. "It feels good [to kill]," Lektor says, "because God has

Gumb's latest victim (Brooke Smith) threatens to kill the maniac's pooch if he refused to let her go.

Gumb a.k.a. "Buffalo Bill" (Ted Levine) puts the finishing touches on the new body he has fashioned for himself out of the skin of his female victims.

power [to kill] and if one does it enough times, one becomes as God is."

The vengeful Lektor exacts his pound of flesh for the free consultation, however, by setting up a coded correspondence with the "Tooth Fairy" through the classified ads of a trashy tabloid called "The National Tattler" and providing the killer with the home address of the FBI man who is hot on his trail. The bureau cracks the code and Graham's family is relo-

cated and kept under close watch.

In return for an exclusive scoop, Graham enlists the aid of an obnoxious "Tattler" reporter named Freddy Lounds to lure the "Tooth Fairy" out into the open. But the plan backfires when the killer realizes a trap has been set for him and he tortures Lounds to death in reprisal. With only six days left until the killer will likely strike another family (he acts when the moon is full), Graham puts his nose to the

Sporting night vision goggles, Gumb (Ted Levine) switches off the lights and plays a tense game of cat and mouse with agent Starling (Jodie Foster), who has tracked him to his lair.

grindstone and tries to figure out how his quarry chose his previous victims and how he knew the interior and exterior layouts of their homes so intimately. He stumbles upon the answer while viewing the home movies and snapshots of one of the dead families over and over and realizes that the killer chose these people and was able to study the layout of their homes because he must have had access to the same movies and snapshots.

This revelation leads Graham to the lab where the film was processed and he at last closes in on his prey—the lab's production controller, Francis Dollarhyde, a tall, powerfully built but facially and dentally deformed man with a sexual identity problem. Dollarhyde is about to claim his unplanned latest victim (a blind female coworker who has seduced the sexually confused and tormented man into a doomed romantic affair) and evolve into the fantasized super-being he calls "Red Dragon" when Graham and his S.W.A.T. team breaks in and shoots him down.

Lambs's sleuth is Clarice Starling, the daughter of a deceased small-town sheriff, who seeks to escape her humble origins by becoming a top agent in the FBI's Behavioral Sciences section. A trainee showing considerable promise, she is assigned by special agent Jack Crawford to persuade the imprisoned psycho-psychiatrist Dr. Hannibal Lecter to fill out a questionnaire designed to probe for information about the mentality of serial killers which the bureau intends to plug into its database. The assignment is a ruse, however, to get the brilliant but twisted Lecter to help solve a baffling case of serial murder in which the killer, known as "Buffalo Bill," starves and tortures his female victims to death, then partially skins their corpses. (Like Francis Dollarhyde, Buffalo Bill, whose real name is Jame Gumb, fantasizes that he too is assuming a new persona through his murders; in this case, he's turning himself into a woman by stitching together the stripped flesh of his female victims and fashioning a new body for himself.)

Lecter, who is even more diabolical and manipulative in this film than in *Manhunter*, takes the young FBI trainee under his wing, plays with her psyche as he did Will Graham's (he even teases her by mimicking her attempt to disguise her rural accent), and guides her in smoking out the identity of Buffalo Bill—a former patient of Lecter's who had been undergoing therapy for a sexual identity crisis.

Lecter's secret agenda is not revenge this time around, however. His ruse is to help Clarice get what she wants (to nail the killer on her own) so that the FBI will help him get what he wants—a transfer to another prison during which he plans to stage an escape. Lecter successfully makes his break and in the nail-biting finish, Clarice comes face to face with Buffalo Bill (unaware at first who he is) in his secluded, dungeon-like digs. Sporting night vision goggles, Buffalo Bill switches off the lights and plays a tense game of cat and mouse with Clarice in the inky blackness. She hears him cock the hammer of his gun at the last second, however, and shoots him first by emptying her own revolver in the direction of the sound.

As the film ends and Clarice receives her FBI badge, she gets a congratulatory phone call from the vanished Dr. Lecter, who concludes his tutelage with the chilling advice, "I have no plans to call on you, Clarice, the world being a more interesting place with you in it. Be sure you extend me the same courtesy." Clarice tells him she can't do that, thus paving the way for a third installment in the saga of Dr. Hannibal "The Cannibal" Lecter which will probably focus on Clarice's hunt (possibly assisted by Will Graham?) for the fiend.

The overall impact of *Manhunter* is diminished somewhat by writer-director Michael Mann's decision to stage the film too much like a glossy, neon-lit episode of *Miami Vice*, the popular TV series he created. It remains a remarkably suspenseful and disturbing thriller, however, largely thanks to the riveting performances of William Petersen, Brian Cox, and, especially, Tom Noonan, whose grotesque Francis Dollarhyde is a chilling tour-de-force.

Its Bedlamesque sets broodingly lit to reflect the dark corners of the psychotic minds it is exploring, *Lambs* goes much more for the gut and is the more relentlessly suspenseful and powerful film of the two. Ted Levine's Buffalo Bill is a scary monster indeed, but we don't get to know him as well as we do *Manhunter*'s Francis Dollarhyde. This is not necessarily a weakness of the film, however, as the main focus in *Lambs* (both novel and film) is the psychological duel between the creepy Dr. Lecter and the determined Clarice Starling (superbly played by Academy Award winners Anthony Hopkins and Jodie Foster) whose frequent, tension-mounting confrontations with one another are guaranteed to raise the blood pressure (and the hackles) of even the most jaded thriller fan.

Supplemental List of Fifty More Great Movie Thrillers

If the fifty thrillers you've just read about have whet your appetite for more nail-biting screen entertainment, keep a sharp eye out for these fifty others, all of them excellent thrillers themselves, which, for reasons of time and space, I couldn't fit into the present volume. Titles are listed alphabetically, followed by the year of release and the name of the director.

ACROSS THE BRIDGE (1957) Ken Annakin
THE ASPHALT JUNGLE (1950) John Huston
    (remade by Delmer Daves as THE BADLANDERS in 1958 , by Wolf Rilla as CAIRO in 1963 and by Barry Pollack as COOL BREEZE in 1972)
THE BIG CLOCK (1948) John Farrow
    (remade by Roger Donaldson as NO WAY OUT in 1987)
BULLITT (1968) Peter Yates
THE COLDITZ STORY (1955) Guy Hamilton
THE COUNTERFEIT TRAITOR (1962) George Seaton
COURT MARTIAL (1954) Anthony Asquith
CRY TERROR! (1958) Andrew L. Stone
DIRIGIBLE (1931) Frank Capra
DIRTY HARRY (1971) Don Siegel
DUEL (1971) Steven Spielberg
ESCAPE FROM ALCATRAZ (1979) Don Siegel
EYE OF THE NEEDLE (1981) Richard Marquand
EXPERIMENT IN TERROR (1962) Blake Edwards
FOURTEEN HOURS (1951) Henry Hathaway
GET CARTER (1971) Mike Hodges
    (remade by George Armitage as HIT MAN in 1972)
HIGH TREASON (1951) Roy Boulting
INFERNO (1953) Roy Baker
KEY WITNESS (1960) Phil Karlson
THE KILLING (1956) Stanley Kubrick
A KISS BEFORE DYING (1956) Gerd Oswald
    (remade by James Dearden in 1991)
KISS OF DEATH (1947) Henry Hathaway
    (remade by Gordon Douglas as THE FIEND WHO WALKED THE WEST in 1958)
THE LADY VANISHES (1938) Alfred Hitchcock
    (remade by Anthony Page in 1979)
LE CORBEAU (1943) Henri-Georges Clouzot
    (remade by Otto Preminger as THE THIRTEENTH LETTER in 1950)

LES DIABOLIQUES (1955) Henri-Georges Clouzot
    (remade by John Badham as a TV movie, REFLECTIONS OF MURDER, in 1974)
THE MAN WHO NEVER WAS (1956) Ronald Neame
MISSING (1982) Costa-Gavras
THE MOST DANGEROUS GAME (1932) Ernest B. Schoedsack & Irving Pichel
    (remade by Robert Wise as A GAME OF DEATH in 1945 and by Roy Boulting as RUN FOR THE SUN in 1956)
NORTH BY NORTHWEST (1959) Alfred Hitchcock
ODDS AGAINST TOMORROW (1959) Robert Wise
ON HER MAJESTY'S SECRET SERVICE (1969) Peter Hunt
PANIC IN THE STREETS (1950) Jules Dassin
PHANTOM LADY (1944) Robert Siodmak
POINT BLANK (1967) John Boorman
A PRIZE OF ARMS (1962) Cliff Owen
THE PROWLER (1951) Joseph Losey
PURPLE NOON (1960) René Clement
SECONDS (1966) John Frankenheimer
SEE NO EVIL (1971) Richard Fleischer
SEVEN DAYS IN MAY (1964) John Frankenheimer
SEVEN DAYS TO NOON (1950) John Boulting
THE SOUND OF FURY (1950) Cy Endfield
THE SNIPER (1952) Edward Dmytryk
THE SPIRAL STAIRCASE (1945) Robert Siodmak
    (remade by Peter Collinson in 1975)
TOPKAPI (1964) Jules Dassin
THE VANISHING (1988) George Sluizer
VIOLENT SATURDAY (1955) Richard Fleischer
WAR GAMES (1983) John Badham
WHILE THE CITY SLEEPS (1956) Fritz Lang
THE WOODEN HORSE (1950) Jack Lee

ABOUT THE AUTHOR

JOHN MCCARTY was born in Albany, New York, in 1944. He has been a movie fan since he was five and started making his own films in his early teens. After graduating from high school in 1962, he attended Boston University where he majored in film and began writing seriously on the subject. Following a stint in the Peace Corps, where he worked in educational television in Bogotá, Colombia, he returned to the States and worked in broadcasting for a number of years, then became an advertising copywriter for General Electric Company. He left that in 1983 and has been a free-lance writer ever since. His affection for the horror film genre (and concern with what was happening to it) led to the writing of *Splatter Movies: Breaking the Last Taboo of the Screen* (St. Martin's Press, 1984). It has become a cult classic. His other books include the horror thriller, *Deadly Resurrection*, and *The Complete Films of John Huston* (Citadel Press, 1991). He lives in upstate New York with his wife, Cheryl, four crazy cats, and a neurotic dog.